Transitioning Into Hospital-Based Practice

Mona N. Bahouth, MD, MSN, was, at the time of this book's inception, the Project Manager for Advanced Practice Nursing at the University of Maryland Medical Center, Baltimore, where she led more than 100 nurse practitioners (NPs) for the promotion of professional growth and development of systems for integrating NPs into hospital practice. From 1998 to 2004, she was the Director for Clinical Programs and Research in the Department of Neurology at the Maryland Brain Attack Center. Dr. Bahouth has extensive experience in developing programs for NPs, dating back to 1999, when she developed the first hospital-wide NP group at the University of Maryland. She has published and lectured extensively on multiple topics including the process of NP transition into hospital-based practice. These experiences were the impetus for the development of this book.

Kay Blum, PhD, CRNP, is a Heart Failure NP and Coordinator for the Cardiac Risk Reduction Center at Southern Maryland Hospital Center in Clinton, MD. She was one of the first few NPs in the University of Maryland Medical System. She has been a researcher, Clinical Nurse Specialist, clinician, continuing educator, and consultant. Dr. Blum has held faculty appointments at the University of Maryland, the University of Texas Medical Branch at Galveston, the MGH Institute of Health Professions, and Clemson University. She is actively involved in NP quality research and advocacy issues in the American College of Cardiology.

Shari Simone, DNP, CPNP-AC, FCCM, is the lead NP for Women's and Children's Services at the University of Maryland Medical Center and Assistant Professor in the Pediatric Acute Care Nurse Practitioner Program at the University of Maryland School of Nursing. She has practiced as a pediatric critical care NP for 15 years and was instrumental in developing the NP role in the pediatric intensive care unit at the University of Maryland. She also holds a faculty appointment at the University of Maryland School of Nursing in the Pediatric Acute Care Nurse Practitioner Program. Dr. Simone has published and lectured extensively on multiple pediatric topics as well as on the role of the NP in pediatric critical care and the NP orientation process.

Transitioning Into Hospital-Based Practice

A Guide for Nurse Practitioners and Administrators

Mona N. Bahouth, MD, MSN
Kay Blum, PhD, CRNP
Shari Simone, DNP, CPNP-AC, FCCM

Editors

SPRINGER PUBLISHING COMPANY

NEW YORK

Springer Publishing Company, LLC
11 West 42nd Street
New York, NY 10036
www.springerpub.com

Acquisitions Editor: Margaret Zuccarini
Composition: Techset Composition Ltd.

ISBN 978-0-8261-5732-4
E-book ISBN: 978-0-8261-5733-1

12 13 14 15/ 5 4 3 2 1

The author and the publisher of this Work have made every effort to use sources believed to be reliable to provide information that is accurate and compatible with the standards generally accepted at the time of publication. Because medical science is continually advancing, our knowledge base continues to expand. Therefore, as new information becomes available, changes in procedures become necessary. We recommend that the reader always consult current research and specific institutional policies before performing any clinical procedure. The author and publisher shall not be liable for any special, consequential, or exemplary damages resulting, in whole or in part, from the readers' use of, or reliance on, the information contained in this book. The publisher has no responsibility for the persistence or accuracy of URLs for external or third-party Internet websites referred to in this publication and does not guarantee that any content on such websites is, or will remain, accurate or appropriate.

Library of Congress Cataloging-in-Publication Data

Transitioning into hospital-based practice : a guide for nurse practitioners and administrators / Mona N. Bahouth, Kay Blum, Shari Simone, editors.
  p. ; cm.
Includes bibliographical references and index.
ISBN 978-0-8261-5732-4 -- ISBN 978-0-8261-5733-1 (e-book)
I. Bahouth, Mona N. II. Blum, Kay. III. Simone, Shari.
[DNLM: 1. nurse practitioners--organization & administration. 2. Nursing Service, Hospital--organization & administration. 3. Organizational Innovation. WY 128]

610.7306'92068--dc23

2012025899

Special discounts on bulk quantities of our books are available to corporations, professional associations, pharmaceutical companies, health care organizations, and other qualifying groups.

If you are interested in a custom book, including chapters from more than one of our titles, we can provide that service as well.

For details, please contact:
Special Sales Department, Springer Publishing Company, LLC
11 West 42nd Street, 15th Floor, New York, NY 10036-8002
Phone: 877-687-7476 or 212-431-4370; Fax: 212-941-7842
Email: sales@springerpub.com

Printed in the United States of America by Bang Printing.

To all of the pioneers who have gone before us and continue to inspire us. . .

Mona N. Bahouth

For Mary Beth Esposito-Herr
Vision where others didn't know to look. Courage where others were afraid to try. . . . You are missed.

Kay Blum

To my personal Community of Practice: Rachel Atkinson, Mona Bahouth, Ellen Clarke, Michael Fisher, Steve Gottlieb, Kathy Mitchell, Janet Moll, Kim Reck, Shawn Robinson, Shari Simone, and Janet Wyman.

Shari Simone

To the nurse practitioners and physicians at the University of Maryland Medical Center who have provided guidance and support over the years and continue to inspire me, but most importantly to the dedicated, talented group of NPs who I have the pleasure of working side by side with every day in the pediatric ICU—Amy Donaldson, Jennifer Nordling, Melanie Muller, Jill Siegrist, Jessica Strohm-Farber, Megan Trahan, Jamie Tumulty, and Anne Vasiliadis—without their support and encouragement this project would not have been a reality.

Contents

Contributors

Alice D. Ackerman, MD, MBA, FAAN, FCCM, Professor and Chair, Department of Pediatrics, Virginia Tech Carilion School of Medicine, Chair and Chief Pediatric Officer, Carilion Clinic Children's Hospital, Roanoke, Virginia

Michael Ackerman, DNS, RN, ACNP-BC, FCCM, FNAP, FAANP, Director, Sovie Center for Advanced Practice, University of Rochester Medical Center, Rochester, New York

Mona N. Bahouth, MD, MSN, Johns Hopkins Hospital, Baltimore, Maryland

Susan K. Bezek, MS, RN, PNP-BC, Associate Director, Pediatric Nursing, Golisano Children's Hospital, University of Rochester Medical Center, Rochester, New York

Robert P. Blessing, DNP, ACNP, Lead NP Neurocritical Care, Associate Professor, Duke University School of Nursing, Wake Forest, North Carolina

Kay Blum, PhD, CRNP, Nurse Practitioner and Coordinator, Cardiac Risk Reduction Center, Southern Maryland Hospital Center, Clinton, Maryland

Cheryl R. Duke, PhD, RN, FNP-BC, Director, Advanced Clinical Practice, University Health System Medical Center, Greenville, North Carolina

Janet Fuchs, MBA, MSN, NEA-BC, Senior Director of Ambulatory Nursing, Cleveland Clinic, Cleveland, Ohio

Elizabeth Fuselier Ellis, DNP, FNP, APRN, BC, FAANP, City of Bryan Employee Health Services Clinic; Provider and Manager, St. Joseph Regional Health Center, Bedias, Texas

April N. Kapu, MSN, RN, ACNP-BC, Assistant Director Advanced Practice, Center for Advanced Practice Nursing and Allied Health, Vanderbilt University Medical Center, Nashville, Tennessee

Ruth Kleinpell, PhD, RN, FAAN, FCCM, Director, Center for Clinical Research and Scholarship, Rush University Medical Center; Professor, Rush University College of Nursing, Chicago, Illinois

Carmel A. McComiskey, DNP, CRNP, Director, Nurse Practitioners University of Maryland Medical Center, Baltimore, Maryland

Tim Porter-O'Grady, DM, EdD, ScD, APRN, FAAN, Senior Partner, Tim Porter-O'Grady Associates, Inc., Atlanta, Georgia

Lisa Rowen, DNSc, RN, FAAN, Senior Vice President and Chief Nursing Officer, Nursing and Patient Care Services, University of Maryland Medical Center, Baltimore, Maryland

Maria R. Shirey, PhD, MBA, RN, NEA-BC, FACHE, FAAN, Associate Professor, Doctor of Nursing Practice Program, University of Southern Indiana College of Nursing and Health Professions, Evansville, Indiana

Shari Simone, DNP, CPNP-AC, FCCM, Lead Nurse Practitioner for Women's and Children's Services, University of Maryland Medical Center, Baltimore, Maryland

Anne Swantz, RN, MS, CPNP, Assistant Director, Sovie Center for Advanced Practice, University of Rochester Medical Center, Rochester, New York

Clare Thomson-Smith, JD, MSN, FAANP, Director, Center for Advanced Practice Nursing and Allied Health, Assistant Dean Faculty Practice, Vanderbilt University Medical Center, Nashville, Tennessee

Jennifer L. Titzer, MSN, RN, RT, RCIS, Nursing Instructor, Baccalaureate Nursing Program, University of Southern Indiana College of Nursing and Health Professions, Evansville, Indiana

Renay Tyler, DNP, ACNP, Director of Nursing, Johns Hopkins Hospital Ambulatory Services, Johns Hopkins Hospital, Baltimore, Maryland

Elizabeth Zink, MSN, CNS, Clinical Nurse Specialist, Neurocritical Care Unit, Johns Hopkins Hospital, Baltimore, Maryland

Foreword

Reflecting on 47 years of the growth of the nurse practitioner (NP) educational and practice programs and on the changes in their integration into the health care sector is a formidable task. From a public health nursing role expansion model in well child care, the model was adapted to fit the needs of many health service venues: schools, clinics, veterans and military services, and so on. Most of these were ambulatory sites; they trained their own nurses to fit their particular needs. Some were newly created while other older ones were adaptable and flexible in their organizational structures. A few neonatal nurseries began to use NPs, but for the most part, the inpatient services were wedded to the Clinical Nurse Specialist model of advanced nursing care.

However, in my combined positions as Dean of the School of Nursing and Director of Nursing at the Strong Memorial Hospital, University of Rochester Medical Center, I became convinced that the NP was the nurse for all settings, including inpatient, acute care hospital settings. From an experience with experimental cardiothoracic NPs, it was obvious that while nurse educators were quite adept at preparing NPs, the major barriers to their successful integration into the total health care sector would require institutional changes in preparation, placement, practice, and policies if the patients and their families were to receive top-quality nursing care from a fully integrated, skilled team of health professionals of which the NP was an integral player. Changing the role of one professional required alterations in many aspects of the so-called "most entrenched, change adverse industry in the US" (Christensen, Bohmer, & Kenagy, 2000).

One of the many factors that escalated the NP into inpatient services was the impending crisis of reduction of surgical resident training funds. This provided an opportunity for NPs to demonstrate their value and worth in inpatient services, not as substitutes for the missing surgical residents, but introduce a comprehensive service of management of the surgical patient, which included continuity; increased communication with the total team of caregivers; coordination of care; patient and family education; support of nursing staff; transitional and follow-up to prevent recidivism and readmission. The NP could improve the safety, quality, patient satisfaction, and education as well as prevent suffering, dissatisfaction, and costly aftercare.

Except for descriptive articles, few guides exist to cover the many facets of inaugurating, implementing, and evaluating the successful integration of the NP into acute care settings. That is what makes this publication a valuable resource for NPs and administrators as well as students, faculty, and health service planners. This reality-oriented and experientially documented guide provides a comprehensive map of the various stages of development from the transitional period to framing the innovation and the evaluative process. It surely will be a major resource of information, referral, and research for some years to come.

Loretta C. Ford, EdD, RN, PNP
Co-Founder of the Nurse Practitioner Model
Dean and Professor Emerita
School of Nursing
University of Rochester

REFERENCE

Christensen, C. M., Bohmer, R., & Kenagy, J. (2000). Will disruptive innovations cure health care? *Harvard Business Review, 78*(5), 102–112.

Preface

The decision to write this book—to call upon the experience of nurse practitioners fresh from the hard work of creating a culture that nourishes and cultivates the best practice—evolved from the desire of the authors to contribute on a larger scale to the well-being of both nurse practitioners and the organizations to which they belong. It is grounded in the fundamental belief that both must prosper or neither will; there must be mutual advantage, mutual reward, and mutual accountability, or the energies of both will be wasted in the struggle to be heard and appreciated. This book provides critical information to the nurse practitioner and supports the successful integration of nurse practitioners into hospital-based practice.

Challenges exist in the integration of nurse practitioners into the organization whether that is a hospital, clinic, medical practice, or tertiary referral center. Societal, political, and economic forces in the environment have led to the hiring of nurse practitioners without planning or thought as to the impact this change would have. The designations of adult, pediatric, neonatal, acute care, and family nurse practitioner and the legal requirements that differ from state to state lead to confusion in the credentialing and privileging that are critical to functioning within an organization. Defining the scope of practice and even naming jobs and creating job descriptions are difficult because the patients we care for cross age and setting categories. Organizing practice, especially in large organizations, is difficult and makes a systematic approach almost an impossible task. Trial and error becomes the most common and the most expensive strategy. This tactic often leaves the participants discouraged and distrustful of the process.

The purpose of this book is to provide a critical summary of resources needed for the nurse practitioners who are entering or refining their role within the hospital setting. The book also helps to facilitate this process for organizations that wish to plan ahead for the integration of nurse practitioners into the models of care. It is also for nurse practitioners who are seeking an environment where they can grow and develop into the best possible providers and have a genuine sense of accomplishment that nourishes them and benefits the patients they care for. We have chosen to take a systematic approach to bring together theory, research, and our experience in a meaningful and pragmatic way. It has been said that there is nothing as practical as a good theory. We have taken that to heart and, just as people use a map to reach a destination they have never traveled to, we see a conceptual framework as a map to guide our journey as advanced practitioners. Conceptual frameworks not only keep us on an efficient path to our destination; they provide a systematic way of examining phenomena that illuminate our way back when we stray, ensure that important components are not missed in our haste, and provide a means of evaluating our progress; they also help us to identify new strategies when old ones have not worked as well as we had hoped.

We have chosen two frameworks to guide the development of this book. First, for organizations, the Diffusion of Innovation Model, initially developed by Everett Rogers in 1962, provides direction for planning and evaluating the introduction of an innovation such as nurse practitioners into an established organization. It suggests strategies for decision making and planning for change (Rogers, 2003). For nurse practitioners and organizations, the Theory of Experiencing Transition suggested by Meleis, Sawyer, Im, Hilfinger Messias, and Schumaker (2000) offers a means of examining the complexity of change in transition and of utilizing supportive strategies to facilitate the transition.

It is our sincere hope that our experiences and the national expertise represented in this book can be useful to our colleagues who are in all stages of transition and who view nurse practitioners as an innovation in the way we care for patients who have sought our help. We believe that respect and collaboration are the fundamentals of practice and that practice must take place in an environment that appreciates and acknowledges the work of nurse practitioners as fully integrated professionals. We believe that successful, productive nurse practitioners see their success as the success of the organization and see the organization's success as part of and not separate from their own success. Our vision for this book is that it will provide guidance for novice and experienced organizations and practitioners and that all can use the information here to develop a dialogue that reflects the common purpose, common language, and common good of organizations and practioners alike.

REFERENCES

Meleis, A. I., Sawyer, L. M., Im, E. O., Hilfinger Messias, D. K., & Schumaker, K. (2000). Experiencing transitions: An emerging middle range theory. *Advances in Nursing Science, 23*(1), 12–28.

Rogers, E. M. (2003). *Diffusion of innovations*, 5th ed. New York, NY: Free Press.

Introduction ████████

Innovation and Transition

Kay Blum

> *He who loves practice without theory is like the sailor who*
> *boards a ship without a rudder and compass and never knows*
> *where he may cast.*
> LEONARDO DA VINCI (1452–1519)

Just as travelers would use a map to get from where they stood to a place they wanted to be, we must use a map to ensure we reach our desired destination of the successful integration of nurse practitioners (NPs) into an organization. This is true for any organization whether a large academic medical center, a community hospital, managed care organization, or private practice. Leonardo da Vinci understood this, and intuitively we all recognize the benefit of a plan or road map to achieve our goals. How then do we identify the right map and then use it to our benefit?

The purposeful introduction of NPs into an organization is innovative. Historically, changes in nursing's scope of practice have epitomized innovation. Florence Nightingale introduced a totally new and innovative definition of nursing in Crimea. Cleanliness, fresh air, and decent food delivered by healthy, attentive, caring women reversed the diseases that killed many more soldiers than battle.

In the 1960s, nurses and cardiologists came together to develop coronary care units. There, specially trained nurses could act quickly to save the lives of myocardial infarction patients without waiting for the arrival of a physician to order them to do what they already knew how and when to do. That innovation was the beginning of today's modern critical care units. The integration of critical care into the fabric and culture of hospitals today, to the point we cannot conceive of a modern hospital without a critical care unit, is the perfect representation of the successful organizational adoption of innovation.

It has been 45 years since Loretta Ford and Henry Silver developed the pediatric NP role at the University of Colorado (Brush & Capezuti, 1996). The issues associated with the rapid development of NP programs in the 1960s and 1970s have continued to foster the evolution of NP specialties and scope of practice. Those issues are access to affordable health care for children and adults, increased subspecialization of physician practice, decreased numbers of physicians, and, more recently, limitations on the number of continuous hours physicians in training can work. In order to fill the needs resulting from these changes, many activities once viewed as the exclusive purview of physicians have progressively become recognized as being within the scope of professional nursing. NPs are hardly new after 45 years of practice; however, the new arenas and developments in practice, health care, and society make NPs an innovation in many acute care settings.

The successful dissemination of these innovations did not happen by chance. Thought, planning, dedication, and even passion went into the hard work of this success. The successful integration of NPs into any organization is and will always be the result of planning and persistence. The planning requires a road map. Rogers's Diffusion of Innovation Model (Rogers, 2003) provides an excellent road map for the integration of NP practice in organizations.

The theoretical model for Diffusion of Innovation (DOI) began as a study of the adoption of hybrid corn species by farmers in Iowa in 1960 (Rogers, 1962). The concept of individual adopters relates to the characteristics of individuals who were quick to try new things (early adopters) versus those who waited longer to see what kinds of problems or successes the earlier adopters had before adopting the innovation themselves. In the 50 years since that study, thousands of studies have been completed using and refining the original model introduced by Everett Rogers (2003). The complexities of looking at individual adopters are dwarfed by the examination of the complexities of institutional or organizational adopters of innovation. Hospitals are examples of organizational adopters. Greenhalgh, Robert, Macfarlane, Bate, and Kyriakidou (2004) reviewed the science in diffusion of innovations applicable to service organizations such as hospitals. The review by Greenhalgh and colleagues and Rogers' evolution of thought presented in the latest edition of his seminal book form the foundation for the use of DOI in the planning and adoption of NPs as an innovation in hospital practice.

The purpose of this chapter is to introduce DOI and explain its concepts as they relate to the adoption of NP practice in hospitals and other organized health care systems. The concepts introduced here will be woven into the fabric of subsequent chapters in order to thread together the practical recommendations provided by content experts who have walked the roads of integrating NPs into the hospital setting. In addition, the Theory of Experiencing Transitions (TET) will be introduced to guide understanding of the challenges and resources that emerge in both organizational and individual transitions.

INNOVATION

What then is an innovation and what is it about NP practice, which is hardly new, that makes that practice innovative? An innovation is a product, technology, procedure, or idea perceived as new. The newness of the innovation is unrelated to the length of time it has been available. All innovation is change, but not all change is innovation. The adoption of any particular innovation is uncertain at best and is not as simple as a decision to implement a new way. Not all innovations are adopted, even if they offer advantages over current practice.

There are five characteristics of innovations that influence adoption. *Relative advantage* is the sense that the innovation is better than what is current practice. *Compatibility* refers to the degree to which the innovation is similar to current practice or consistent with the goals and culture of the organization. *Complexity* refers to the difficulty one might have in understanding, implementing, or incorporating the innovation. *Trialability* refers to the ability to "try it out," to implement the innovation in a stepwise manner, or to experiment with the use of the innovation. *Observability* is the ability to see the benefit or outcome of using the innovation.

DIFFUSION

Diffusion is the communication of the innovation over time throughout the social system. Some authors distinguish between the passive diffusion of the innovation and active dissemination of the innovation (Greenhalgh et al., 2004). Rogers does not make this distinction, but has acknowledged the evolution of thought about diffusion as more than the passive communication of ideas. Whether the diffusion of the innovation is active or passive, the newness of the innovation guarantees that there will be some risk or uncertainty in rejection or implementation. Rogers asserts that diffusion is social change and the result is a change in both the structure and function of the organization. The risk and uncertainty associated with the adoption of any innovation should not be taken lightly; however, respecting the lack of predictability of all aspects of the change improves the likelihood that the innovation will meet desired goals.

The bulk of the research in DOI and the majority of Rogers's books (2003) are related to individual adopters of innovation and to the traditional model of innovation Figure I.1 diffusion reflects this research. However, some aspects of organizational innovation depart from Rogers' original work (1962), which portrayed diffusion of innovation as a linear process.

DIFFUSION OF INNOVATION IN ORGANIZATIONS

Organizations are relatively stable systems of people who work toward common goals through a "hierarchy of ranks and a division of labor"

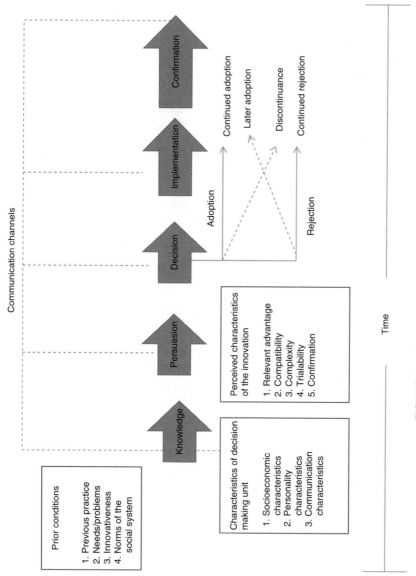

FIGURE I.1 Original duffusion of innovation model.

(Rogers, 2005, p404). An organization functions through rules, regulations, formal roles, and agreed-upon goals. Organizations are relatively stable, but, like living organisms, change on a continuous basis. Some of these changes are evolutionary and some are innovative. Hospitals are such organizations and, in addition to internal forces for change, there are external regulatory, financial, political, societal, and scientific forces that contribute to an internal and an external environment of change.

The innovation process for organizations is represented in Figure I.2 (Rogers, 2003). For organizations adopting an innovation, the implementation decisions may be more prominent than the decision to adopt the innovation. Several factors have been shown to have positive and negative effects on the implementation of organizational innovations. Strong individual leader characteristics have a positive effect on implementation. Internal organizational characteristics such as complexity of the organization, interconnectedness within the organization, organizational slack (flexibility of roles and resources), and size of the organization have all been positively associated with successful implementation. Centralization of decisions and formal or rule-oriented cultures are less successful in implementing innovative solutions to problems. System openness is a positive external characteristic for innovation success.

Prior conditions associated with individual decisions as well as the perceived characteristics of the innovation itself are still relevant for organizational innovation. Most of the DOI research on individual adopters looked at technology or procedure, neither of which was expected to change significantly over the adoption period. These innovations were also assumed to be consistent across individuals and context. These assumptions cannot be safely held in relation to the NP as innovation nor can they be assumed within organizations where culture may differ from division to division.

Planning can help to mitigate undesired changes and create an atmosphere or culture that is prepared to exploit positive unintended consequences while minimizing the effects of negative consequences.

IMPLEMENTATION OF NP PRACTICE AS AN ORGANIZATIONAL INNOVATION

For any model to be useful, it must first have the concepts operationalized so that the model makes sense within the context. See Figure I.3. There are basically three time-related concepts. These periods—Initiation, Decision, and Implementation—are presented as linear in the model and each has its tasks. In reality, they are nonlinear and different tasks may be revisited as the final stage of routinization or sustainability is reached.

6

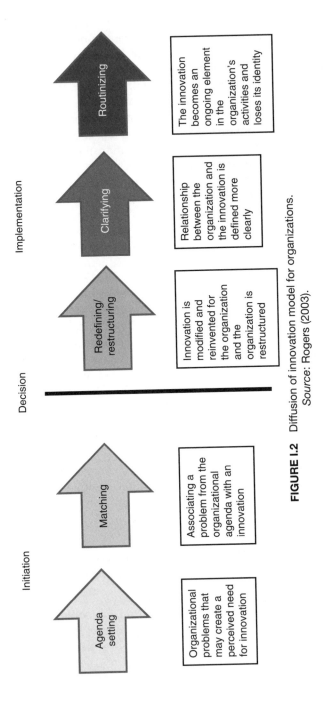

FIGURE I.2 Diffusion of innovation model for organizations.
Source: Rogers (2003).

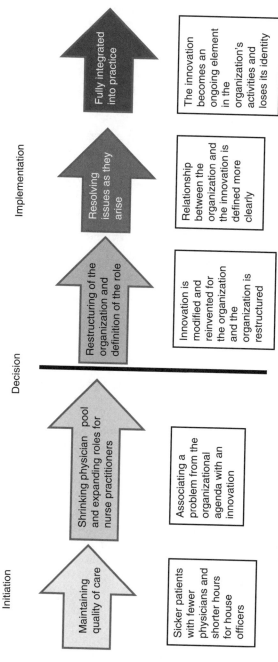

FIGURE I.3 Five stages of the innovation process for nurse practitioners in organizations.
Source: Rogers (2003).

Agenda Setting

For most organizations, the decision to integrate NPs into clinical practice has been the result of changes in medical practice. The most recent trends include fewer physicians, fewer physician specialists, and a mandated decrease in work hours for house officers. The latter relates predominantly to academic medical centers and hospitals that depend on residents and fellows for their around-the-clock care. These recent changes in work hours have created several issues as organizations strive to maintain an adequate quality and continuity of care.

Hospitals struggle with the financial bottom line, which affected by series of complex multifactorial issues. Timely discharge of patients from the hospital is critical to the financial stability of the organization since it makes beds available to new admissions and increases the likelihood that reimbursement will cover the expense of care. Hospital readmission is often not reimbursed at all. Unnecessary testing increases the cost of care in a climate of reduced reimbursement. This testing is often the result of poor communication between provider groups or at the time providers change services in teaching hospitals. Consequently, even if staffing of physicians is not an issue, the financial bottom line may be the agenda item that leads the organization to explore innovative ways to maintain or improve quality of care at a reduced cost.

Matching

Once the agenda setting is complete and the problem is clearly defined, the decision makers embark on a search for possible solutions to the problem. It is critical that the problem be clearly defined so that reasonable and accomplishable outcomes can be identified. Without these outcomes, the search for a solution—an innovation—will be inefficient and ultimately unsuccessful.

In the case of a shortage of physicians and a desire for a team-based approach to maintaining quality patient care, the match is intuitive. As with many things, however, assuming that everyone has the same intuition about team-based care and the practice of physicians and NPs will lead to a less than satisfactory solution. A critical part of the matching is determining whether the culture of practice in the institution is one that will foster collaboration or competition. If the prevailing climate is one in which physicians may see NPs as competition, there is no match even if the innovation makes sense from a purely objective view. Realistic and frank discussions must occur at this stage in the process before any innovation is selected. The expense and investment in NP practice in an organization is not to be taken lightly, and identifying and addressing potential negative consequences up front will increase the likelihood that the integration will be successful in meeting the organizational goals.

In determining the adequacy of the match, the prior conditions as well as the perceived characteristics of the innovation that are described in Figure I.1 continue to hold true for organizational decisions about the adoption of an innovation. Prior conditions include previous practice, both the way medical practice is delivered, governed, and reimbursed, and the relationship of medical practice with any previous NP practice. An unsuccessful attempt to integrate NPs into hospital practice will make a future new decision more difficult to implement. The degree of respect and collaboration between physicians and staff nurses or NPs is a powerful influence on the success of a decision to fully implement NP practice in an organization. Organizations such as hospitals are social systems with their own social norms, and any decision to implement an innovation must consider the social order within the organization as it is and not as the decision makers wish it to be. An honest assessment of the social environment prior to the decision to implement NP practice will enable the decision makers to avoid a number of pitfalls and will improve the likelihood of success.

The personal characteristics of the decision-making body, individually and collectively, are significant factors in the success of the matching and of the ultimate success of the innovation in achieving organizational goals. Of the three characteristics listed, personality and communication characteristics have the most impact on the decision to implement NP practice in the organization as a strategy to alleviate the physician shortage and maintain quality care. The personalities of the decision makers contribute to cooperation and power sharing within the group and powerfully affect their consideration of unexpected consequences of the innovation. Communication within the decision-making group and between that group and the organization members affected by their decision to implement NP practice is critical to success. If the group or the organization has a history of control of information and a top-down, hierarchical communication style, the innovation is unlikely to be well accepted and therefore is unlikely to succeed (Rogers, 2003).

The perceived characteristics of the innovation are critical to both the decision to implement NP practice as well as the strategy for implementation. It seems intuitive that there should be a perceived relevant advantage to NP practice. The relevant advantage of NP practice must relate specifically to the goals and outcomes specified in the agenda. NPs must realistically be able to achieve the goals in a cost-effective way within the organization. Their ability to accomplish these tasks in other organizations reported in the literature is important, but the decision-making body must be convinced that those same outcomes are not just possible, but probable within their own organization as a fundamental step in the matching process.

Once the decision makers establish that the implementation of NP practice in the organization is a match for their goals they must decide whether NP practice is compatible with the culture and social environment of the organization. This is not a simple task and should involve stakeholders and champions as well as careful planning for when and where implementation has the best chance of success within the organization. Timing is critical here as well. Compatibility decisions are often made on the basis of familiarity rather than careful analysis. Moreover, there may be a misconception that everyone defines NP practice the same way and has the same vision. Discussions at this point about definitions and expectations can preempt a number of often expensive problems down the line.

The complexity of the innovation has a direct effect on the success of its implementation (Rogers, 2003). Large, complex organizations are capable of absorbing innovation, even complex innovation. NP practice is quite complex and is regulated by the state practice act, organizational bylaws and organizational culture. Furthermore, no two NPs are alike—each comes with his or her individual clinical experience and education. The individual characteristics of the NP are not separate from the collective in terms of importance and likelihood of success. While each individual NP must demonstrate ethical, knowledgeable, professional practice, there must be a collective identity that demonstrates the same qualities. It is the development of a community of NPs that provides the mentoring, socialization, support, and encouragement that elevates the practice of all. The community is more than and different from a group of people who happen to practice in the same organization. It is the mutuality of the individual and the community or "collective" NP identity that ties the success of the individual to the community and the success of the community to each individual member. Furthermore, the success of the individual/community identity of the NPs is interdependent with the success of the organization in achieving the purpose for which it adopted the NP innovation. This mutuality compounds the complexity of the innovation. The combination of individual, collective, and organizational capacity for variability make this a very complex innovation, and utilizing the full capacity of the NP is not always an easy task. This requires knowing the scope of NP practice as well as knowing the individual hired to meet the needs of the unit/organization.

Unfortunately, in an attempt to simplify the complexity, decision makers may use analogy or establish practice based on previously known roles. For example, if they have worked with nurses or house officers—what health care professional has not?—they may translate their experiences and understanding of that relationship to the relationship with NPs. This underestimates the contribution NPs are prepared to make within their scope of practice, limits their productivity, and can lead to significant dissatisfaction with the innovation. Ultimately this may result in failure for both the institution and the NP if the situation is not remedied.

Any organizational innovation potentially involves large investments of human and financial capital. The matching stage is critical to the stewardship of that capital. When the innovation requires the addition of a whole new category of providers, which includes recruitment, orientation, development and governance, the decision makers have a duty to engage in the difficult discussions. These difficult discussions involve clear definitions of the role and how it will be implemented in a way that both achieves organizational goals and nourishes the NP. The failure to achieve organizational goals or to provide a work environment that promotes stability and successful NP practice can usually be traced back to failure in this matching stage. The best innovation will fail if implementation and adaptation of that innovation to one's own organization is not adequately planned. Even with excellent planning, a period of trialability will allow the organization to further redefine and restructure the innovation to best succeed in the organization.

Redefining/Restructuring

Rogers details the evolution of thinking about innovation from the studies of individual adopters of innovation in which the innovation does not change with its adoption, to complex, variable, adaptable innovations that are remodeled and reinvented to fit the goals of an organization. (Rogers, 2003). Organizations such as hospitals are systems of organizations within organizations, and a one-size-fits-all approach is shortsighted and suggests a misunderstanding of the complexity of organizations. Considering these complexities is important as one envisions how the organization will respond to any change, especially the addition of a new group of personnel. The honest assessment of the organizational culture and expectations that went into the matching process provides some guidance for how the innovation—NP practice—should be designed within the organization, as well as where to begin and what kind of education and preparation needs to be completed prior to the implementation if it is to be successful. A careful examination of the project management process that goes into the implementation of a new computer system for the entire organization is a good way to envision the scope of the work necessary to implement NP practice within an organization. No one would consider implementing and electronic health record throughout a hospital by just installing it and letting people figure it out by trial and error. Yet, this is often the level of planning for implementation of human innovations such as NP practice.

Planning takes advantage of another characteristic of innovation, *trialability*. Selecting one or more venues to "try out" the planned practice can provide valuable information about how the practice will work in the organization and can explore the cultural and social changes that occur within the organization and identify some of the unintended consequences that always attend innovation. It may also become obvious that one definition or practice guideline that works well in one area does not work at all in another. These trials clarify the advantages and challenges that can be addressed in a timely and productive way.

Clarifying

Clarifying is that stage where the innovation is fine-tuned to the organization. During and after the trial and initial implementation, responses to and consequences of the change will become obvious. It is not humanly possible or financially feasible to try to predict every consequence of an innovation decision. In the Redefining and Restructuring stage, the decision team has tried to foresee any obstacles or barriers to success and address them in the initial project plan. Contingency plans are just good business, but given the complexity of the innovation and the organization, issues will arise that were not predicted. Plans made ahead of time may not be effective in achieving the goals originally set and thus require clarifying. Clarification is the time for working out those problems before full implementation and routinization.

Routinizing

The notion of sustainability of the innovation is a concept that only recently appears in Rogers' writings (Rogers, 2003). Routinization is the full integration of the innovation into the culture and social fabric of the organization. In some organizations this never occurs, and the innovation is eventually rejected as unworkable or it changes to something less than the original plan because there were too many barriers to successful implementation. Still others adopt the change permanently. Even after the innovation becomes part of the fabric of the organization, it must be nurtured, guided, and generally attended to in order to grow and be productive in achieving the goals of the organization. Evaluation is ongoing to be sure that innovation continues to meet the goals of the organization even if the goals have changed.

Organizations are much like living organisms in that there is little in the way of a steady state. Organizations and the individuals within the organization must respond to the constant change in the environment from trends in technology, political and economic forces, and even globalization of life. Hospitals in particular are subject to many forces outside the organization that influence the survival of the organization and the professionals and patients who make up the human side of the organization's purpose in being. The ongoing role of decision makers in organizations such as hospitals is to keep vigilant for new problems and trends that initiate the Diffusion of Innovation cycle. The cycle begins with agenda setting. The infinite potential for complexity, organization, and change guarantees that agendas will continue to be set that require innovation in thinking and acting. It has been said "Change is the only constant;" for the living organism that is a hospital, that is very true. That change is both evolutionary and revolutionary; over time, the organization transitions to something new. Transition is more than change. It is change that creates a profound difference, sometimes only recognized in retrospect. Transition occurs in both the organization and in the individuals who make up the organization.

TRANSITIONS

Transitions may be deliberate or forced upon us by forces outside our control. Transition involves a new path, a new vision, a new story. For early adopters of an innovation, transition may be more reflective of Frost's "road less travelled" as they often must use trial and error as they find their way. As pioneers, they map the wilderness of the change so that others can follow more assuredly and safely. Just as the Diffusion of Innovation Model helps with the safe passage of decision making and Integration of NPs into the organization, a model that reflects the predictable and unpredictable aspects of personal and organizational transitions will facilitate the success of those transitions. The Theory of Experiencing Transitions (TET) is such a model (Meleis, Sawyer, Im, Hilfinger Messias, & Schumacher, 2000).

THE THEORY OF EXPERIENCING TRANSITIONS

Nature of Transitions

The TET (Figure I.4) describes types, patterns, and properties of transitions. Types of transitions include developmental, situational, health/illness, and organizationalones. Developmental transitions are those somewhat predictable transitions that occur as one grows and develops, in the case of NPs, professionally, personally, and socially as they mature as individuals. Situational transitions are those predictable and unpredictable transitions as NPs become part of the organization and as they move from being new to the organization to organizational veteran. Organizational transitions occur at the individual, group, and organizational levels. Organizational transitions involve the movement of the organization from the identification of the agenda item to the full integration of the innovation, in this case the NP. This organizational transition is a mutual, symbiotic process that involves the adaptation, success, evaluation, and growth of both the NP and the organization, and one cannot successfully transition without the success of the other.

Meleis and colleagues (2000) also describe six patterns of transition. Transitions may occur as single, multiple, sequential, simultaneous, related, and unrelated events. Both the NP and the organization will experience multiple, sequential, simultaneous, related and unrelated patterns of transition. It would be rare to have only a single transition occurring at any time.

14

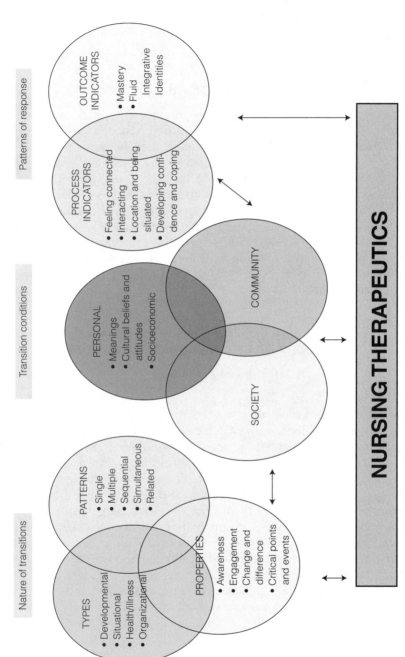

FIGURE I.4 Reconceptualization of the theory of experiencing transitions.

The properties of transitions distinguish transitions from simple changes. First, there must be an awareness of the transition. Transition results in a change in the essence of the person or organization. Transition often begins before there is awareness, so awareness is not necessary for the transition to begin. However, for successful resolution of the transition, awareness of the process and the difference is critical. Another property that helps to distinguish transition from change is engagement. Transition is an active rather than a passive process. Change occurs without the requirement for active participation by the person affected by the change, but transition in response to the change requires the engagement of the person or organization in the transition. The fifth property of transitions is that of critical points and events. Not all transitions have clearly identifiable critical points and events; however, many times they are obvious more in retrospect than real time.

Transition Conditions: Facilitators and Inhibitors

A host of personal, community, and societal transition conditions contribute to the success of the transition. Personal factors such as the meaning or purpose the individual attaches to not only the transition but also the situation itself have great impact. The individual's cultural beliefs and attitudes—those personal ones gleaned from the life experiences of that individual in addition to those of the nursing education process and matched with the culture of the organization—may determine the success of the NP and that of the organization. The individual's socioeconomic status and the knowledge and experience that individual brings to the organization heavily influence both the person's decision to stay or go and the success of the integration within the organization.

A community is a group of people who have common goals and similar beliefs who come together for a common purpose. Communities and the larger society that we live and work in are defined by and define the members. NPs may draw strength from their perception of membership in a community of NPs—strength in numbers—or support from more experienced NPs within the community. The same NPs may feel gratified by the opportunity to give back to that same community. With each individual transition, the essence of the community evolves and develops as well. Support or disapproval from those communities and society are strong influences on both NPs and organizations as they work toward successful transitions that mark the successful integration of NP practice into the organization.

Patterns of Response

The TET describes both process and outcome indicators that reflect the success of the transition. Process indicators include a sense of feeling connected. Connections develop among individuals, community, and society.

That feeling of connectedness is the foundation for interacting and a sense of being in the right place at the right time—belonging. The sense of belonging is the pattern referred to as location and being situated. A natural reflection of these patterns is the pattern developing confidence and coping.

Feeling connected, interacting, location, and being situated represent a complex destination for the transitioning NP. Perhaps this destination is best understood in contrast to that first day of work, whether the person is a new NP or a seasoned NP in a new organization. The anxiety of not knowing where things are or who to call, and not knowing organizational politics can be overwhelming. Questions of "What have I done? Can I do this job?" plague the new NP. Then one day, that NP realizes, "I do know where things are, who to call, and I know that I am exactly where I am supposed to be and doing my job well." Over some individually determined period of time, that NP has made this transition, one of many recognized only in retrospect. Upon looking back, the pattern of events that led to this confidence in one's abilities and in one's colleagues is clear, as are the coping mechanisms that have developed along the way.

Outcome indicators are *mastery* or competence and fluid integrative identity. As the NP examines an individual transition trajectory, there are identifiable tasks and challenges that have been mastered. The TET designates fluid integrative identity as that level of mastery where competency is "second nature," that is, so much a part of who the NP is that there is no question of one's ability. The ultimate outcome then is seamless integration of the role, changes in the story of who the individual is, and the sense of competence that defines successful transition.

Nursing Therapeutics

The fundamental assumption of the TET is that interventions to enhance facilitators and minimize the barriers to successful transition are possible. The model is not explicit about what those interventions are, but the model does offer suggestions about how those strategies can be identified and implemented. Although the model is not explicit about the strategies that facilitate the successful transition of NPs in practice, the purpose and content of many of the chapters in this book are precisely that. Recruitment, orientation, mentoring, coaching, develoment, governing, credentialing and much more make up the interventions that determine the success or failure of transition.

NP TRANSITIONS

Regardless of the number of years a NP has practiced, there are still developmental changes. Arguably, the NP never stops growing and developing. Whether this development is actually part of a transition or just individual growth is less clear. There are clear transitions, however, described in the literature. The transition from novice to expert NP and the transition from new hire to full integration within the organization are two transitions that are common to all NPs who work within organizations. From the perspective of TET, the transition from novice to expert is a developmental transition and the transition to full integration in the organization is a situational transition. Along the path of any professional transition are personal developmental, situational, health/illness, and organizational transitions. A new NP may be engaged in the novice to expert transition as a clinician while progressing through the situational transition of a new organization. The situational transition may be a new role—for instance, NP in the same organizations where the NP was a staff nurse. Even seasoned NPs may experience the organizational transition of a new role as a lead NP or administrator or educator that changes the NP's practice significantly enough that the NP no longer views himself or herself as only a care provider.

One of the most difficult situational transitions for new NPs is the transition from expert staff nurse to novice NP. To experience the professional validation of being the person everyone looks to for the answers to their questions and help with difficult situations as staff nurse; and then to have to prove oneself all over again can be overwhelming. In many ways, this is not so much a transition as a new beginning.

It is obvious from the types of transitions described above that any one NP may be experiencing multiple sequential, simultaneous related and unrelated transitions all at the same time. Feeling overwhelmed may be the catalyst to awareness of the transitions that the NP is experiencing. Awareness can be heightened and facilitated by a mentor or other interested person whom the NP respects. Once the NP is aware of the transitions, he or she can make choices about the priority of engagement in each. The mentor can help the NP explore true transition and differentiate it from change and can help to set goals that optimize the transition time. Professional development that includes an individualized orientation and preceptorship can facilitate the developmental transition and improve the efficiency of the situational transition within the organization. Setting intermediate goals can help the NP consciously benchmark critical points and events in the transition.

Personal, community, and societal factors facilitate or inhibit the successful transition for each individual NP. The individual NP attaches meaning to everything in his or her life, including the transitions in the role, transitions in personal life, and each event that transpires over the course of the NP's life. These meanings are the attachment of purpose to the roles and events that make up the NP's personal and professional trajectory. The NP who sees the role as an escape from the perceived oppression and lack of autonomy of the staff nurse role will view the transition, the organization, and the role differently than the NP who sees the role as the next step in his or her professional nursing development. The NP's cultural influences as well as the culture of the organization influence the success of the NP within the organization. The NP who attaches an emancipatory meaning to the NP role, but chooses to work in an organization where the culture is one that marginalizes NPs to very dependent roles, will be faced with a paradox that causes tremendous dissonance. If that dissonance is not resolved positively, the NP will likely leave or become disruptive.

Dissonance can be an especially significant factor for new NPs, who may feel after graduation that they are not adequately prepared and knowledgeable enough to assume the role for which they have been hired. This "imposter syndrome" can lead to the failure of the NP to successfully transition into a seasoned, integrated member of the organization if it is not addressed early. Again, the presence of a mentor can help new NPs adjust expectations and explore the meanings that they have brought to the transition in a way that facilitates the success of the NPs. Being part of a community of NPs within the organization or within a professional organization can mitigate some of the dissonance that naturally accompanies unmet expectations. And even more important, having a forum to discuss all of the changes through the transition period with peers who are experiencing a similar phase of transition is an additional support. The larger society has a less direct impact on the successful transition of the individual NP, but it is not insignificant. Society's expectations of NPs, nurse/physician relationships and the role of health care in people's lives all influence the success of the NP, but it may be more obvious in relation to NPs as a group than it is for any one NP.

Process indicators of a successful transition include a feeling of being connected and interacting with other NPs as well as other care providers. The NPs' sense of developing confidence in the role and in the organization as well as the development of strategies for dealing with new situations are important indicators of the progress of the transition process. Ultimately, a sense of being in the right place to be successful (location and being situated) develops. These are internal benchmarks for the transitioning NP. The community, the mentor, and other members of the team of providers the NP works with are important in increasing the awareness of the NP that he or she is moving along the continuum from new to seasoned, novice to expert, and new employee to fully integrated member of the organization. The sense of being a part of the organization, and of the NP community and the provider team, and a sense of mastery of the requirements of the role are key outcomes of the successful transition. A sense of mastery and belonging do not imply that learning and growing in the role are done. The transition is one of accomplishment and is the completion of a portion of a lifelong journey.

ORGANIZATIONAL TRANSITION

The transition of the organization is inevitable with the adoption of an innovation (Rogers, 2003). Like the transitions of individual NPs, the organization may experience multiple simultaneous and unrelated transitions while integrating the innovation of NP practice. It is critical when the decision is made to adopt the innovation that the organizational decision makers are aware that the organization will transition into something new and that they prepare for the concept of a new and improved system of care. An institution that is prepared and welcoming to the concept of change will have more chance for success. The recognition must lead to engagement in the process, both for the successful transition of the organization and for the successful transition of the NPs who will practice there. The successful transition of each is dependent on the successful transition of the other. Part of the trial that occurs in the redefining/restructuring and clarifying stages in the DOI is the development of strategies and tactics that will promote the success of the innovation and the mutual transitions of the organization and the individual NPs.

The TET can provide some guidance as the organization develops these strategies and tactics. As part of the agenda setting and matching process of the DOI, the ideal process would include a careful examination and clarification of the meanings for the organization that NPs and their practice represent. It is easy to assume that everyone in the organization has the same agenda and beliefs about NP practice, but it would be naive to make this assumption. The culture of the organization and the attitudes of the stakeholders can facilitate or sabotage the success of any innovation, and the polarization that can develop around NP practice requires careful consideration and attention in order to make the successful transition. Socioeconomic factors often drive decisions within large organizations such as hospitals, and the adoption of NP practice as an economic decision without attention to the social and cultural aspects can doom the process before it starts. Many of the advantages can be enhanced and the barriers mitigated by adequate preparation and knowledge. First, the organization must know itself. The matching process described earlier emphasizes the organizational assessment and a candid evaluation of the culture and the attitudes of stakeholders, mainly physicians, nurses, and administrators related to NP practice. If that information is ignored or dismissed, then the successful transition to NP practice will be more difficult than necessary and may not be successful at all. However, careful examination of this assessment information can be incorporated into the strategic plan, and tactics such as education, orientation, trialability, and refining of the plan can address problems before they threaten the success of the overall innovation.

It is in the organization's best interest to promote community within the organization, planning ahead for the developmental transition needs of the NPs as a group and as individuals. For the individual NP, the community that is formed among NPs, as well as the larger team of care providers, facilitates the transition of the NP who is new to practice or to the organization. The conscious engagement with an existing community such as an Advanced Practice Nurse (APN) network, or the development of a community as a new entity such as a peer support group, can facilitate the developmental transition through mentorship and support. For the organization, conversations and the development of a community of organizations that are integrating NP practice provide the same support. The acceptance of NP practice by the larger society as a whole is important. The acknowledgment of goals and missions of patients as well the acknowledgment of as other disciplines, medicine in particular, is extremely influential in the realization of the full scope of practice for NPs and for the mutual success of the organizations that have decided to integrate NP practice. Community is important for the organization as well. Problem solving and sharing of information about successes and failures among organizations that have adopted NP practice improves the likelihood of success for all involved. In addressing societal issues around NP practice, the organization has an obligation to the customers of the organization—patients, families, communities—to educate and inform the public about the nature and quality of NP practice. The influence of these organizations on public policy and on reimbursement can promote the success of NP practice as well.

The measurement of the success of the organization's transition depends a great deal on the clarity and measurability of the organizational goals set out at the beginning of the process. The goals of adopting NP practice as an innovative approach to maintaining the quality of care provided by the organization are the clear, measureable outcomes that are critical to both the clarifying stage and ultimately to the routinizing or sustainability of the innovation. The ultimate goal of the DOI of a sustainable innovation is consistent with the outcome indicators of the TET. Mastery of the innovation and the fluid integration of NP practice reflect a new organizational culture that now includes NP practice, not as a trial or as a temporary solution, but a fundamental, identifiable characteristic of the organization.

Figure I.5 summarizes the relationships between Diffusion of Innovation and the Theory of Experiencing Transitions. This discussion is meant to be a road map reflecting multiple paths to the same end, namely successful integration of NP practice in organizations such as hospitals. The remainder of the chapters in this book will elaborate on these processes and explore in more detail the challenges and rewards of the integration of NP practice. Four very important themes have come up in this discussion, and will be explored in more detail.

- The decision to implement NP practice in an organization is a huge and expensive undertaking and must be planned in detail after much candid, frank discussion.

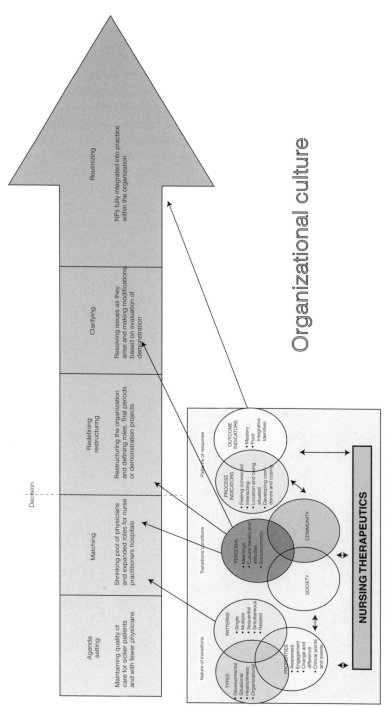

FIGURE I.5 Combined diffusion of innovation and theory of experiencing transitions in organizations.

- NP practice, like any successful innovation, must be adapted, tested, and refined to the needs, goals, culture, and resources of each organization.
- Each NP progresses at an individual pace through multiple transitions and benefits from and provides benefit to a community of NPs.
- The success of NP practice and the success of the organization are interdependent and mutual. One cannot succeed without the other, and the measure of that success is the sustainable integration of NP practice into the culture of the organization.

REFERENCES

Brush, B. L., & Capezuti, E. A. (1996). Revisiting "a nurse for all settings": The nurse practitioner movement, 1965–1995. *Journal of the American Academy of nurse practitioners, 8*(1), 5–11.

Greenhalgh, T., Robert, G., Macfarlane, F., Bate, P., & Kyriakidou, O. (2004). Diffusion of innovations in service organizations: Systematic review and recommendations. *Milbank Quarterly, 82*(4), 581–629.

Meleis, A. I., Sawyer, L. M., Im, E., Hilfinger Messias, D. K., & Schumacher, K. (2000). Experiencing transitions: An emerging middle-range theory. *Advances in Nursing Science, 23*(1), 12–28.

Rogers, E. M. (1962). *Diffusion of innovation*. New York, NY: Free Press.

Rogers, E. M. (2003). *Diffusion of innovation* (5th ed.). New York, NY: Free Press.

1

Forces Affecting Nurse Practitioners in Hospital-Based Practice

Kay Blum and Elizabeth Fuselier Ellis

We live in a complex world where shifting and often conflicting forces affect our lives. These forces weave their way into the tapestry of our personal and professional lives individually, collectively, and organizationally. We may welcome them, push back against them, or react passionately or powerlessly against the effects of these forces, but we cannot ignore them.

This chapter will discuss many of the significant forces influencing the practice of nurse practitioners (NPs) in a hospital setting. Many of these issues can be generalized to other settings, but for the purpose of this chapter, will remain focused on hospital-based practice. While some attempts to explain these relationships have reduced them to simplicities that trivialize their significance, they must be understood in dynamic relationship to be fully meaningful.

Adler, Kwon, and Heckscher (2008) describe a model of three forces that affect professional work. The three forces they describe are market forces, hierarchical (regulatory) forces, and community forces. These forces are not mutually exclusive and change in relation to each other, affecting professional work over time (Figure 1.1). This chapter will use Adler's model to describe how these forces and their contributing issues affect NPs and hospitals. The interrelationship between these forces helps explain both difficulties and successes in implementation of the role in complex organizations.

MARKET FORCES

It is easy to think of market forces such as the economic and financial forces associated with reimbursement, health care services, or cost of care. There are also political, sociological, demographic, ethical, legal, geographical, and meteorological forces that can affect health care markets. These forces may have a direct, acute effect on health care markets as happened with Hurricane Katrina, or may have a more prolonged, chronic effect, as happens with the aging of the population.

Critical Forces

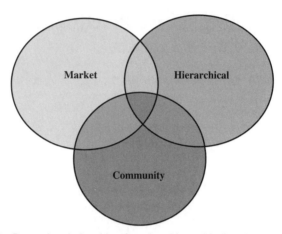

FIGURE 1.1   Dynamic relationship of market, hierarchical and community forces.

Market forces are basically defined by the tension between the demand for resources and the availability of resources to meet that demand. The availability of resources is defined by both the quantity and quality of those resources. In health care, the demand for those resources may arise from not only the real need defined by health care problems but also by sociological demands, ethical demands, and cultural demands of how health is defined. The availability of health care providers in terms of the individuals who are available to provide that care and their educational preparation as well as the equipment, pharmaceuticals, and facilities, independent of the quality of those resources, determine much of the care that is provided. In the past, the quantity of resources, number of facilities, number of providers, and the availability of technology services and pharmaceuticals were based on fee-for-service calculations and were the metric of choice in determining adequacy of resources. This has resulted in huge increases health care services costs and has led to discussions about changes in how we purchases and pay for health care in the United States. Those discussions have led to changes in the way the largest purchasers of health care services in the United States, Medicare and Medicaid, will pay for those services in the future. In the past Medicare and Medicaid have led the way for third-party payers, therefore everyone is paying close attention to the results of new strategies for identifying quality and value in health care and how that is reported.

Although there are an infinite number of forces that are acting together to affect current health care market services there are a few major influences that are affecting the market long term. These forces include the aging of the population, including health care provider

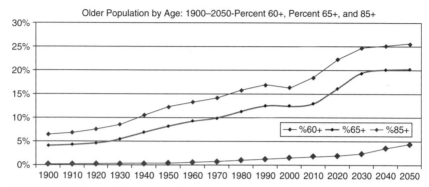

FIGURE 1.2   Aging of the population.
Source: Administration on Aging, http://www.aoa.gov/AoARoot/Aging_Statistics/future_growth/future_growth.aspx

shortages, changes in the way we deliver and pay for health care; the Affordable Care Act the current methods of reimbursement for physicians, NPs, and other providers of care; and the global recession. These key forces will be discussed in greater detail.

Workforce

Aging Population

Much has been written about the aging of the population in the United States. The US Department of Health and Human Services Administration on Aging projects that by 2020, 25% of the population will be 60 years of age or older; 17% of the population will be 65 or older; and approximately 3% of the population will be 85 years of age or older (Figure 1.2). The aging of the population is significant for a number of reasons. With aging of the population come a greater number of patients with chronic disease, as well as increases in other age-related acute problems such as heart disease, cancer, and stroke. These patients at advanced age use more resources, both as outpatients and inpatients; require more pharmaceuticals; require more procedures; and have more hospitalizations than younger persons.

Aging Workforce

Not only is the population in general aging, but also so are the providers of care for these persons who are aging. It is reported that the average age of the practicing nurse is 43 years old (Fleming et al., 2003). The average age of practicing physicians has not been reported. However, Young, Choudhry, Rhyne, and Dugan (2011) report statistics on currently practicing physicians and noted that one-fourth of all physicians practicing now are 60 years old or older and half of all physicians are 50 years old or older.

Decreasing Numbers of Providers

Aging of the workforce is one factor that has been reported for the decreased number of providers of primary care. Aging has also been suggested as a cause of the inadequate numbers of nurses available for bedside care. In addition to aging, poor working conditions, lack of time for family and nonwork pursuits, work stress, poor sense of fulfillment, and decreasing relative earnings have all contributed to decreasing numbers of persons entering the workforce.

For NPs, the issues are likely somewhat different from those for bedside nurses. Salaries increased 5.9% from 2004 to 2009 (American Academy of Nurse Practitioners, 2011). Since nurse practitioners need at least a master's degree, the shortage of faculty to teach at the graduate level remains a limiting factor for NPs. The shortage of faculty is the result of two major factors, inadequate numbers of NPs with doctoral degrees who are eligible for graduate faculty appointments, and faculty salaries that are significantly lower than those for practicing NPs. For both physicians and NPs, the length of time for study limits the numbers of practitioners that can be produced to address the shortages.

Changes in Education Programs

Doctor of Nursing Practice. The American Association of Colleges of Nursing (AACN; 2004) has taken the position that the entry level for NPs should be the Doctor of Nursing Practice (DNP) by 2015. This position is not without controversy (Chase & Pruitt, 2006). Statistics published by the American Association of Colleges of Nursing (2011) indicate that there are currently 153 programs that had enrolled students in their DNP program with 160 programs in the planning stages. As of 2011, 37 states and the District of Columbia have programs and eight states have more than five programs currently enrolling students. There is great controversy and concern about the requirements for the Doctor of Nursing Practice as entry level into practice for NPs by the projected date of 2015. Concerns that have been voiced including the limited number of faculty to teach in these programs; the longer period of education that is necessary to graduate with a doctorate; the concerns that there will be fewer positions willing to pay salaries for nurses with doctoral degrees, and that the graduates will be overeducated for the positions that are available. There are also territorial concerns from our medical colleagues. The major concern that has been voiced by some physicians is that role confusion on the part of patients is occurring as the patient may not understand the difference between a nurse who calls herself doctor and a physician who is a medical doctor. There are also unfounded concerns by NPs that they will be forced to return to school for a DNP in order to continue to practice. Concerns have been voiced by a number of nurses and nursing faculty as well about diluting the educational value of the doctoral degree in nursing by yet another degree, referencing the past in nursing where there were multiple research doctorates—the DNS, the DSN, the PhD, and the DNSc— which led to confusion. Another concern is that the degree will not be rigorous enough to be a legitimate entry into the doctoral world and will detract from the gains that nurses have made in the world of academic legitimacy. The conversation is ongoing, but the American Association of Colleges of Nursing, through their regulatory arm, the Commission for Collegiate Nursing Education, the CCNE, has developed clear criteria for the accreditation of Doctor of Nursing Practice programs.

Changes in Medical Education. There are currently a number of controversies in medical education as well. In 2009, Medicare invested $9.5 billion in graduate medical education. Medicare is the largest single payer for graduate medical education for physicians. The Medicare Payment Advisory Commission (MedPAC) recently conducted a review of graduate medical education and of the graduate medical education system to evaluate how well clinicians are being trained in the use of cutting-edge technology and the provision of quality health care to severely ill or injured patients. There was some concern that current methods of education were not maximizing the provision of skills for the use of evidence-based practice and quality measurement, cost awareness, and care coordination as well as the leadership of interdisciplinary teams to ensure shared decision making (Hackbarth & Boccuti, 2011).

At the request of MedPAC, the RAND Corporation surveyed 25/381 eligible internal medicine program directors to review their curriculum and their methods of preparing internal medicine physicians (Kane, Diemer, & Feldman, 2011). The survey identified problems with three Accreditation Council for Graduate Medical Education (ACGME) core competencies.

Those three core competencies are:

- Practice-based learning and improvement, to include evidence-based medicine, quality improvement methods, and using clinical decision aids.
- Systems-based practice, specifically across provider handoffs in the hospital and other settings, and communicating and coordinating discharge.
- Interpersonal and communication skills—communicating with other providers and communicating with patients; communicating with special populations; and communicating about End-of-Life issues.

Although these are not all of the issues that were raised in the RAND report, these are the specific issues that are of interest for hospital-based NPs. Methods used to teach nurses and physicians for centuries, primarily Socratic and didactic methods and apprenticeship methods that have served well when the amount of information that needed to be distributed was limited, are no longer the most advantageous in today's explosion of information that needs to be disseminated, integrated, and used on a daily basis. This approach is no longer ideal when attempting to educate clinicians about the highly technical modalities of our current health care environment.

For nurses, physicians, and all other members of this team, poor inter-disciplinary communication, poor communication between inpatient and outpatient providers, poor communication during handoff between provi-ders at different times within the same institution, poor communication with patients and their caregivers decrease quality and safety for patients and even for providers. The safety and quality concerns decrease the value of the health care that is provided and increase the cost not only to patients, to insurers, and to other payers, but to each of us as taxpayers through government-sponsored programs such as Medicare and Medicaid. Consequently, there is a close relationship between regulators, the regu-lations and laws that they pass to try to control costs, safety, and work-force issues that have just been discussed.

The Global Economy

The private National Bureau of Economic Research announced that the United States, economic recession began in December 2008 and ended in June of 2009. It ended, not with a return to economic health, but with an end to the economic slide (*New York Times*, 2010). In examining the recovery from that low point in June of 2009, the Federal Reserve Bank in St. Louis (2011) published graphs of four leading economic indicators: industrial production, retail sales, employment, and real income.

Over 30 months following the reported end of the recession in June of 2009, there were gradual increases in both industrial production and retail sales. In spite of this improvement in sales and production, real income stayed completely flat for 10 months longer. It was 21 months before any improvement in employment began to emerge.

The recession, the subsequent unemployment, and lack of real income growth affected the health care market in a number of ways. Of real signifi-cance is the fact that much of private health insurance is offered through employers. When people are unemployed, their ability to afford health care is very limited and they often put off treatment for real and acute health care problems and certainly for preventive care. This leads to more expensive care for problems that have become more difficult and more expensive to treat, which could have been treated earlier for less cost, or prevented altogether. It also means that more expensive emergency room care must be provided when less-expensive primary care may have been provided if the person had insurance or had the money to pay for the care then. It may also mean that people are unable to afford medications to treat chronic problems that now have become poorly controlled because medications were unavailable to maintain a steady state.

Increased unemployment, increases in poverty, and decreases in real income lead to poor nutrition and poor sanitation, resulting in decreased resistance to disease and a greater burden on the health care system. Unemployment and the inability to care for one's family and provide for one's children may also be associated with higher incidence of depression, alcoholism, drug abuse, trauma, domestic violence, and suicide. All are factors that increase the cost of care for everyone.

Health Care Costs

The Centers for Medicare and Medicaid Services (CMS) projected that 2009 National Health Expenditures (NHE) would grow by 5.7%, reaching $2.5 trillion even though the economy was still in recession (2012a). Martin Lassman, Washington, and Catlin (2012) report that U.S. health care spending did, in fact, reach $2.5 trillion in 2009, and $2.6 trillion or $8,402 per person in 2010. While this is still a mind-numbing figure, rates grew more slowly in these 2 years than in any other of the 51 for which records have been kept. Private health insurance spending for in-hospital care declined while Medicare and Medicaid spending on inpatient care increased 28% and 19%, respectively (Martin et al., 2012).

Private insurance pays for 46% of provider and clinical services with Medicare accounting for 22%. Out-of pocket expenses increased about 10% in 2010. Last-minute action by a divided Congress prevented a 27% decrease in Medicare payment rates for physicians and therefore for NPs due to the Sustainable Growth Rate (SGR) provisions (Centers for Medicare and Medicaid Services, 2009). The SGR is designed to control health care costs, but it cuts indiscriminately, satisfying no one, provider or legislator. Attempts to change the law have been unsuccessful and legislative "Band-Aids" have been used to mitigate its effects.

The Patient Protection and Affordable Care Act

Throughout history and in all cultures, there have been segments of society that have been less able to care for themselves because of illness, disability, poverty, social status, or perhaps just bad luck. Those societies, through philanthropy or legislation, cared for this segment of the population through almshouses, debtors' prisons, veterans' benefits, or old age pensions. Many modern societies, most notably Canada and Europe, provide a nationalized, one-payer health insurance for their citizens, guaranteeing a minimum level of care for all citizens.

Even in colonial times, the ruggedly individual American colonists provided for those less fortunate (Social Security Administration, 2011). This assistance often came at a price for the recipients in the form of wearing a letter "P," much like the adulterer's scarlet letter. The shamefulness of poverty persists into the 20th and 21st centuries, with stories of "welfare queens" and "class wars." The debate rages between conservative calls for the poor to "pull themselves up by their bootstraps" and liberals, cry of "we must protect the weakest of us all," and the truth, as it often does, lying somewhere in between.

Social Security was approved by Congress in response to the worst depression in U.S. history (Social Security Administration, 2011). Reading the history of this act is enlightening, particularly in relation to the current discussion of health reform. Although Social Security made a significant difference in the lives of older Americans, it was not until 1965 and passage of legislation creating Medicare that real improvement in health care for older Americans became a reality (Centers for Medicare and Medicaid Services, 2005). Most people have likely forgotten the huge opposition by physician groups and insurers to the passage of Medicare at the time.

Over time, Medicare has expanded to include those with disabilities, and programs have been developed for those in poverty (Medicaid administered through states) and for children (Child Health Insurance Program, CHIP, also administered through state grants). Other major government-managed health care programs include the military health system for active-duty military, the Veterans Health Care System, and Tricare, for military families and retired military. After consideration of all these government-managed health care systems and private insurance, there remain a large number of citizens without any health insurance. They often work for wages that are inadequate to afford individual policies, which tend to be very expensive, and work for employers that do not provide health insurance. They may have preexisting conditions that are excluded or prevent them from finding insurance. Hospitals and taxpayers bear the burden of their health care.

The last of the modern industrialized societies to address universal health care for all of its citizens, the United States passed the Patient Protection and Affordable Care Act and President Obama signed it into law on March 23, 2010. The key provision that all citizens have health insurance was immediately protested and has been before the Supreme Court. The Supreme Court ruled that the individual mandate is constitutional and therefore can be enforced. The Court's decision raised other questions, however, by suggesting that states were not required to expand Medicaid to cover larger numbers of low income individuals and families, even though the federal government would be covering the increased cost fully for three years and at 90% after that. As a result of this ruling, a number of state governors have announced that they will not be participating, leaving many of their citizens and the health care systems in those states without access to many of the provisions of the ACA.

Many of the provisions will not be law until 2014, but some key provisions allow children to continue on their parents insurance until age 26 and place increasing emphasis on value-based purchasing of services for Medicare and Medicaid (Kaiser Family Foundation, 2011). In spite of the results of the Supreme Court decision, the remainder of the Affordable Care Act will be implemented in 2019, adding millions to the health care system (Kaiser Family Foundation, 2011).

For hospital-based NPs, several key components of the Affordable Care Act offer opportunities for expansion of practice. The emphasis on value-based purchasing, team-based care, and preventive care offer fertile areas for NPs to bring together their nursing background and their medical acumen and critical thinking to the patient-centered care for which they are best prepared.

Value-Based Purchasing

The original rules under which Medicare pays for hospital care were derived from the traditional means of billing for care that were in place when it was approved in 1965. Under that program hospitals billed Medicare for whatever they would ordinarily charge and Medicare paid for a percentage of that charge. As those charges increased over time, the fees and the cost of Medicare increased phenomenally and Medicare changed to the current prospective payment system in 1983 based on diagnosis-related groups or DRG. Under this system, a hospital was paid a fixed amount, based on the diagnosis group that was submitted for payment.

This system was problematic in that hospitals that routinely treated the sickest of the sick received the same payment as a hospital that routinely treated only the easiest cases and transferred the sicker patients to tertiary referral hospitals. In response, Medicare developed a new DRG system that accounted for the sicker patients. However, when patients acquired hospital-related or iatrogenic complications, the DRG was enhanced and payment for the hospital-related or iatrogenic complications increased the cost of Medicare for poor quality care. In response to this problem of paying for poor quality care, Medicare rules have again begun to change, based on three principles.

The reforms suggest that:

• Medicare should pay for care that is reasonably more expensive because of complications to the patient.
• Medicare should pay more for care that is evidence based.

- Medicare should pay less for care that is of low quality. This is the beginning of what has now become law and is labeled *pay for performance*. (Box 1.1, page 32, lists conditions Medicare associates with low quality, which it will no longer pay for when not present on admission.)

Furthermore, patients readmitted within 30 days of discharge have been targeted as an area for improvement in terms of quality for Medicare patients. The Affordable Care Act provided for $500 million for community-based transition programs (CCTP) to reduce 30-day readmissions for patients with chronic diseases—in particular, heart failure, acute myocardial infarction, and pneumonia. The community-based transition programs are administered out of the Center for Innovation at CMS and are awarded to collaborative centers who are able to take proven programs such as Naylor's Transitional Care Model (Naylor et al., 2004) and apply them specifically to their own populations. The desired outcome of each of these programs is to reduce 30-day readmissions and therefore reduce costs for Medicare. These goals are consistent with the goals of other programs, to improve communication between providers both within the hospital and between providers within the hospital and within the community. It also increases the transparency of care, which is consistent with the Affordable Care Act's goals. The goals of all of these programs come together synergistically for patient-centered care. The focus on patient-centered care models seeks to focus care away from providers and settings and onto whatever is necessary to meet the needs of patients and caregivers. Figure 1.3 contrasts traditional care, delivered in settings that operate independently of each other with limited communication, with the patient-centered approach. NPs are seen as agents of greater communication and continuity, both within the inpatient units and between hospital settings, leading to better patient outcomes and fewer complications. NPs bring not only their advanced education and practice skills, but their practice wisdom and experience as RNs at the bedside which, although it is a different experience, informs and enriches the NP practice.

BOX 1.1   Eight Conditions Medicare Will Not Pay for if Not Present on Admission

1. Object left in patient during surgery;
2. Air embolism;
3. Blood incompatibility;
4. Catheter-associated urinary tract infection;
5. Pressure ulcer;
6. Vascular catheter-associated infection;
7. Mediastinitis after coronary artery bypass grafting;
8. Fall from the bed.

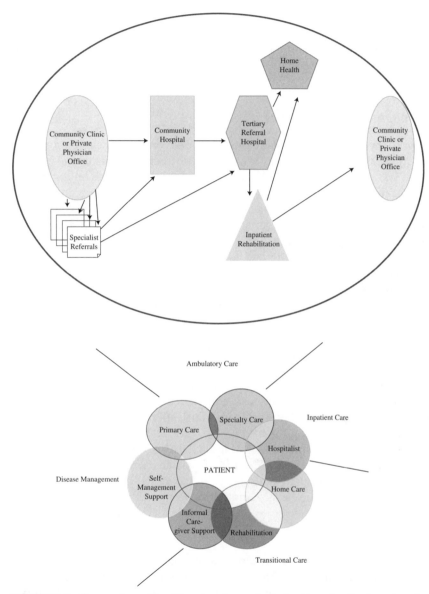

FIGURE 1.3   Comparison of traditional system-oriented care and patient-centered care models.

Care Delivery Models

A nurse or physician transported from 1980 to 2012 would be unable to function in today's technological and informational environment. Most of the medications and therapeutic and diagnostic procedures are more scientifically and technologically advanced, and yet our care delivery models remain essentially the same as they were in the 1960s and 1970s. The exceptions are additional care providers such as respiratory therapists, NPs, and physician assistants, rather than new models of care. There are a few other exceptions.

Hospitalists and Intensivists

Prior to the mid-1990s the same physician delivered inpatient and outpatient medical care to patients known to that physician, unless the hospitalization was the first contact with the health care system. The emergence of physicians whose sole practice was acute inpatient medicine and, in the case of intensivists was critical care medicine, met several needs. Hospitalists were often the agents of managed care plans in decreasing length of stay and minimizing cost of care, which also benefitted hospitals by increasing patient flow and improving bed availability (Schneller & Epstein, 2006). Many were not only agents of managed care companies, but also were their employees. Hospitalists benefited patients by being more readily available, usually onsite 24/7, and were more versed in evidence-based therapies, more current on clinical literature, and more experienced and practiced in procedures and emergency response, compared to generalists.

Acute care nurse practitioners (ACNP) have been certified by the American Nurses Credentialing Center (ANCC) since 1995 (Rosenthal & Guerrasio, 2009). ACNP competencies were written by the National Panel for Acute Care Nurse Practitioner Competencies in 2004 and the American Association of Critical-Care Nurses in 2006 to specifically address the scope of practice for NPs caring for adults with acute and complex chronic illness (Kleinpell, Hudspeth, Scordo, & Magdic, 2012). There is an effective and safe collaboration between NPs and physicians working as hospitalists and intensivists in patient-centered care (Cowan et al., 2006) even when the contributions of the NP are limited by design (Ettner et al., 2006).

Transitional Care

Transitional care is a loose, umbrella term that has evolved out of a very specific model called the Transitional Care Model (Naylor et al., 2004), developed and tested to facilitate the discharge of patients with heart failure from the hospital to home and to reduce readmission to the hospital. This model uses a combination of patient education, discharge planning, home visits, and follow-up employing NPs to engage patients and their caregivers in self-care and self-management of their heart failure. Transitional care has emerged in response to the realization that in-hospital care can no longer be delivered without reference to the care that came before and that which comes after. There must be continuity among providers and the continuation of a plan of care between settings for any lasting benefit; this is particularly true for chronic diseases characterized by cycles of compensation and decompensation. Transitional care, and the philosophy of collaboration, communication, and patient centeredness that forms its core, is on the crest of a wave of new initiatives that bring together the CMS Center for Innovation; the Institute for Healthcare Improvement; the Agency for Healthcare Research and Quality (AHRQ); as well as the RAND report on internal medicine education; the Institute of Medicine Report on the Future of Nursing; and the (Advanced Practice Registered Nurse) APRN Consensus Model.

Chronic Disease Care

Recent studies have challenged whether hospital nurses know what to teach heart failure patients (Albert et al., 2002; Dickson & Riegel, 2009) and whether teaching patients about their care without teaching them how to self-manage has any effect on outcomes (Lee, Moser, Lennie, & Riegel, 2009). These studies in transitional care and in heart failure self-care management reflect two critical trends that have significant importance for hospital-based NPs and for the health care marketplace in which they work, far beyond what they report about heart failure:

- The escalating prevalence of all chronic disease
- The increasing expectation that there are informal caregivers available to provide care in the home for the person with one or more chronic diseases.

The prevalence of chronic disease increases dramatically with increasing age. The elderly are also more likely to have multiple chronic co-morbidities, and chronic disease disproportionately affects the poor and disadvantaged (Bodenheimer, Chen, & Bennett, 2009; Boult, Green, Bult, Pacala, Snyderm, & Leff, 2009). Even the lay literature and newspapers are replete with stories of the epidemics of obesity and diabetes, in addition to increasing numbers of persons with heart failure, Alzheimer's disease, and chronic mental illness. Often forgotten in the discussion are children living with congenital and genetic disabilities and acquired problems of asthma and diabetes. Many congenital abnormalities that formerly led to early demise in infancy or childhood today are treated with sufficient success for those same persons to see adulthood, requiring close follow-up and specialized health care. Rarely spoken of are the new veterans of the wars in Iraq and Afghanistan with the physical and mental wounds of amputation, traumatic brain injury, and chronic posttraumatic stress disorder. The definition of chronic health problems for these veterans must be expanded to include homelessness, depression, suicidal ideation, domestic violence, and chronic mental illness. Because of their youth, and because the complexity and impact of their injuries is still not completely understood, the contribution of their injuries will continue to be a significant factor in the burden of chronic disease.

Caregiver Burden

The truth of chronic disease is that it cannot be cured and must be managed. The fact that symptoms and limitations of chronic disease can be managed is the upside. The potential downside is that the individual with the chronic disease can seldom manage alone, especially as the disease progresses. Throughout time, extended families have taken on the responsibilities of family members who, through age or disability, required help or supervision to guarantee their safety or well-being. Today, the extended family is rare and the nuclear family, often a blended or single-parent family, is more common. When elders are a part of a family, the caregiver is often a woman, daughter, and daughter-in-law, who has children of her own, sandwiched between generations, who may also have a job outside her home and is stretched to meet more responsibilities than she has hours in a day (Blum & Sherman, 2010).

The greater burden that is placed on patients and their informal caregivers to manage symptoms and manage their disease process outside the hospital has also increased the burden on providers, especially NPs, to partner with patients. Hospital performance measures publicly reported by CMS in Hospital Compare (www.hospitalcompare.hhs.gov/), the Joint Commission Core Measures, and the Hospital Consumer Assessment of Healthcare Providers Survey (HCAHPS) survey of patient experiences are all impacted directly or indirectly by how well patients and their caregivers are prepared to manage their care at home post-discharge, and how well they understand their instructions and responsibilities, and make arrangements for follow-up. Meeting these requirements, is impossible without clear communication provided at a literacy level understood by the patient and caregiver; the hospital-based caregiver's responsibility for continuity does not end at the hospital door. The promotion of Accountable Care Organizations (ACOs) and medical homes in the Patient Protection and Affordable Care Act, and funding for the CCTP and the Primary Care at Home program at CMS, are examples of the government's commitment to funding new care-delivery models that recognize the changes in the marketplace for health care. Patient-centeredness, continuity, comprehensiveness, value, and prevention are the watchwords of the marketplace going forward.

HIERARCHICAL (REGULATORY) FORCES

There are a number of hierarchical or regulatory forces that affect individual and collective NP practice. The most direct are regulation of licensure, certification, and privileges controlled by Boards of Nursing, accrediting organizations, and the hospitals that hire NPs. The details of acquiring licensure, certification, and prescriptive privileges are described in other chapters, but the issues underlying the significance of these important procedures will be discussed here. In addition to the regulation of NPs, there are specific regulations of, most notably, the physicians-in-training that have had a profound influence on the practice of NPs in hospitals.

Licensure, Accreditation, Certification, and Education

The first NPs who completed certificate programs in the mid-1960s were not regulated or licensed outside of their RN license. As they became more prominent and became recognized as an answer to the shortage of primary care physicians, especially in rural and underserved areas in the 1980s, state Boards of Nursing began to have serious discussions about regulation of advanced practice nurses within their mission of protecting the safety of the public. Professional organizations, certifying bodies, and practicing NPs who found it difficult to move from state to state shared many of the same concerns, if not for the same reasons, as the state Boards of Nursing about the inconsistencies in education, scope of practice, and licensure for advanced practices, nurses (Ballard, 2006; Hartigan, 2011; Kleinpell, Hudspeth, Scardo, & Magdic, 2012; McCabe & Burman, 2006; Philips, 2012; Stanley, Werner, & Apple, 2009).

From the fall of 2004 through July of 2008 the APRN Consensus Work Group labored to produce the consensus document for licensure, accreditation, certification, and education, or LACE for short. This APRN regulatory model standardizes scope of practice, educational requirements, certification examinations, and licensure, based on APRN roles and populations. It localizes the expertise of the NP in the needs of the patient, not in the location of the patient. Figure 1.4 is the Consensus APRN Regulatory Model. McCabe and Burman (2006) movingly describe their dilemma when patients in their clinic have a problem outside the usual description of their practice such as depression in primary care, or hypertension in a community psychiatric practice that begs for treatment but is outside the strict purview of the NP seeing that patient. The Consensus Model rejects arbitrary designations for practice based on location or subspecialty. The Consensus Regulatory Model attempts to meet the National Council of State Boards of Nursing's duty to protect the public and to protect the nursing profession's need to organize care delivery in a way that is patient centered and rejects arbitrary divisions and classifications that interfere with access to care rather than facilitating it.

There is evidence that restrictive prescribing practices and requirements for physician supervision of practice or proscriptive protocols limit not only the numbers of practicing NPs in a state (and therefore access to needed health care), but also restrict enrollment in educational programs that graduate NPs (Kalist & Spurr, 2004). Extremes of difference exist in scope of practice from state to state, making mobility difficult. Advanced practice nurses that practice near the border of two or more state and see

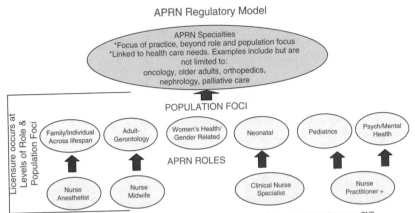

APRN Regulatory Model

APRN Specialties
*Focus of practice, beyond role and population focus
*Linked to health care needs. Examples include but are
not limited to:
oncology, older adults, orthopedics,
nephrology, palliative care

POPULATION FOCI

Licensure occurs at Levels of Role & Population Foci

| Family/Individual Across lifespan | Adult-Gerontology | Women's Health/Gender Related | Neonatal | Pediatrics | Psych/Mental Health |

APRN ROLES

| Nurse Anesthetist | Nurse Midwife | | Clinical Nurse Specialist | Nurse Practitioner + |

+The certified nurse practitioner (CNP) is prepared with the acute care CNP competencies and/or with the primary care CNP. competencies. At this point in time the acute care and primary care CNP delineation applies only to the pediatric and adult-gerontology CNP population foci. Scope of practice of the primary care or acute care CNP is **not setting specific** but Is based on patient care needs. Program may prepare individuals across both sets of roles, the graduate must be prepared with the consensus-based competencies for both roles and must successfully obtain certification in both the acute and the primary care CNP roles. CNP certification in the acute care or primary care roles must match the educational preparation for CNPs in these roles.

FIGURE 1.4 Advanced Practice Registered Nurse Consensus Model.
Source: National Council of State Boards of Nursing, https://www.ncsbn.org/aprn.htm

patients from multiple states may need to have licenses in each state. Each of those licenses may have different scopes of practice, licensing requirements, and collaboration/supervision requirements, with physicians.

Scope of Practice

In 2010, the Robert Wood Johnson Foundation in conjunction with the Institute of Medicine released their report on the future of nursing (Committee on the Robert Wood Johnson Foundation Initiative on the Future of Nursing, 2010) recommending that nurses, and—of significance for this discussion—NPs be allowed to practice at the full extent of their education and training. The full extent of their education and training is defined by law in each state as scope of practice. The scope of practice defines who can be seen by the NP, in what setting and under what circumstances as well as what guidance and/or supervision must be in place and by whom. Scope of practice also determines the limits and privileges of licensure, the ability to bill for services, and the limits of liability. The limits of liability determine the need for and the required limits of malpractice insurance. Currently, scope of practice for NPs, unlike physicians, is different from state to state (Klein, 2005). Furthermore, scope of practice for hospital-based NPs has some special requirements (Kleinpell et al., 2012).

Credentialing and Privileging

When a hospital hires an NP, there is an obligation—a duty—to perform due diligence in relation to the veracity of the NP's credentials and competency. The staff bylaws will describe a procedure for this process and it is reviewable by the Joint Commission. NPs usually are subject to the same process as physicians unless there are sufficient numbers or there is an organization of NPs with its own process and bylaws that are subject to the same rigor and review as Joint Commission standards. The hospital process may be more rigorous than the individual state's Scope of Practice requirements, but may not be less so (Kleinpell et al., 2012). If the NP is to perform procedures, there must be a process in place to document competence, with reviewable records. This process may or may not be reviewable by the Board of Nursing, depending on the state requirements.

ACGME Hour Limitations for Residents

The first restrictions of medical resident work hours in 2003 and the revision with updated restrictions in 2010 were clearly a catalyst for the increased utilization of NPs in hospital-based practice (Pastores et al., 2011). This rapid introduction of NPs was often accomplished with little planning or thought as to how their practice would be integrated into the units or how they would be evaluated and by whom. Because they were nurses, they were often included with staff RNs reporting to nurse managers who did not understand the NP role. The NPs often worked in settings where their education and abilities were not appreciated and, since they were replacing interns and residents, they were seen as such and were given low-level responsibilities and seen as peers of student physicians rather than as licensed, autonomous practitioners with experience and critical thinking skills. These two factors have contributed to job dissatisfaction and high turnover in some settings. In other settings, NPs had already made an inroad in hospital practice and there was experience with their abilities and scope of practice that could guide the expansion of the numbers that grew in response to the ACGME requirements.

HANDOFF AND INTERPROFESSIONAL COMMUNICATION

One very clear and significant issue persists however, independent of the amount of planning that went into the integration of NPs into hospital-based practice. That issue is handoff from one provider to another. When residents were in the unit for 36 to 40 hours at a time, there was rarely a need to hand off the care of their patients to someone else. Their responsibility to know everything about that patient was clear and there was little uncertainty about what was expected of people. Now, hour restrictions, limited involvement in planning discussions, the need to trust others to provide care for their patients, and the uncertainty of increased frequency of handoffs can lead to frustration and even hostility if steps are not taken to reduce the uncertainty. The uncertainty can be reduced by being clear about responsibilities and expectations; having a clear, standardized, systematic handoff routine; and providing regular opportunities to evaluate issues with communication.

COMMUNITY FORCES

The NP in hospital-based practice holds membership in multiple communities, some more loosely organized than others. Hospitals and other large organizations are communities of communities. Communities are more than groups and are organized around common goals, passions, and purposes. In nursing academia, there has been acknowledgment of communities of scholars who have come together to advance research and theoretical knowledge. Parse and Rogerian scholars have forged recognizable community identities that foster knowledge development and mentor new scholars into their society. These are the goals and purposes of communities.

Communities of practice (Adler et al., 2008; Li et al., 2009; Kislov, Harvey, & Walshe, 2011) have been described in business organizations and management research for over 30 years as a way of studying and describing the communication of knowledge. More recently, communities of practice (CoP) have been proposed as a way of examining the dissemination of information (Li, Grimshaw, Nielson, Judd, Coyte, & Graham 2009) and collaboration (Adler et al., 2008; Kislov et al., 2011) in health care.

Communities of practice may arise spontaneously and informally and communicate the culture and social norms of the organization to new members and novice NPs. This informal information transfer and socialization has the potential for good or bad outcomes depending on the culture of the organization.

The good news is that communities of practice do not have to be left to chance. They are effective and useful management tools. Citing Saint-Onge and Wallace, Li and colleagues (2009) note three major components of a community of practice. Those components are people (the members), practice (what they do), and capabilities (their shared advantages). Furthermore, they describe three different levels of CoP. There are informal groups, which develop somewhat spontaneously around shared interests and self-identified learning; supported groups, which have formal acknowledgment and support from management to build learning; and structured groups, which are developed and managed by the organization and aim to advance the organization's business. This last CoP best is exemplified by administrative councils of directors and lead NPs, described in other chapters of this book, which provide self-governance structure for NPs within the organization.

Dissemination of Knowledge

Health care is a knowledge industry. It is more than and different from the sum of all that knowledge. It is the infinite combination of multidisciplinary knowledge and practice wisdom of countless years of provider experiences, passed down from provider to provider in formal and informal teaching sessions. Health care knowledge is as significant for what we do not know as for what we do know. In a world of clinical practice where disciplines—medicine, nursing, respiratory therapy, nutrition—worked in independent silos with only physician orders to communicate between them, knowledge acquisition, dissemination, and utilization was discipline specific and limited to the silo. Even in multidisciplinary teams, much of the silo mentality is maintained. However, in a true interdisciplinary philosophy of teamwork, those silos are broken down and knowledge acquisition, dissemination, and utilization is shared by all members of the team without regard to discipline. There is mutual respect and acknowledgment of each team member's contribution to the work of the team because the patient is the focus, not the rank of the team member.

Professional Socialization

It is in this way that new professionals are socialized. The communities in which they seek and gain membership professionally, whether they are professional associations aligned with the clinical specialization they have chosen for their work or general professional associations chosen for advocacy for professional issues, socialize the new professional by disseminating social norms. These social norms include the issues that the community prioritizes, the behaviors it values, and the people whom it esteems from the membership. Whether or not NPs participate in professional organizations, or even belong to them; participate in or originate research; write for publication; precept or mentor new NPs; or participate in advocacy efforts for the profession is determined by the professional socialization they receive by the community to which they belong. Their professional behavior is most influenced by the first community to which they belong.

The same is true within the hospital organization. When a new NP joins the group, the social norms of the NP group are communicated to the new NP in much the same way. Because the group is much smaller than a professional organization, the new NP's decision to conform or not to the professional social norms of the group will be obvious quickly and will often determine the new NP's success at the hospital. A healthy organization will promote healthy social norms and will provide multiple opportunities for professional socialization for new NPs, whether they are new graduates who not only need socialization to the organization's social order, but to the role or are seasoned NPs who are well socialized to the role, but not to the organization. The introduction to research groups, writing groups, and education or advocacy groups within the organization can foster successful behaviors in the new member and lead to a professional life that is varied and engaged.

If you are the first NP in an organization, or one of the first, you have the opportunity to determine how this professional socialization process will occur. If you are creating a formal NP organization within your hospital, there are a number of specific things you can do with orientation and mentoring to facilitate this process. These strategies are discussed in detail in other chapters.

Cultural Norms

Cultural norms are related to professional socialization, but are often more insidious. A culture within an organization is more like the personality of the organization, and it can be characterized as a macro-culture made up of many micro-cultures. Organizational cultures range on a continuum from open to closed. Open cultures are welcoming and receptive to new people and ideas. Closed cultures cling to old ways and change very slowly or imperceptibly. In reality, these extremes rarely exist, and true cultures fall along the continuum between the extremes.

Cultures that exist on the more closed end of the continuum tend to make it very difficult for new people to establish their worthiness to belong. When the culture of an organization fosters or permits relational aggression, bullying, or discounting (Dellasega, 2011; Duffy, 2009; Martin & Hutchinson, 1999), the outcome of the socialization is marginalization of new NPs, whether novice NPs or experienced NPs new to the organization. The result is expensive turnover for the organization and compromised access to care for patients. Even worse is the shattered trust of the NPs who are emotionally and professionally battered by the experience. When the undermining or bullying behavior comes from a manager or supervisor, it can be even more emotionally destructive, and even economically devastating (Resvani, 2012).

On the other hand, a culture that is open and welcoming offers a safe haven for new graduates and seasoned NPs alike to grow and develop. A healthy environment for providers contributes to better care for patients by allowing the full attention of the provider to be on the patient and not on the NP's own survival and safety. Furthermore, that safe and nurturing environment promotes creativity and innovation, which benefits the organization as well.

Clinical Knowledge

Clearly, no one comes out of an educational program knowing all he needs to know to be an expert practitioner in any area of practice. Learning is a lifelong endeavor. Clinical knowledge and the evidence-base for practice are growing exponentially. Without question, the pooled knowledge of a team of providers is more powerful and helpful in the care of patients than the knowledge of a single provider or discipline alone.

Interdisciplinary Collaborative Communities of Practice

It is important from a legal standpoint for NPs to establish that they are licensed independent practitioners who function autonomously to provide care for patients. This legal designation is critical for so many reasons, but specific to this discussion, it buys a seat at the table where decisions are made about the provision of health care. In the delivery of that health care, that independent practitioner designation allows NPs peer status for collaboration. Providers at any level can cooperate to provide care for patients and certainly, cooperation is a necessary though not sufficient condition for collaboration. For true collaboration, there must be a level of mutual respect and acknowledgment of the fundamental value of the contribution of each of the individuals involved in the collaboration. There can be no hierarchy of value, no sliding scale of merit to the contributions of the collaborators. Interdisciplinary collaboration is discussed fully in another chapter.

Social Media as Community

For professionals, there are opportunities to connect and stay connected with Facebook and LinkedIn as well as with many professional organizations that have developed communities within that organization's website for special interests. These specialized connections promote closer ties and unite people with common interests and goals who, in the past, would have had difficulty finding each other. These opportunities will only expand as technology and demand increase. These sites are so ubiquitous that even the Centers for Medicare and Medicaid Services (CMS) and the AHRQ, as well as many other agencies important to health care, have links to them.

For anyone searching for employment today and even more so in the future, a strategically placed resume or curriculum vitae on LinkedIn will bring you to the attention of potential recruiters and employers. Social media can be a double-edged sword, however, if youthful indiscretions or careless postings have left pictures or comments that are uncomplimentary to your character for potential employers to find. These are forces that newer NPs may face, which more seasoned NPs never had to be concerned with.

The opportunities to use these sites as well as Twitter to form virtual support groups, coaching opportunities, patient education delivery models, gaming for patient education, and endless other applications are unlimited.

Many organizations committed to patient and community education and outreach already have a presence on these sites and are taking advantage of the market penetration.

Developing Technology to Expand our Definition of Community

One of the biggest threats to patient safety and preventable readmissions is poor patient adherence to medication regimens. Patients rarely set out to miss medications, however, they often just forget. Almost everyone these days has a mobile phone. Apps are available to help patients remember to take their medications, and to know what their medicines are and what they look like. They can get reminders about diet, exercise, and symptom management. We have only just begun to tap into the use of mobile phones, interactive television, and telemedicine to increase the opportunities to benefit patients and their caregivers. Consider the future in which some ambulatory patient appointments or post-discharge follow-ups might be completed using Skype.

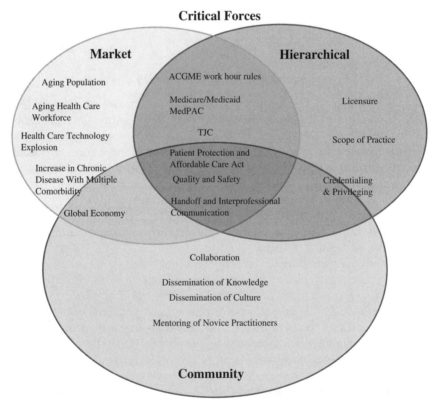

Critical Forces

Market — Aging Population; Aging Health Care Workforce; Health Care Technology Explosion; Increase in Chronic Disease With Multiple Comorbidity; Global Economy

Hierarchical — Licensure; Scope of Practice; Credentialing & Privileging

Market/Hierarchical overlap — ACGME work hour rules; Medicare/Medicaid MedPAC; TJC; Patient Protection and Affordable Care Act; Quality and Safety; Handoff and Interprofessional Communication

Community — Collaboration; Dissemination of Knowledge; Dissemination of Culture; Mentoring of Novice Practitioners

FIGURE 1.5 Dynamic model of market, hierarchical, and community forces on NPs, with major influences.

SUMMARY

This chapter has introduced a few of the forces that are in dynamic interaction and that affect the practice of NPs. Market, hierarchical, and community forces are not mutually exclusive, as we have seen, and in particular, market and hierarchical forces related to licensure and workforce are closely bound to each other. Other chapters will develop these ideas more completely so that there are specific strategies for making NPs' practice and the organizations in which they practice mutually successful. Figure 1.5 brings together all these forces within Adler's model to form the context for later discussions.

REFERENCES

Adler, P. S., Kwon, S. W., & Heckscher, C. (2008). Professional work: The emergence of collaborative community. *Perspective Organization Science, 19*(2), 359–376.

Administration on Aging, United States Department of Health and Human Services. Projected future growth of the older population. Retrieved January 17, 2012, from http://www.aoa.gov/AoARoot/Aging_Statistics/future_growth/future_growth.aspx

Albert, N. M., Collier, S., Sumodi, V. et al. (2002). Nurses' knowledge of heart failure education principles. *Heart and Lung, 31*, 102–112.

American Academy of Nurse Practitioners. (2011). *2009–10 AANP National NP Sample Survey: Income & benefits.* Retrieved January 29, 2012, from http://aanp.org/NR/rdonlyres/AC773A15-35BA-4AAC-9734-56516ACE8142/0/OnlineReport_Compensation2.pdf

American Association of Colleges of Nursing. (2004). AACN position statement on the practice doctorate in nursing. Retrieved January 18, 2012, from http://www.aacn.nche.edu/publications/position/DNPpositionstatement.pdf

American Association of Colleges of Nursing. (2011). Media relations. Retrieved January 18, 2012, from http://www.aacn.nche.edu/media-relations/fact-sheets/dnp

Ballard, K. A. (2006). National council of state boards of nursing's paper on the regulation of advanced practice nursing: Is this really a vision? *Policy Politics Nursing Practice, 7*(2), 114–118.

Blum, K., & Sherman, D. W. (2010). Understanding the experience of caregivers: A focus on transitions. *Seminars in Oncology Nursing, 26*(4), 243–258.

Bodenheimer, T., Chen, E., & Bennett, H. D. (2009). Confronting the growing burden of chronic disease: Can the U.S. health care workforce do the job? *Health Affairs, 28*(1), 64–74.

Boult, C., Green, A. F., Boult, L. B., Pacala, J. T., Snyderm, C., & Leff, B. (2009). Successful models of comprehensive care for older adults with chronic conditions: Evidence for the Institute of Medicine's "Retooling for an Aging America" report. *Journal of the American Geriatric Society, 57*, 2328–2337.

Centers for Medicare and Medicaid Services. (2005). Key milestones in Medicare and Medicaid history, selected years: 1965–2003. Retrieved January 19, 2012, from https://www.cms.gov/HealthCareFinancingReview/downloads/05-06 Winpg1.pdf

Centers for Medicare and Medicaid Services. (2009). National Health Expenditures Projections 2009–2019. Retrieved January 18, 2012, from https://www.cms. gov/NationalHealthExpendData/25_NHE_Fact_sheet.asp

Centers for Medicare and Medicaid Services. (2012a). NHE Fact sheet. Retrieved January 18, 2012, from https://www.cms.gov/NationalHealthExpendData/ 25_NHE_Fact_sheet.asp

Centers for Medicare and Medicaid Services. (2012b) *Value-based purchasing*. Retrieved January 20, 2012, from https://www.cms.gov/QualityInitiatives GenInfo/downloads/VBPRoadmap_OEA_1-16_508.pdf

Chase, S. K., & Pruitt, R. H. (2006). The practice doctorate: Innovation or disruption. *Journal of Nursing Education, 45*(5), 155–161.

Committee on the Robert Wood Johnson Foundation Initiative on the Future of Nursing, at the Institute of Medicine (2010). *The future of nursing: Leading change, advancing health.* Retrieved January 22, 2012, from http://www.iom. edu/~/media/Files/Report%20Files/2010/The-Future-of-Nursing/Future% 20of%20Nursing%202010%20Report%20Brief.pdf

Cowan, M. J., Shapiro, M., Hays, R. D., Afifi, A., Vasirani, S., Ward, C. R., & Ettner, S. L. (2006). The effect of a multidisciplinary hospitalist/physician and advanced practice nurse collaboration on hospital costs. *Journal of Nursing Administration, 36*(2), 79–85.

Dellasega, C. (2011). *When nurses hurt nurses: Recognizing and overcoming the cycle of nurse bullying.* Indianapolis, IN: Sigma Theta Tau International.

Dickson, V. V., & Riegel, B. (2009). Are we teaching what patients need to know? Building skills in heart failure self-care. *Heart & Lung: Journal of Acute & Critical Care, 38*, 253–261.

Duffy, M. (2009). Preventing workplace mobbing and bullying with effective organizational consultation, policies and legislation. *Consulting Psychology Journal: Practice and Research, 61*(3), 242–262.

Ettner, S., Kotlerman, J., Afifi, A., Vazirani, S., Hays, R. D., Shapiro, M., & Cowan, M. (2006). An alternative approach to reducing the costs of patient care? A controlled trial of the multi-disciplinary doctor-nursed practitioner (MDNP) model. *Medical Decision Making, 26*(1), 9–17.

Federal Reserve Bank of St. Louis. (2011). Tracking the global expansion: Economic indicators—United States. Retrieved January 18, 2012, from http://research. stlouisfed.org/economy/us/us_monthly.pdf

Fleming, K. C., Evans, J. M., & Chutka, D. S. (2003). Caregiver and clinician shortages in and aging nation. *Mayo Clinical Proceedings, 78*, 1026–1040.

Hackbarth, G., & Boccuti, C. (2011). Transforming graduate medical education to improve health care value. *New England Journal of Medicine, 364*(8), 693–695.

Hartigan, C. (2011). APRN regulation: The licensure-certification interface. *AACN Advanced Critical Care, 22*(1), 50–65.

Kaiser Family Foundation. (2011). Focus on health reform: Summary of new heath reform law. Retrieved January 20, 2012, from http://www.kff.org/healthre form/upload/8061.pdf

Kalist, D. E., & Spurr, S. J. (2004). The effect of state laws on the supply of advanced practice nurses. *International Journal of Health Care Finance and Economics, 4*, 271–281.

Kane, G. C., Diemer, G., & Feldman, A. M. (2011). Commentary: Preparing internists for the 21st century: A response to the recent RAND survey of internal medicine education. *American Journal of Medical Quality, 26*(6), 505–508.

Kislov, R., Harvey, G., & Walshe, K. (2011). Collaborations for leadership in applied health research and care: Lessons from the theory of communities of practice. *Implementation Science, 6*(1), 64–74.

Klein, T. A. (2005). Scope of practice and the nurse practitioner: Regulation, competency, expansion and evolution. *Topics in Advanced Practice Nurse eJournal, 5*(2): Retrieved from http://www.medscape.com/viewarticle/506277.

Kleinpell, R. M., Hudspeth, R., Scordo, K. A., & Magdic, K. (2012). Defining NP scope of practice and associated regulations: Focus on acute care. *Journal of the American Academy of Nurse Practitioners, 24*(2012), 11–18.

Lee, C. S., Moser, D. K., Lennie, T. A., & Riegel, B. (2009) Event-free survival in adults with heart failure who engage in self-care management. *Heart & Lung: Journal of Acute & Critical Care, 40*(1), 12–20.

Li, L. C., Grimshaw, J. M., Nielsen, C., Judd, M., Coyte, P. C., & Graham, I. D. (2009). Evolution of Wenger's concept of community of practice. *Implementation Science, 4*(1), 11–19.

Martin, A. B., Lassman, D., Washington, B., & Catlin, A. (2012). Growth in US health spending remained slow in 2010; Health share of gross domestic product was unchanged from 2009. *Health Affairs, 31*(1), 208–219.

Martin, P. D., & Hutchinson, S. A. (1999). Nurse Practitioners and the problem of discounting. *Journal of Advanced Nursing, 29*(1), 9–17.

McCabe, S., & Burman, M. E. (2006). A tale of two APNs: Addressing blurred practice boundaries in APN practice. *Perspectives in Psychiatric Care, 42*(1), 3–11.

National Council of State Boards of Nursing. *Campaign for APRN consensus.* Retrieved January 29, 2012, from https://www.ncsbn.org/aprn.htm

Naylor, M. D., Brooten, D. A., Campbell, R. L., Maislin, G., McCauley, K. M., & Schwartz, J. S. (2004). Transitional care of older adults hospitalized with heart failure: A randomized, controlled trial. *Journal of the American Geriatrics Society, 52*(5), 675–684.

New York Times (2010). Recession. Retrieved January 18, 2012, from http://topics.nytimes.com/top/reference/timestopics/subjects/r/recession_and_depression/ index.html

Pastores, S. M., O'Connor, M. F., Kleinpell, R. M., Napolitano, L., Ward, N., Bailey, H., … Coopersmith, C. M. (2011). The Accreditation Council for Graduate Medical Education resident duty hour new standards: History, changes and impact on staffing of intensive care units. *Critical Care Medicine, 39*(11), 2540–2549.

Philips, S. J. (2012). APRN consensus model implementation and planning. *The Nurse Practitioner, 37*(1), 23–45.

Resvani, S. (2012). Why mean girls grow up to be meaner bosses. *The Washington Post,* January 29, 2012.

Rosenthal, L. D., & Guerrasio, J. (2009). Acute care nurse practitioner as hospitalist: Role description. *AACN Advanced Critical Care, 20*(2), 133–136.

Schneller, E. S., & Epstein, K. R. (2006). The hospitalist movement in the United States: Agency and common agency issues. *Health Care Management Review, 31*(4), 308–316.

Social Security Administration. (2011). *Brief history*. Retrieved January 19, 2012, from http://www.ssa.gov/history/briefhistory3.html

Stanley, J. M., Werner, K. E., & Apple, K. (2009). Positioning advanced practice registered nurses for health care reform: Consensus on APRN regulation. *Journal of Professional Nursing, 25*(6), 340–348.

Young, A., Choudhry, H. J., Rhyne, J., & Dugan, M. (2011). A census of actively licensed physicians in the United States, 2010. *Journal of Medical Regulation, 96*(4), 11–20.

2

Organizational Assessment and Development of the Business Plan

Janet Fuchs and Kay Blum

The decision to adopt and implement an innovation is complex and time consuming. Extensive planning prior to the adoption can increase the likelihood that the adoption and implementation will be successful and decrease the likelihood that money and resources will be wasted on an effort that has little or no chance to succeed. It is critical that the innovation align with the resources, culture, and goals of the organization if the innovation is to succeed. When the innovation is as complex as adding a group of practitioners, the complexity itself is a factor in the success of the innovation.

A frank and candid exploration of the organization, its culture, its resources, and its ability to respond to change and innovation will assist the decision makers in making the best possible decision about whether they should implement the innovation and whether or not the innovation is a good match for the organization. Rogers (2003), in her classic book *Diffusion of Innovation*, discusses the concept of reinvention. Reinvention is the act of reshaping or changing the innovation to match the needs, abilities, and culture of the adopter, the organization in this case. There is an increased likelihood of success when the innovation is reinvented or adapted to match the organizations needs, culture, and goals. This chapter gives an overview of the areas that need to be assessed and developed prior to implementation of nurse practitioner (NP) practice within a hospital organization. Other chapters will explain in detail some of these areas where decision makers and those charged with the implementation process may have less experience or need more help in identifying the details of the process. This chapter is divided into three sections. First, the status of the organization is assessed to identify the current reality. Second, the steps required to develop the proposal will be discussed. The last section will discuss factors to consider for facilitating and shepherding the change process within the organization.

ORGANIZATIONAL ASSESSMENT

Within the Diffusion of Innovation Model (Rogers, 2003), the decision to adopt an innovation is the result of two prior steps in the process: agenda setting and matching. Both of these process steps include various aspects of organizational assessment. The types of assessment that need to be done do not vary, but the formality of the assessment pieces may vary by the size and complexity of the organization in which the assessment occurs.

Agenda Setting

Agenda setting refers to the reason a decision maker or group of decision makers considers the adoption of an innovation. The two major categories of reasons one might consider for integrating NPs into the organization are the identification of problems for which NPs are proposed as a potential solution and the identification of NP practice as a trend that represents and evolutionary/revolutionary change in the delivery of health care. Part of agenda setting is clarifying the organization's goals in considering the adoption of NP practice in the organization, as well clarifying as the goals for the practice in achieving the mission of the organization. These are often confused and they are not the same.

An example of conflict in these goals happened in a hospital organization that identified NPs as the answer to reducing 30-day readmission rates for heart failure. However, the attending physicians and residents on the teaching services, who were not involved in the decision to adopt this innovation, refused to collaborate with the NPs because they saw this as a conflict with the teaching mission of the organization. This could have been avoided by identifying all stakeholders and bringing them into the discussion.

Matching

Matching is the process of examining the possible solutions to the problem that was identified in the agenda setting or studying the particular trend that is being considered for adoption. Although all hospital organizations share attributes and characteristics, each is unique in some way. Mostly, the uniqueness is because of the people who make up the organizations and create the complexities that characterize them. For that reason, NP practice is never exactly the same from place to place although it is similar enough that certain generalizations can be made that will allow organizations and NPs to learn from each other. The matching process as Rogers (2003) describes it involves examining the strengths and weaknesses, goals, resources, and constraints of the organization, and reinventing the innovation to fit within that organization.

CURRENT REALITY

The current reality assessment can be compared in principle to a patient's history and physical exam. Depending on the size and scope of the innovation being considered, it can be comprehensive or focused. The size and scope of the assessment, who should carry it out, when and how it should be completed, and under whose authority emerges from a number of decisions made in the agenda setting and matching processes. Although the graphic image of the Diffusion of Innovation Model for Organizations (Rogers, 2003) depicted in the Introduction chapter shows linear process, the decisions are not linear, but rather are iterative in nature. One or more decisions lead to reconsideration and revision of others until the innovation is well matched to the needs and resources of the organization.

Once an adequate match is approximated and a decision to adopt is made, a business plan is constructed that allows for testing the match. This plan includes clear, measurable indicators of success that can be evaluated at a specific time point. At that time point, the plan can be further revised, if necessary, to increase the likelihood of long-term success within the organization.

Size and Scope of the Assessment

Several things go into the decision about how extensive the organizational assessment needs to be. First, how big is the organization and how many NPs are being integrated into it? The items that need to be assessed do not change; however, the complexity of the process does. For example, a small community hospital seeking to add NPs to the Internal Medicine Hospitalist Service may be able to collect the data it needs to perform the assessment through informal requests to people they know personally. For them, the challenge may be identifying what data they need to collect. In a large organization, the challenge may be in identifying who to contact to obtain the required information. The purpose of this section is to suggest some solutions to the identification of data and data sources that will facilitate these assessments, regardless of the size of the organization and complexity of the scope of the assessment.

Scope of the Innovation

It is always difficult to think and speak about a nonlinear process with linear language. What we mean by this is that we tend to think about processes in steps that follow 1-2-3. However, in a nonlinear process such as this, you might start at 2 and do 3 and 4 and have to do 3 again. Exhibit 2.1, gives an example of how this could happen when just starting out. In looking at this example and the financial assessment, it is hard to imagine that the problem could have been identified without some of this assessment having already been done; however, it is not clear that all of it has been

EXHIBIT 2.1   An Organizational Assessment and SWOT (Strengths, Weaknesses, Opportunities, and Threats) Analysis

DECISION-MAKING GROUP

Chief of Cardiology, Catheterization Laboratory Manager, Cardiovascular Service Line Manager, Chief Nursing Officer (CNO), Catheterization Recovery Nurse Manager, Coronary Care (CCU) Nurse Manager, Medical Director Coronary Care Unit

AGENDA SETTING

The problem is patients are backing up in the recovery room and not being discharged or admitted in a timely way. The result is increased overtime in the recovery room and pressure on the recovery room nurse manager to reduce her budget variance; and delayed discharge from the CCU leading to longer than average LOS and loss of revenue due to ED drive by, threats to STEMI center status, and reimbursement denials for unnecessary days, with pressure on the CCU nurse manager to push the cardiologists to make discharges a higher priority.

MATCHING

The group has explored a number of potential solutions including

- Pressure from the Chief of Cardiology on the other cardiologists about patients with denied days
- Reminders in the eHR each time a cardiologist signs on that he or she has patients in recovery
- Reminders from the Nurse Managers when patients are waiting to be discharged
- NPs for the CCU and the recovery room
- Hiring a hospitalist physician to cover the inpatients in the CCU and cover the recovery room when the interventionalists are tied up in the catheterization laboratory

OBJECTIVES

- Reduce recovery room overtime by appropriate timely discharge or hospital admission
- Reduce CCU denied days by timely discharge
- Reduce ED drive-by hours by increasing CCU bed availability

(Continued)

EXHIBIT 2.1 *(continued)*

ORGANIZATIONAL ASSESSMENT

Financial assessment

- CCU days, CCU LOS, CCU denied days for the previous 6 months by month (or by year if that is more appropriate for your discussions)
- Number of patients discharged from CCU after 11 a.m. (or whatever the cutoff is for a new day charge)
- Average cost per CCU day
- Overtime costs per month for the catheterization recovery room by month for the last 6 months
- Number of hours and days per month the ED was on drive-by by month for the last 6 months

	JAN	FEB	MAR	APR	MAY	JUN	JUL
CCU denied days	60	52	64	68	62	64	66
RR overtime hours	80	76	82	88	84	84	82
ED drive-by hours	15	18	22	24	30	32	36
CCU beds	24	24	24	24	24	24	24
CCU days	744	672	744	720	718	732	744
CCU daily cost	$3,957	$3,957	$3,957	$3,957	$3,957	$3,957	$3,957
Estimated overtime cost	$3,600	$3,420	$3,690	$3,960	$3,760	$3,760	$3,690
Estimated lost revenue from denied days	$237,430	$205,764	$253,248	$269,076	$245,334	$253,248	$261,162

System Assessment is about taking stock of the processes and infrastructure of the organization to determine what is and is not in place to support the diffusion of this innovation.

(Continued)

EXHIBIT 2.1   (*continued*)

Organizational Chart for Cardiovascular Service Line

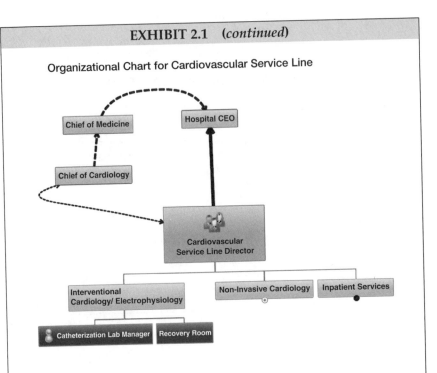

Discussions with the service line director and managers in the Catheterization Lab, Recovery Room, and CCU indicate that they have decision-making authority and responsibility for their budgets, staffing, hiring and firing decisions, and general operations. There is little interference from directors, and they feel that there is good support from the director when conflict arises with staff or physicians. Most feel that communication is good and is bidirectional. The consensus of managers is that the late discharges are related to the number of cases the cardiologists are performing in the catheterization labs. They just cannot be in two places at one time.

In the past, the cardiologists have been reluctant to embrace any changes. Upgrades in equipment, changes in procedures, and differences in routines have been met with hostility, complaints, and work slowdowns by some physicians. They have purposely been left out of the discussions and this is a real problem. The process cannot go much further until this group of stakeholders is included in the discussions. In spite of reminders embedded in the eHR and personal reminders by nurse managers the actual numbers of discharges have not changed. Although these activities have improved discharges for some physicians at the time the nurse manager approached them about a particular patient, the strategy did not result in any global change in behavior. Investigating the cost of hiring hospitalist physicians to cover these two units demonstrated that the salary costs would be at least 50% higher and the requirements of the units would not use the physicians full scope of practice.

(*Continued*)

EXHIBIT 2.1   (*continued*)

The organizational culture assessment instrument was used to assess the culture in the different units of the Cardiovascular Service Line (http://gsbc.colorado.edu/student_tools/documents/8bOCAIWorksheet-Second2004.doc). There was close agreement between the Now and Preferred segments and the culture was described as follows:

- The organization is very results oriented. A major concern is with getting the job done. People are very competitive and achievement oriented.
- The leadership in the organization is generally considered to exemplify coordinating, organizing, or smooth-running efficiency.
- The management style in the organization is characterized by teamwork, consensus, and participation.
- The glue that holds the organization together is loyalty and mutual trust. Commitment to this organization runs high.
- The organization defines success on the basis of the development of human resources, teamwork, employee commitment, and concern for people.

There are currently 15 other NPs working in the hospital. There are 10 working in various surgical services and five in pediatric and neonatal ICU roles. Human resources have experience in recruiting NPs and there is a process in place to credential and privilege them through the hospital Medical Staff Office. All of the NPs work within the service line for which they are hired rather than for a central advanced practice administration or nursing service. There is currently no formal NP orientation program. NPs attend hospital orientation and the service line is responsible for any other orientation or mentoring that occurs.

There is very limited space in either the recovery room or adjacent to the CCU. There is a small area currently used by staff as a secondary lounge that can be wired for computers and outfitted with cubicle style desks that could be made into an office with privacy for one to three NPs with ready access to both clinical areas.

The catheterization labs schedule patients Monday through Saturday 8 a.m. through 6 p.m. with the first patients arriving at 6:30 a.m. for preparation for an 8 a.m. start. NPs would be scheduled for 12-hr shifts, 6 a.m. to 6 p.m., Monday through Saturday in the recovery room and daily in the CCU. This scheduling would require a minimum of five NPs cross-trained for both areas.

UNIT ASSESSMENT

The high numbers of hours of overtime are beginning to take a toll on both the morale of the staff and their willingness to pull together to care for patients. At first, the extra money was viewed as a good thing and staff looked forward to a few extra hours each pay period. Now each person works 20 to 40 overtime hours every pay period and they are tired. The average age of nurses in the

(*Continued*)

EXHIBIT 2.1 *(continued)*

catheterization lab and recovery room is 48 and they feel that the extra work is too demanding. They have indicated that they will have to look for other jobs if the overtime does not decrease soon.

In the CCU, the burden is less since the unit is staffed for full occupancy. The stress there comes from no downtime since all of the beds are full all the time. There is a lot of patient frustration from not being able to get access to physicians in a timely way when they are in the catheterization laboratory. The Nurse Manager is concerned about the staff, but feels powerless to get the patients out in a timely way.

INDIVIDUAL-BASED ASSESSMENT

Hospital-wide evaluations are completed yearly, and yearly increases are tied to merit. The system was developed in house. Merit is determined by the unit manager and is based on a percentage of the previous year's salary. There are no bonuses based on volume of work.

SWOT ANALYSIS

Strengths

A responsive, flat organizational structure that supports decision making and accountability at the unit level. There is a minimum of bureaucracy. These issues have arisen out of a strong financial situation with a heavy patient flow.

Weaknesses

Physicians are a key group of stakeholders who have not been part of the discussion and have not historically been receptive to change. They need to be brought on board quickly and helped to see the advantages if the program is to be successful.

Opportunities

The salary and benefits for five NPs is less than half the cost of the denied CCU days for the patients waiting for discharge. The opportunity for the hospital to increase its revenue and turn over beds, as well as improve access for patients who now must be routed to more distant hospitals, is great.

Threats

The potential for turnover and bedside nursing shortages for both the CCU and the recovery room staff is great. The sooner the problem of overtime and constant full capacity can be addressed, the sooner the issue of burnout can be remedied. Other strategies for addressing these problems must be considered as well.

completed. The complete set of data is necessary to support the decision and implementation of the innovation. There are many ways to organize the scope of the innovation in order to discuss the associated organizational assessment; this is only one of them, but it is a fairly simple and straightforward way. We will look first at some organization-wide variables, at unit specific variables, and then at some individual-specific variables that should be part of the assessment prior to implementation of NP practice or the trial of NP practice. Obviously, if you are considering NPs for only one unit, the trial and the implementation are the same thing.

Organization-Level Assessment

Organization level assessment for this project starts with the *financial assessment*. In small hospitals these data are available, usually through your financial officer, who may also be over the business office or have several titles. It is computerized even in small hospitals now, and you can request the information in a report, but you should be very specific about the information and the time period for which you are requesting data. You should also be aware that finance and data processing professionals use the same words, but often with different meanings than nurses so it is helpful to provide an Excel spreadsheet or a table of the variables you would like information about as a starting place. A face-to-face conversation can be helpful as well.

The specific data that you request will depend on the nature of the objectives you are trying to accomplish with the introduction or organization of NP practice. This is really pretty practical. If you are trying to reduce length of stay because of denied days, then you need to collect data about the number of denied days, the cost of those days, the cumulative cost of those days, and the cost of those lost days compared to the cost of an NP. If there are NPs in the organization already, then the mean or median salary range for your organization can be used for salary cost projections in the business plan. Planning for the first NPs for the organization? The American Academy of Nurse Practitioners (AANP) surveys practicing NPs on a regular basis to estimate regional salaries around the country, and they post these salaries on their website (www.AANP.org). If the NP costs less, or the NP costs the same, but you can identify added value of the NP for the same cost in your business plan, then you have justification for the cost. Financial analysis is about justification of cost.

System Assessment

System Assessment is about taking stock of the processes and infrastructure of the organization to determine what is and is not in place to support the diffusion of this new innovation. *Processes* include reporting relationships and decision-making authority as well as formal and informal power or influence. *Infrastructure* refers to the provision of those things necessary for the practice to happen. This includes procedures and personnel for recruiting, hiring, orienting, precepting, credentialing, developing, mentoring, evaluating, and providing administrative support for the NPs when they are integrated into the organization. Infrastructure also includes adequate space for the NPs to have private workspace, private telephone conferencing space that is HIPAA compliant, and computer access. As a matter of policy, will NPs have access to physician parking, dining rooms or lounges, and other perks that have previously been reserved only for physicians?

Begin by examining the organizational chart. Is it flat? Deep? Balanced? Are there many layers of management between bedside caregivers and Chiefs of Service? Where are decisions made? Do first-line managers have the power to control their own budgets and make autonomous decisions or do they have to seek layers of approval before even simple changes can be made at the bedside? The answers to all of these questions will have substantial influence on the success of any attempt at integrating NPs into the hospital. Rogers (2003) has noted that the organization that is more complex, more flexible and responsive, and less bureaucratic is more likely to be successful in adopting an innovation. The purpose of the assessment is not to change what is or to judge what is, but rather to describe what is in place in order to include the characteristics of the organization's structural complexity in the implementation strategy.

Stakeholders are those persons who stand to win or lose based on the success of the innovation. When forming workgroups to solve problems or bring about change, membership is often selected based on the likelihood that the members are going to support the change and benefit from it. Consequently, the arguments against the change are often not heard and are not taken into consideration. This results in two big problems and innumerable potential problems. First, those who have not been included in the discussion because they are not viewed as supportive of the change feel validated in their lack of support and more entrenched in their position. Second, that validation can easily become justification for obstruction and sabotage if the organizational culture fosters that behavior.

Knowledge of the stakeholders and their positions is not a mystery in any organization; however, many assumptions are made about them based entirely on previous experience. While previous experience is a good predictor of current reality, it is not a perfect predictor of current reality. Consequently, due diligence is still necessary, even when people think they know what the position of a stakeholder will be. For example, the fact that Dr. X has been opposed to NPs in general in the past does not mean that under certain different, specific circumstances, he be would again. His position must be assessed.

Even if a hospital already has NPs in practice, there can be no assumption that the infrastructure components of personnel and procedures for recruitment, onboarding, credentialing, orientation, precepting, developing, and supporting are in place or that they are adequate. For those planners that have never had NPs practice in their organizations, the assessment conclusion that those infrastructure components are missing from their organizations will send them to other chapters in this book for help in creating them.

Adding a professional or a category of professional practitioners means that significant resources are necessary to support them. These resources are often forgotten in the planning, if there is any planning prior to the decision to hire NPs. These resources include workspace, preferably away from the unit if the NP is unit-based, so that the NP has privacy to talk with patients, family, and other caregivers without violating patient privacy. There needs to be a computer, printer, and telephone that can be used privately for the same reasons. If the NP's job expectation includes research, publication, advocacy, or other professional activities, there needs to be space away from the clinical work area where the NP can do this work without constant interruption and with access to reference materials to support the work. The lack of these spaces and equipment can contribute to burnout and turnover, increasing recruitment and hiring/orientation costs, which far exceed the cost of this equipment.

Unit Assessment

Unit assessment could mean the physical unit the NP will be working on or the work unit the NP will be part of. Sometimes this is the hardest of assessments to make. There are, however, some clues as to problems that might exist, but are ignored and might create problems or opportunities for NP practice. High turnover, frequent errors, low patient satisfaction scores, high numbers of falls, complications, or complaints from patients and families are clues that the culture or climate of a unit is not healthy. The relative health of the unit per se is neither an indication nor contraindication for the institution of NP practice but another factor for the strategy.

History is important here as well. In the bigger picture of implementing an innovation, successful innovation in the past is associated with being more open to innovation in the future (Rogers, 2003). When considering the introduction of NPs to a unit or team that has tried NPs or PAs in the past and abandoned that practice, it is critical to understand why it did not work so that any addressable problems can be corrected.

Individual-Oriented Assessment

The key question here is whether or not there is room for individual excellence. Are all employees treated equally versus fairly? This is reflected in a longevity-based reward system versus a merit-based reward system. Are there opportunities to identify individuals who excel in certain leadership qualities for leadership development and positioning for future leadership roles in the organization? Organizations that have a formal program in place to identify and develop their future leaders and managers guarantee continuity through succession.

ANALYSIS AND INTERPRETATION

Once all the data are collected, they must be analyzed. There is no single correct way to do this. Rather than searching for a single, comprehensive statement about the organization, the purpose in doing the assessment is to identify strengths, weaknesses, threats, resources, and constraints that will affect the success of NPs introduced to the organization. There are a number of authors who advocate for the strengths, weaknesses, opportunities, and threats or SWOT analysis method, but there is nothing magical about this form of analysis over any other. As with any of the theories and tools taken from business and industry where there is a concrete product that is manufactured, marketed, and sold, the translation to the knowledge/service industry of health care is not exactly a perfect one. For instance, the definitions of opportunity and threat are different for a nonprofit hospital than for a for-profit one, even though the market for both is the same.

The most important thing here is to be very systematic, transparent, comprehensive, and honest with yourself and with each other about the realities of the organization. Ignoring uncomfortable relationships, power struggles, noncompetitive programs, or toxic environments in the hope that they will either not matter or will change on their own can only lead to more problems later on. Putting an NP into the middle of someone else's power struggle will likely make it impossible for the NP to be successful as an individual and will threaten the success of collective NP practice in the organization.

It is very difficult to tell someone how to analyze an organizational assessment. There are, of course, principles and models, as we have indicated. The Agency for Healthcare Research and Quality (AHRQ) has developed a guide for organizations that are implementing innovative ways to improve the quality and safety of the care they deliver. This guide includes a number of helpful resources and tool kits to help assess the organization's resources, culture, readiness to adopt the innovation, and impact of the innovation once it is adopted. This resource offers a very helpful tool kit for assessing the value and significance of the evidence you have collected in the organizational assessment, and it offers direction and structure for ordering and analyzing your findings to support your decision. This AHRQ guide is available at www.innovation.ahrq.gov/WillItWorkHere.pdf. It may still be instructive to demonstrate an example. Exhibit 2.1, gives an example of an organizational assessment that starts with agenda setting and moves through the analysis of an organizational assessment as an exemplar of one way it might be done.

The result of this assessment should be the conclusion, based on the evidence collected in the assessment, that the introduction of NPs into the organization can be supported, and furthermore, that the introduction of NPs into the organizations has one or more clear, measurable objectives by which the success of their integration and their value to the organization can be measured. Without these things, NP practice is not sustainable and the organization will have made a substantial financial and human resource investment with little or no return. The vision of how NPs are a part of the mission of the organization and the clear measurable objectives by which their value to patients and to the organization is demonstrated make up the core of the business plan.

DEVELOPING THE BUSINESS PLAN

The Vision Statement

Once the assessment has been completed, you will need to develop your formal proposal and business plan so that it can be vetted by senior leadership for approval and financial support.

A well-thought-out plan often begins with a vision statement. A vision statement embodies a picture of the future, incorporating the improved processes and outcomes, and it will clarify the general direction for change motivating and helping to coordinate others. Kotter (1996) has identified the following six characteristics of an effective vision. It must be imaginable; desirable; feasible; focused; flexible and easily communicated (see Exhibit 2.2).

An example of a potential vision statement involving the incorporation of an NP into the hospital service can be found in Exhibit 2.3. The vision statement should always begin with the organizational assessment and identified needs. If your organization is focused on reducing the length of stay; ensuring that quality measures are met; and that readmissions are minimized in the management of patients with congestive heart failure (CHF), the addition of a CNP to the hospital service could be visualized as: It is our goal to become a national leader in the care of patients with

EXHIBIT 2.2   Characteristics of an Effective Vision
Imaginable
Desirable
Feasible
Focused
Flexible
Easily communicated
From Kotter (1996).

> **EXHIBIT 2.3   Addition of a NP to Optimize Treatment of Patients with CHF**
>
> It is our goal to become a national leader in the care of patients with congestive heart failure (CHF). This will be achieved through the incorporation of a certified nurse practitioner (CNP) into the multidisciplinary care team, whose role will be to educate patients and care providers, provide care coordination and post-discharge follow-up, ensuring compliance with core measures and quality metrics related to CHF. The addition of this CNP will result in improved patient satisfaction and a shortened length of stay for patients on the CHF service within the next 2 years.

CHF. This will be achieved through the incorporation of a CNP into the multidisciplinary care team, whose role will be to educate patients and care providers, provide care coordination and post-discharge follow up, ensuring compliance with core measures and quality metrics related to CHF. The addition of this CNP will result in improved patient satisfaction and a shortened length of stay (LOS) for patients on the CHF service within the next 2 years. This vision statement provides focus (improve care of CHF patients), points specific to areas requiring improvement (LOS, quality scores), and states a specific measurable target (decreased length of stay for CHF patients within the next 2 years). It is desirable and is easily communicated. Development of an accurate and concise vision statement can be difficult but is critical to success of the proposal. An accurate vision statement takes time to develop and will require input from the team as they give feedback and offer revisions.

Developing the Proposal

Once the vision has been developed, you are ready to begin building the proposal. Your proposal should include, and build upon, recognized strengths identified in your assessments or SWOT (strengths, weaknesses, opportunities, and threats) analysis. Weaknesses can be mitigated by building in support structures or processes that will counteract the identified weaknesses. If there are external threats in the environment, acknowledge them in the proposal as such, developing processes for mitigation if possible. Build upon and enhance the opportunities as identified in the organizational assessment. Identify and outline the direct and indirect impacts of the CNP's role on care delivery. Who will be impacted? How will the outcomes or success be measured?

The proposal to add NPs to a hospital service will require you to review several factors specific to NP practice:

1. Review and understand the scope of NP practice in your state;
2. Assess the availability of properly educated NPs to meet your clinical needs;

3. Evaluate your environment and whether it will accept a new role such as the NP;
4. Assess your institution's ability to mentor and specialty-train the number of NPs that is being proposed.
   Be sure to factor these into your proposal as they may impact your ability to operationalize the innovation.

The projected revenue as well as costs and other resources must be identified and incorporated into the proposal's budget. Be sure to factor in the cost of benefits such as health insurance, paid time off, or continuing education, as well as salaries, when estimating the expenses associated with the NP role. Factor in the cost for coverage if the NP is off and administrative support if required. Estimate professional and technical revenue generated from billable procedures as applicable, based upon the proposed model of care and historical data. Will the CNP be billing professional charges? If so, how often? Will they be performing technical procedures for which the CNP can bill? If so, how frequently will these procedures be performed?

Once the proposal is developed, it is often helpful to seek out and gather feedback and support with both formal and informal leaders prior to presenting your proposal. They may alert you to an unanticipated concerns or unforeseen circumstances or outcomes that you might have overlooked in your planning and proposal, which can then be addressed.

Assessing Organizational Fit

Once you have developed your draft proposal and have vetted it with a number of associated clinical staff, you will next need to assess it for organizational fit. Brach et al. (2008) in the AHRQ publication titled *Will It Work Here? A Decision Makers Guide to Adopting Innovations* (2008) may be helpful to you in this analysis. This guide will take you through a series of steps outlining the various discussion points you should answer to test your innovations for congruence and organizational fit. The sections include: Does the innovation fit? Should we do it here? Can we do it here? and How will we do it here? The guide may be used to further assess or clarify the proposal for the organization.

Development of the Business Plan: Implementation and Resources

The actual proposal is often spelled out in business plan format and is discussed below (see Exhibit 2.4). The business plan begins with an Executive Summary or overview. The Executive Summary will include a brief discussion of the problem, a brief summary of current opportunities based upon the assessment, and an overview of your proposed solution. The

---

EXHIBIT 2.4   Components of the Business Plan

I. Executive Summary
II. Body
  Needs Assessment
  Marketing Plan
  Operational Impacts
  SWOT Analysis
  Space Equipment Requirements and
  Financial Feasibility
  Implementation Plan
  Metrics for Success
  Exit Strategy
  Risk Assessment/Regulatory Implications
III. Summary

Source: Cleveland Clinic (2011)

---

proposal should closely align with organizational objectives or strategies and compatible with the organization's mission and vision.

The body of the business proposal should include an overview of the following elements: the needs assessment; the marketing plan as applicable; operational impacts; results of the SWOT analysis; equipment or space requirements; financial feasibility and opportunities; an implementation plan; key metrics to measure program success; and an exit strategy and associated costs, if applicable. A risk assessment, including legal impacts, regulatory impacts, and tax consequences may also be included as applicable. The business plan will conclude with a recommendation and recommended next steps. Further discussion regarding each of these required elements is included below.

- The needs assessment provides a discussion of the current process, the identified problem or concern, and it provides the *WHY* of the proposal. Include a discussion of the current processes and issues, current baseline data, and outcomes, as applicable.
- The marketing plan section includes information related to the promotional aspects of the business plan. This may be needed if you are adding a new service or marketing an expanded program. Include marketing objectives, strategies, tactics, and marketing budget, as applicable.
- The operations section of the business plan will describe the *HOW* of the plan. Include information about the current organization and management and include information about the proposed organization and management, as applicable. Be sure to include the projected impact on other departments or facilities as part of the operational assessment. Current and required staffing (including available talent, anticipated recruitment, and hiring challenges) should be included in this section.

- The SWOT analysis is included, as well as an explanation of any major findings. The SWOT analysis should include information from the marketing, operational, and financial aspects of the proposal and should discuss how identified issues or concerns will be mitigated. You should also include a discussion on any other initiatives within your department or organization that are planned or underway that could have an impact upon your proposal.
- Space and equipment requirements such as office space or computer access.
- The financial feasibility section depicts the financial implications of the program implementation. Include estimations of the cost of staffing requirements, space and equipment requirements (if associated with the program), as well as any revenue projections associated with the program. Analyze the current state and develop a financial model of projected results once the program is implemented.
- The implementation plan outlines the *WHEN* of the proposal. Include a review of how the project will be managed, estimated timelines, tracking, and key metrics that will be assessed as a result of the program implementation.
- You should consider including an exit strategy and a risk assessment, as applicable. The exit strategy outlines the potential steps required to exit the program along with projected costs associated with the exit. The risk assessment should include an analysis of the legal impacts, the regulatory impacts, and tax impacts associated with the project.

Adapted from Cleveland Clinic Business Plan template (2011).

The Approval Process

Once the proposal has been finalized, it will need to be vetted by senior leadership for approval and financial support. As a manager, you may be involved in presenting the formal presentation to senior leadership. Presentations should be concise, comprehensive, and professional in appearance. Articulate the need clearly, aligning the proposal with the hospital's mission and strategic objectives. Discuss the rationale for the addition of the NP, including a discussion on weaknesses and threats and how they will be mitigated. Include measures of success and discuss how these will be measured. Include the projected revenue as well as expenses. Summarize the presentation by reviewing the need and the proposal, and end with a time for discussion and questions.

Implementation of the Proposal

Once the proposal has been approved by senior leadership, the working group or team is often charged with carrying out the implementation. Inclusion of members of the working team in the development of the action plan will help to ensure buy-in and avoid overlooking important steps in the process.

The action plan should identify each of the following components: objectives of the proposal; actions required to meet each objective, including steps and timelines; designated personnel for each of the steps; organizational resources that will be required; and how results will be measured. These objectives should be clearly articulated, well defined, and measurable. A commonly used acronym for goal setting is SMART. Smart goals are specific, measurable, attainable, results oriented, and time bound (Kinicki & Kreitner, 2008). The action plan should incorporate a series of SMART goals that build upon others, culminating with the program implementation and a proposal for ongoing evaluation.

It will be necessary to identify the steps needed to accomplish each key component. A timeline or Gantt chart should be established to ensure that the proposal stays on target. Beginning and ending dates for each step also help to provide structure and accountability for each of the identified steps. This helps to assure that all necessary components have been identified and addressed (Swayne, Duncan, & Ginter, 2008).

Developing the action plan can be challenging. It is often difficult to get agreement and buy-in from all involved parties. Each step may raise further discussion, questions, concerns, or controversies. Leaders need to be adept at consensus building and decision making. They must also be flexible enough to recognize when something is not working and be willing to step back and look at the proposed process for required changes or improvements.

Fostering Change

Transformational leadership is defined by the ability to create a compelling vision and by creating an environment that supports exploration, experimentation, risk taking, and sharing of ideas (Jung, Chow, & Wu, 2003). Successful leaders need to not only develop new ideas or innovations but also to implement them and assure their ongoing success. The transformational leader has the ability to clearly communicate the vision, yet remain open and flexible enough to see the big picture, maintaining the flexibility needed for a change-oriented organization.

Leaders can help employees adapt to change through implementation of the change commitment process advocated by Conner (1992). In the preparation stage, employees hear about the change through staff meetings and personal contact and discussion. In the acceptance stage, leaders help the employees understand the full nature and impact of the proposed change, focusing on the positive aspects of the change. The third stage represents the commitment stage and involves installation and institutionalization. Installation may be a trial or pilot project, which give leaders the opportunity to assess the impact of the change and identify concerns or problems that were previously unrecognized or were not planned for. In the final step of institutionalization, employees accept the change as part of their normal workday and process.

To foster the acceptance of the CNP role, it will be important to include all members of the health care team in the discussion about the NP role, their function, and role expectations. It may be helpful to have members of the multidisciplinary care team included in the interview process. The new NP should be oriented to all members of the team and should be told about their roles in the care of the patients, in order to help facilitate the NP's acceptance into the team and to help ensure success.

Daft (2007) has identified a number or potential barriers that may be encountered during the change process, including an excessive focus on cost, failure to perceive benefits, lack of coordination and cooperation, uncertainty avoidance, and fear of loss. Leaders need to be alert to and aware of these concerns and barriers and must build plans into the programs to counteract these as part of the proposal and implementation planning and process.

CONCLUSION

This chapter has focused on the organizational assessment that is required prior to the development of a proposal for an innovation. Factors to assess have been reviewed along with the process for analysis and interpretation. Finally, the process of developing a business plan has been discussed along with factors to be aware of when fostering change within the organization.

REFERENCES

Brach, C., Lenfestey, N., Roussel, A., Amoozegar, J., & Sorensen, A. (2008). *Will it work here? A decision maker's guide to adopting innovations.* Prepared by RTI International under Contract No. 233-02-0090. Agency for Healthcare Research and Quality (AHRQ) Publication No. 08-0051. Rockville, MD: AHRQ; September 2008.

Cleveland Clinic. (2011). Business Plan Narrative. Cleveland, OH: Author.

Conner, D. (1992). *Stages of commitment to change.* New York: Villard Books.

Daft, R. (2007). *Organizational theory & design* (9th ed.). Mason, OH: Thomson South-Western.

Jung, D., Chow, C., & Wu, A. (2003). The role of transformational leadership in enhancing organizational innovation: Hypotheses and some preliminary findings. *The Leadership Quarterly, 14,* 525–544.

Kinicki, A., & Kreitner, R. (2008). *Organizational behavior: Key concepts, skills & best practices* (3rd ed.). New York: McGraw-Hill/Irwin.

Kotter, J. (1996). *Leading change.* Boston, MA: Harvard Business School Press.

Rogers, E. (2003). *Diffusion of innovation* (5th ed.). New York: Free Press.

Swayne, L., Duncan, J., & Ginter, P. (2008). *Strategic management of health care organizations* (6th ed.). West Sussex, England: Jossey-Bass.

3

Developing a Model for Centralized Nurse Practitioner Leadership

Carmel A. McComiskey, Renay Tyler, and Lisa Rowen

The tertiary medical system is complex, comprised of many departments, processes, and systems. These include adult and pediatric patient care units, medical departments, surgical departments, and those that support patient care service (e.g., dietary, materials management, central supply, housekeeping, and information technology). There are additional departments that provide ongoing service support (e.g., safety, quality improvement, human resources, and informatics). Each of these provides value to the patient, but must be interwoven by an effective leadership team that incorporates initiatives and builds a synergistic model in order to support a common goal: a safe and positive patient care experience. The acute care nurse practitioner (ACNP) role is well suited for this environment. The nurse practitioner (NP) is frequently the glue that synchronizes the many aspects and levers necessary to drive the care experience for each individual patient admission. The goal of this chapter is to describe the process of developing and implementing a leadership model for the NP workforce in an academic medical center. It will include the important stages of integrating the NP into the organization, the NP professional community, and the health care team.

SETTING THE STAGE

Expanding Numbers of NPs in the Hospital Setting: Need for Leadership

Safe, efficient, cost-effective, and quality care are the health care goals for the new millennium. Porter-O'Grady and Malloch (2007) suggested that medical errors offer opportunity for organizational leaders to improve the processes and systems within health care. The traditional academic medical model (Figure 3.1) relied on an apprenticeship hierarchy that allowed for a slow, methodical teaching from the attending physician to the medical student. It utilizes a chain of command that takes its time

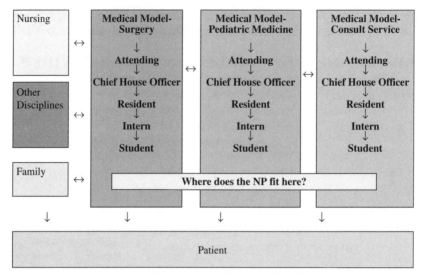

FIGURE 3.1   Classic academic medical center model.

to make decisions. Changing the medical team in academic medical centers from an apprenticeship model to one of interprofessional collaboration and teamwork, which uses best evidence to drive patient care decision making, does not happen merely by the introduction of the NP to the team. This apprenticeship model of care continues to allow fragmented care to be delivered by inexperienced providers, and although NPs fill the gap, there continues to be competition for who directs patient management and confusion about independent decision making. Although education of physicians about NP practice continues, many physicians still expect to utilize the NP as a resident substitute. NPs' collaborative ability is well known and respected. However, in some instances, their infusion into the medical model has resulted in duplication of work product and effort as well as confusion about patient care decision making.

The Nurse Practitioner as an Innovation in Health Care: The Changing Landscape

The nurse practitioner is a key interface in the relationship between the family, the patient, the nursing staff, and the medical/surgical team. There are hundreds of teams within health care organizations whose shared goal includes the delivery of safe patient care. Although each of these teams attempts to share expertise, they often compete rather than collaborate to "control" the patient care environment. Leaders are challenged to embrace the complexity of this environment in order to create a seamless creative patient care experience that focuses on each unique patient. Quality and safety initiatives have identified challenges that include the need for improved provider handoff and for improved communication among team members and between teams. NPs are well positioned to lead these quality improvements. A recent systematic review by Newhouse et al. (2011) reported the results of published literature about NP outcomes between 1990 and 2008. This review provides strong evidence that NPs in collaboration with physicians had outcomes that were similar to, and in some cases better than, physician outcomes alone. The results indicated that NPs provide high quality and effective patient care, have a role in improving the quality of health care, and help address concerns about whether the NP can augment the care provided by physicians in order to meet care needs.

Scope of Practice

With the Accreditation Council for Graduate Medical Council's (ACGME) recommendation mandating the reduction of work hours by residents, NPs have been recruited to provide inpatient care. Robles and colleagues (2011) recently reported that adding a NP to an academic surgical service improved the utilization of resources. This need is highlighted now in an era when medical and surgical training hours are changing to provide coverage in a shift-like way, where service and duty hours are counted, while the work of patient care often occurs, even though surgical education is focused in the operating room. NPs are being recruited to fill the gaps: to improve throughput, the discharge process, communication, and real-time problem solving; to decrease readmission; to provide patient education and continuity; and to improve satisfaction.

While the shift from residents to NPs seems logical, the shift has been made sporadically. For example, some medical departments might have expected the NP workforce to replace the house staff, assuming that the NP would merely function as a physician extender. Many practitioners were hired to staff in the critical care setting. Alternatively, NPs have been hired to augment service lines. As a result, the role of the NP has become, in some instances, dependent on the need that the position was created to meet, rather than restructuring the work. This paradigm shift could be streamlined by testing the old models with process improvement initiatives that might challenge the status quo and develop new ways of working. In fact, Reay, Golden-Biddle, and Germann (2003) reported the results of a survey that challenged managers of NPs to: clarify the reallocation of tasks, manage the work within the teams, and work with the teams to develop roles.

Fitting the NP into the traditional medical model of health care delivery (Figure 3.1) as the sole solution to the mandated reduction in resident work hours has not been efficient and has contributed to NP turnover. The NP's entry to the medical team has highlighted the complexity of the system and magnified inherent flaws in the apprenticeship model that allows the most junior in experience to work without adequate supervision. The NP role on the interprofessional team addresses the Institute of Medicine's (IOM) recommendations for change. These include delivering patient-centered care, working as part of an interprofessional team, practicing evidence-based medicine, focusing on quality improvement, and utilizing informatics (Institute of Medicine, 2003). In a more recent report, the Committee on the Robert Wood Johnson Foundation Initiative on the Future of Nursing (2010) has recommended that nurses be allowed to practice to their full scope in order to meet the patients' needs in an ever-changing health care environment that has a greater emphasis on reducing error and decreasing cost. As health care reform occurs, it will become necessary to utilize this workforce to the full scope of practice in order to efficiently meet the care delivery needs and collaborate with, rather than compete with other health-care providers for the work.

Making the Case for a Centralized Leadership Model

Recruitment and Retention

Recruitment and retention of NPs into the tertiary environment has been problematic. Inefficiencies in the recruitment process have led to increased cost, fragmented patient care processes, and staff frustration. Additionally, the process of hiring a new NP staff member (onboarding), credentialing, role development, and service orientation requires additional time and expertise. Integration into the medical team may be fragmented. Many times, the role is new to the medical team and little thought has been given to how to integrate the NP, what the NP work might look like, and who will be responsible to train the NP about the population-specific diseases and management strategies required in order to provide expert tertiary care. At some health care organizations, NPs have reported that they received little or no orientation; others have been encouraged to attend the nursing orientation, which provides little or no provider-focused information. Often, the NP has developed an orientation that has been service-driven or self-directed where no formal orientation existed.

Recruiting and retaining NPs should include developing standardized hiring and salary/benefit packages that ensure internal NP salary equity within the entire environment, credentialing the NP providers with established delineation of privileges, developing collaborative agreements or attestation, if necessary for licensure, doing background references checks, and providing assistance with the "basics" (see Chapter 5). A centralized leader who can focus on these issues provides an active solution for many of these problems. Morse and Brown (1999) identified

Advanced Practice Nurse (APN) credentialing as one of five critical obstacles to APN satisfaction. When hired by service line administrators in medicine or surgery practice offices, there remains confusion regarding how to credential this professional group.

Credentialing challenges

Challenges exist within complex organizations that may unwittingly hinder the successful integration of the NP into the system. Departmental clerical staff lack knowledge and are unable to support NP credentialing, often failing to process paperwork. There can be a lack of knowledge about the NP role among other support systems and therefore an unwillingness to assist the practitioner with tasks, such as when administrative assistants refuse to transcribe practitioner notes, stating that they only work for physicians. Even credentialing departments lack experience about the advanced practice provisions and often fail to grant appropriate delineation of privileges to the NPs. The integration of this new role into the complex system can be hindered at all levels. Centralizing the process to provide leadership of the NP workforce is needed to educate, foster relationships, promote retention of expert staff, and to provide support.

Retention of NPs continues to be difficult. Although advocates for the NP role exist within the traditional medical model, there may little motivation to foster the development of a collaborative practice model. The traditional hierarchal personnel management continues to flourish, and NPs continue to be positioned in an outmoded organizational chart where they might find themselves "supervised" by a nonclinical administrative leader. However, in those subspecialties where senior NP leadership exists, collaboration and partnership with physicians occurs and the NP model flourishes, thus proving that mentoring of new NPs can be expected and planned, when time to explore partnerships and to build expertise is provided and these actions are embraced. The centralized NP leader provides mechanisms to support these activities which promotes retention of expert staff.

Performance Measures

Although NPs are licensed independent providers who can practice in a variety of care settings, it is crucial to establish descriptive and objective metrics that will measure the performance as well as establish guidelines for practice in new roles. Without established and understood performance expectations there remains the possibility of underutilization of the NP resources within the institution. Inequity as well as delay in NP performance evaluations can occur and lead to frustration as well as wage disparity among NPs performing similar jobs when there is no centralized way to monitor salary or mentorship of NPs by NPs. When

NPs report to a combination of supervisors with varying educational preparation (administrators, physicians, nurse managers, other NPs) confusion occurs around practice metrics, goal setting, and accomplishments. Prior to 2008, at one academic medical center, 40% of NPs reported to physicians who were not, themselves, employees of the hospital. The majority of those evaluating NP performance may have little if any understanding of the NP role or the scope of practice, or any understanding of how to describe NP quality related to patient outcomes, and thus unwittingly may potentially discount their contribution to the system. This directly relates to NP job satisfaction and retention. The NP leader must focus on means for measuring success across the institution in order for the NP and the institution to continue to thrive.

CENTRALIZING THE PROCESS

Establishing a System for Self-Governance

The current health care climate's emphasis on quality and safety has encouraged such organizations as the American Nurses Credentialing Center to develop the Magnet™ designation, an award for those hospitals who meet the highest nursing standards. Inherent in the Magnet framework and required of Magnet designated organizations is the self-governance model. As NPs practice in a variety of services and settings and many do not report through traditional nursing chains, the development of APN councils in many organizations may be the first opportunity to address the gaps that exist in NP practice. These councils are, for many organizations, the first means to establish advanced practice nursing leadership. The council members begin to explore the contributions of the workforce and to identify the support necessary to APNs' successful integration. The advent of APN councils begins as a collaborative self-governance body of experienced APNs who establish a dialogue with nursing, medical, and hospital leadership in order to address the successful integration of this growing workforce into the bigger health care organization. These early councils quickly identify practice challenges. Establishment of this support system allows the NP to become an empowered and informed team member and should be one goal of the organization's leadership team (Porter-O'Grady & Malloch, 2007). The goal of these groups is to establish a framework that directs advanced practice nursing initiatives; and setting these priorities as a strategic document helps to establish credibility (Figure 3.2).

Developing a centralized NP model allows NPs to lead and foster, mentor and guide advanced practice nursing. Once this council development process begins, council members may address issues in an efficient fashion. These early self-governance councils identify unique organization-specific barriers that prevent successful practice. These may include

The Advanced Practice Nurse (APN) Council provides strategic direction and innovative ideas for developing, implementing and evaluating APN practice models, as well as for suggesting solutions to APN related clinical issues at University of Maryland Medical Center. This council assists Senior Leadership in setting the practice environment and provides an advisory role for operational issues that affect clinical practice. The council has a collaborative role with the University of Maryland School of Nursing (UMSON) as well as with other disciplines within the practice setting.

Key Responsibilities:
- Provide support for advanced practice nursing issues.
- Advance the provision of nursing care delivered at the bedside to improve patient care outcomes.
- Encourage and support use of evidenced-based practice and research by advanced practice nurses.

Key Strategies:
People:
- Build and foster maintenance of strong relationships between APNs and other nurses, as well as health care professionals from other disciplines.
- Provide a forum for APN communication for the purposes of information sharing and learning.

Service:
- Provide consultation in areas regarding the role of APNs and in clinical topics where specific APNs are expert.
- Foster a collaborative relationship with the (UMSON) University of maryland school of nursing regarding didactic and clinical curriculum.

Safety and Quality:
- Foster safe and high-quality patient care by promoting the use of evidence-based best practices and strategizing about changes that encourage optimal patient outcomes.

Stewardship:
- Encourage efficient and cost-effective clinical practices that help to achieve optimal patient outcomes.
- Consider policies and legislative issues affecting the APN role.

Innovation:
- Provide innovative ideas for developing, implementing and evaluating APN practice models and for suggesting solutions to APN-related clinical practice issues.

FIGURE 3.2 Adaptation of the University of Maryland Medical Center's APN Council Strategic Goals.

recruitment problems, lack of understanding of the NP role, lack of clarity about NP contributions, lack of appropriate role development or job descriptions, lack of orientation or mentoring of new graduates, lack of professional advancement opportunities, inability to establish a networking and support system, and finally, difficulty in establishing metrics and effective standards to guide performance.

Once a group of advanced practice nurses agrees that oversight is needed or the organization identifies this need, early grassroots discussions can take place. During these meetings, the NPs usually can identify many common themes and challenges. The appointment of a senior NP leader organizes the process and accelerates advancements needed for this group of providers. This leader gathers the NP stakeholders together and seeks to understand the institutional challenges and opportunities. One can then develop forums for brainstorming possible solutions, creating strategic plans, and testing the climate for the readiness for change. It is recommended that the leader identify other senior NPs and develop a partnership in order to organize goals and implement strategies to identify common themes, assess the environment, develop short- and long-term goals, and evaluate the benefits of working as a more formalized team. This small but efficient group can take important first steps to gain momentum toward the establishment of a broader leadership system and establish a foundation of resources to increase the chance for success of this developing leadership system. The next step includes the development of a high-profile APN council—including a senior clinical nurse specialist (CNS), certified registered nurse anesthetist (CRNA), senior certified nurse midwife (CNM), and faculty from the partnering school of nursing. Together this group of APNs can utilize each other's strengths and learn from the prior mistakes of each group in order to develop systems for all APNs in the institution. Typically the NP group represents the largest proportion of APN providers and therefore several NP representatives from a variety of practice settings will be needed. Communication with executive leadership about potential solutions for the gaps that exist in practice, role, salary, onboarding, and performance is essential during this process. It may take several years of work for an individual lead NP to garner the support for a centralized reporting structure. Evolution takes time, and committed leadership is requisite in order to overcome the initial inertia of preexisting/marginally functioning systems. The timing of the proposal of such a model should be selected carefully.

Engaging Stakeholders

There are many stakeholders during this process whose perspectives, opinions, and needs drive the conversations. These include the NPs who make up the workforce. At the University of Maryland Medical Center (UMMC), this workforce rapidly grew from approximately 35 NPs to greater than 80 in a 3-year period. These NPs were employed by three distinct employers—the hospital, the physician practice, and the medical school. Initially, no school of nursing faculty NPs shared dual appointments, although work was beginning that would forge that relationship as well. NP salary, benefits, policies, and procedures varied among employers. Presently there are over 200 advanced practice nurses employed by the medical center; the number of NPs employed by the faculty practice has decreased to 29, which we attribute to the model's success.

Paramount to success when gathering the NPs together is to communicate and gather support from physician leaders, current NP administrators, and nursing leaders. Each group has its own priorities and each holds beliefs about the NP role that deserve consideration as the NP group establishes its agenda. For example, depending on the reporting structure that exists within the health care organization, any group may misunderstand the goals of the initiative. Physician colleagues, especially in academic medical centers, have rigid reporting hierarchies that must be addressed in order to assure they will support the initiatives. If a centralized reporting structure becomes a reality, the physicians must understand the collaborative and strategic intention of the model and must be assured that the individual NP/MD relationship will be encouraged and supported. Nursing leadership may also need to understand the benefits of partnering with this workforce. Our experience has shown that nurse managers and directors were uncomfortable leading APNs; many reported a lack of experience and lack of confidence when challenged to support the expanded scope of practice.

The centralized leadership model gains support only when the medical and nursing executives recognize the need. The formally appointed APN leader should fully engage fellow nursing executives at the leadership table and be authorized to provide the NP link to the medical leadership. Self-appointed leaders lack formal authority and often lack the support of their constituents to effect any real change. Finally, the position has greater chance for success with fiscal responsibility for NP resources. This is an essential lever when there is a request for NP resources and positions are allocated.

Engaging NPs

The early response to a centralized model of NP leadership from the APN workforce may be surprising. New graduate NPs struggle with role development and knowledge acquisition as well as with navigating the transition from expert RN to novice NP to expert NP, so these novices welcome support from a designated leader focused on their professional development. Senior NPs may resist this initiative. Many excuses can be offered, which include reports that they have little time in their workday to collaborate with NP colleagues from other services or units, or that their physician partner does not support the initiative, or that they lack any interest to change the structure for fear that the new model will not improve the status quo. Three chief levers influence the paradigm shift: satisfaction, recruitment/retention, and role confusion. Gathering and analyzing both NP and physician satisfaction data offers evidence to support a change. Surveys are easy ways to gather the data that support the need for change.

ROLE OF NP LEADERSHIP IN THE MEDICAL CENTER

Developing a leadership model that embraces, supports, and values the NP's vision and autonomy addresses only one issue of blending the NP into the inpatient medical team. Richmond and Becker (2005) reported eight characteristics important to creating an NP-friendly environment. These include: clarity of vision and values, commitments, communication, collaboration, credibility, contributions, confidence, and complexity.

Van Soeren and Micevski (2001) evaluated the barriers to the implementation of an acute care NP role, which include lack of mentorship, lack of knowledge from colleagues about the role, and lack of support from administration and physicians. NPs reported improving patient care, paying attention to patient care issues, and enhancing quality and consistency of care. Respondents also reported that mentorship and development of purpose and value of the role would ease the acute care NP into the health care team.

Successes in Similar Organizations

Many tertiary academic centers have developed centralized leadership models to support APN practice. Chapter 4 provides the description of a model leadership program. These centralized leadership structures focus on education, professional development and coaching, practice development, and credentialing. Bahouth and colleagues (2012) reported on the need for a centralized process to support advanced practice providers by describing similarities among six large health systems across the United States. Of these, five of six reported greater than a 100% increase in the number of NP roles within a 4-year period, underscoring the need for centralized leadership. These authors reported common challenges that are summarized in Table 3.1.

The Role of the Director

Several academic medical centers have established the creation of an advanced practice director or chief advanced practice officer. This leadership position is designed to lead an APN leadership team to develop a strategic initiative that incorporates the mission of the organization in order to lead the changes that ensure the successful integration of the NP into inpatient practice. In several models, the director leads a team of NP leaders who manage NPs who are focused around specific patient populations (Figure 3.3). These leaders have responsibility for up to 20 NPs and have developed a foundation for mentoring novice practitioners and also challenging the expert NPs to explore opportunities to initiate evidence-based improvements to their practices. With this level of supportive leadership, this provider workforce can be integrated more effectively into the complex system. Broad role descriptions of the APN Director and Lead NP are listed in Table 3.2.

The leader of this workforce should be an advanced practice nurse who can champion the role and articulate the advantages of new practice models. The leader has to understand the policies that govern systems within the organization. The leader needs to pay attention to the

TABLE 3.1 Common Challenges in a Decentralized Advanced Practice Nursing Leadership Model

CHALLENGES	POSSIBLE NEGATIVE OUTCOMES
Fragmented reporting structures	Ineffective communication between NPs and both nursing and medical leadership
Lack of standardized process for hiring, credentialing, and orientation	Lack of clarity for the NP role Ineffective utilization of the provider Lack of accountability
Multiple entry points into practice within the campus	Lack of accountability for a standardized APN scope
Variable scope of practice among NP	No institutional awareness regarding role development or scope of practice alignment
Inefficiencies in addressing NP professional issues	Lack of consistent and clear APN expertise to guide and standardize expectations
Difficulty with recruitment and retention	Costly turnover Unsafe staffing patterns
Lack of centralized budgeting and resource utilization, creating duplication and waste	Underutilization of existing resources
Lack of a professional ladder	Two-tiered status within some academic centers
Role confusion	Physician/organizational confusion and dissatisfaction Unclear, unsafe accountability

Source: Bahouth et al. (2012).

relationships within the medical leadership of the organization and be empowered to engage the physicians in dialogue and decision making about the NP role. The NP leader must understand and communicate effectively; the physicians must engage this person and respect his or her ability to understand the issues, bridge gaps, gain consensus, and be successful in creating change. The NP leader must be approachable and knowledgeable

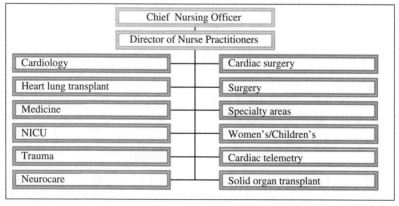

FIGURE 3.3 University of Maryland Nurse Practitioner organizational chart.

TABLE 3.2   Role Differentiation Between the APN Director and the Lead NPs

APN DIRECTOR	LEAD NP
Strategic planning	Team planning
Organizational representation of APN providers	Represents a team of NPs who are responsible for a patient-focused population
Responsibility for hiring lead NPs, contributing to model development, leading NP mentoring	Manager responsibility for hiring, orientation, annual appraisal, corrective action, mentoring
Fiscal direction and accountability for salary, market analysis, salary equity, professional advancement, credentialing process, medical staff office and risk, quality and safety reporting	Local team responsibility for managing moonlighting and allocation of manpower within the teams
Utilization of the NP provider role across departments	Utilization of the NP provider role within teams

and willing to share a vision that will transform the environment in order to improve care by the addition of NPs to the workforce.

The goals of a centralized NP leadership support the NP's entry into the academic medical center. The leadership team can standardize NP practice, identify quality indicators for practice, develop HR policies, identify new practice opportunities, partner with physician and organizational leaders to create new NP roles, recruit the most appropriate applicants, and create a mentorship program for novice NPs so they might gain expertise, surrounded by support that allows them to flourish. Bahouth and colleagues (2012) identified goals crucial to the success of centralizing the APN leadership model: streamline the reporting structure, improve NP productivity, and simplify the work environment. These authors describe teams of experienced NPs who continue to identify processes to address the NP's entry into the acute care environment, as well as giving ongoing support that fosters relationships and provides resources that allow full participation in building a new health care team. The teams have improved other multidisciplinary relationships by teaching a new awareness of NP scope of practice, and the leaders continue to partner with the physician/nursing leadership to ensure that individual NPs are supported and that the environment exists to promote individual, autonomous, and collaborative care wherever there is NP practice. A process to manage and evaluate individual performance is used that enhances job satisfaction, encourages self-evaluation, and promotes job advancement.

Leadership Philosophy

The goal of the leadership model is not to micromanage individuals but to create environments where NPs can be successful. It is intended to shift the locus of control to the individual practitioner, to develop a practice

TABLE 3.3   Common Obstacles and Challenges in Developing a Leadership Model

- NP opposition
- Lack of executive leadership support
- Physician opposition
- NP anxiety about the change in reporting
- Fragmented hiring practices
- Multiple entry points into the system (faculty practices, hospital employment, schools of nursing and medicine)
- NPs' lack of formal human resources and budgetary training

model that supports collaboration, fosters and facilitates independent practice, and coordinates patient-centered care. It is not intended to be a decision-making hierarchy, but instead a model to support the evolution of strong and collaborative members of the health care team who can make independent decisions based on sound team principles, advance the patient's plan of care, and ensure the safest and best outcomes for the patient.

Crucial for the success of this model is the director's philosophy about leading a professional workforce. The notion that the leader is, in fact, someone who "supervises" from the top down is outmoded and may contribute to the failure of this system to sustain success in the future (Lichtenstein et al., 2006). The NP director will likely champion the NPs' independence and work toward the goal of interprofessional collaborative practice models. The NP leader might well focus on relationships rather than on owning or directing. That leader will unite NPs who practice within individual teams by supporting their growth and networking capability to strengthen individual performance within the interprofessional model.

Hazy (2006) describes five leadership areas or levers necessary to support sustainability in complex systems. These include working for collaborative benefit, improving process effectiveness, promoting and sharing learning and knowledge, innovating and nurturing powerful ideas, and balancing investment and risk. By doing this, the NP leader establishes a stronger, more sustainable organization. Encouraging autonomous individuals to practice for the collective benefit strengthens the system. This channels the individual's effort toward the organizational framework.

Team Building

The same is true for facilitating team dynamics, in order to improve effectiveness and promote the team's accountability. Leaders who promote process effectiveness send cues to the members that allow them to self-organize. This encourages teams to work together to combine resources and improves the financial goals of the organization. Leaders who nurture innovation will enable the adoption of new ideas to survive. Respect for innovation and the opportunity to create and explore new ways of thinking and working will strengthen the organization. Finally, leadership that defines a consistent mechanism for project selection adds value to the organization and reduces risk. This is important when defining new roles for the NPs, especially as competing areas clamor for more support. The criteria for NP resource allocation can be monitored in a manner that supports the financial strength of the organization, thus assuring quality care to services that can document the need and the appropriate utilization of the role.

Comprehensive Recruitment Strategy

Centralizing the NP workforce allows for streamlining recruitment strategies. The process of interviews and decisions about hiring should be accomplished in the same way with the same criteria across the organization. Salary, benefits, schedules, and advancement opportunities are managed with a strategy that looks at the needs of the team, the patients, and the individual employees to encourage job satisfaction and fairness. Internal salary equity can be assured; salary packages are standardized based on experience and without bias. Having a centralized way to measure the way of working, salary metrics, and individual service needs also allows for fair and equitable resource allocation and standardized performance evaluation.

Development of an orientation program ensures the NP's successful integration into the team and assures everyone that the individual has the knowledge, skills, and abilities that are necessary to practice. Establishing a standardized approach to orientation (Chapter 6) ensures accountability and safety and encourages a culture of ongoing learning, clear expectations, and role development. The leadership model encourages the physicians to collaborate and provide expert medical knowledge about a defined patient population. The NP leader ensures that the new or novice NP has the opportunities to master the elements of the broadened scope of practice, and can monitor the steps necessary to demonstrate procedural competency. The leader is a key mentor, providing verbal and written feedback along the continuum and, together with the NP, should plan a course that allows the NP to develop an ongoing and goal-oriented career trajectory.

Professional Advancement

Once the NP leadership model has resources to establish and develop an environment that supports advanced practice, there is an opportunity to develop strategic planning that includes professional advancement. NP advancement models encourage evidence-based practice, practice-based expertise, continued academic commitment, preceptor opportunities, and legislative roles in health care reform. This environment challenges the NPs at every phase of their careers promotes a scholarly environment of continued growth, and enhances retention of these expert advanced practice nurses.

How to Operationalize the Leadership Structure

Once the CNO and senior hospital administrators recognize the need and garner the necessary support for the role, appointment of the formal leader can occur. In the University of Maryland Medical Center model, the director was empowered with fiscal responsibility and given authority to develop and implement the model. Moving the NP budget into a centralized cost center model took a full year. During this time, plans to align the existing workforce into functional teams began. There were two NP clinical program managers, formally appointed prior to this management realignment, and the rest of the team was appointed and promoted into a similar preexisting job description that mirrored what had been established by the trauma and cardiology services. The remaining positions were delineated to align NP teams around patient populations and NP certifications. For example, all pediatric NPs were designated together; all neonatal NPs were cohorted; NPs who had neurocare scope of practice were cohorted, and medicine and surgical service lines were established. Small but focused NP specialty areas were cohorted together; for example: our PREP center, Palliative Care NP, and our NP-Ambulatory Zone, an innovative NP-only model in the emergency department. This created a model that required 12 lead NPs. Additional funding was allocated to allow for promotion of these leaders. The NP lead salary offered 5% to 20% more remuneration than the most senior team member. The leadership team organizational structure is outlined in Figure 3.3 (page TK).

NP Leads or Program Manager Selection

The University of Maryland experience included a promotion process in order to allow for NPs to apply for lead positions, especially when there were areas with many experienced providers. The criteria for promotion were based on clinical expertise, maturity, leadership potential, ability to garner stakeholder support, and traits that exhibited the emotional intelligence that would be necessary as the model was conceived. Training for the group of NPs with identified leadership potential began years prior to the inception of the formalized centralized leadership model. This developed the leadership skills for a larger group of NPs and provided foundational skills in areas such as communication (active listening, crucial conversations, providing feedback), conducting a performance evaluation, and leading a meeting. Once the leaders from internal and external sources were hired, two intensive leadership retreats occurred with the support of organizational development experts from the hospital's human resources (HR) department. Finally, an HR specialist was identified who would partner with this new management team; she was charged with teaching and mentoring these new managers about the knowledge, skills, and abilities to assure their success. Ongoing support for this development continues. A leadership team retreat occurs every 6 months. Recently, the leaders participated in a talent assessment. These results will drive the next leadership retreat that will focus the group's development as well as fill individual gaps. Considerable anxiety exists around communication, giving positive and negative feedback to employees who were formerly peers, and establishing metrics for performance improvement. Early in the process, the NP leaders self-identified challenges regarding the need for effective communication. This has resulted in ongoing support from the director as well as creating ways to provide learning opportunities that focus on formalized communication techniques.

Time Management

One remaining challenge that exists is to strike a balance of clinical and administrative time. All leaders, including the director, maintain active clinical practices. Although this reinforces their credibility as experts in the provision of advanced practice nursing, it certainly challenges their time management and organizational abilities. With a variety of competing priorities, there is little time for problem-solving or creative strategic planning. This challenge is ongoing in a financial climate that requires efficient use of personnel to manage patients' clinical needs.

Fiscal Advantages to Planned Integration of NPs Within the Organization

The nurse practitioner director can be instrumental in planning for and ensuring the system's resources are maximally utilized. Exploration of reimbursement for the care of this licensed independent provider can occur, which will further offset the cost of care. Other fiscal advantages to the organization include broad visioning and strategic allocation of NP resources with a shared vision for the NP role. Prior to the model, NP positions were allocated with variability, service favoritism, and without consideration of what the work was and how it should best be accomplished.

Fiscal advantages to the individual NP employee include standardizing the salary matrix and insisting it be built upon years of nursing and advanced practice nursing experiences. When different departments and different administrators could independently negotiate salary, NPs could likely be underpaid or overpaid; salary was not standardized and internal equity was not ensured. Reversing this has a positive effect on retention, provides fairness to the entire NP workforce, and has improved satisfaction.

FUTURE CHALLENGES

Development of the Interprofessional Care Delivery Model

One critical component of success as we move ahead is to actively engage and implement a new patient care delivery system that might include the development of an interprofessional health care model. The NP is positioned perfectly to lead this team as well as to synthesize and deliver a plan of care as encouraged by this IOM recommendation: deliver patient-centered care by members of an interdisciplinary team, emphasize evidence-based practice, continuously improve quality, and maximize informatics.

NP roles have been described as "disruptive innovation" by Dr. Uhlig in 2006 (Pogue, 2007). As such, they have the potential to be the impetus in the process of achieving a transformed health care system. Outcomes of NP care must continue to be planned and measured. NPs already provide patient-centered care, but metrics to measure their value must be established in order to validate their contribution as well as to meet regulatory requirements of health care agencies that measure quality and safe provision of health. In order to accomplish this, individual NP outcomes need to be tracked and reported.

One of the challenges of providing patient-centered care by a multidisciplinary team occurs when the mission of the organization includes education. The tertiary health care system's mission also includes providing expert, specialized care to critically ill patients with complicated medical and social problems. This can highlight the conflicting values of providing traditional educational experiences while still providing comprehensive and streamlined multidisciplinary evidence-based care. Utilizing the NPs' roles and ensuring their efficiency and effectiveness must be intentionally woven into the delivery system with the intention of bridging these goals. The NP, as the consistent licensed independent provider, must ensure ethical and cost-effective care despite the hierarchy that is inherent in the teaching model. NP patient management is cost effective, ethical, and safe and it ensures that the care is appropriate, reducing duplication and error that can occur with inexperienced novice decision making. Within all disciplines there remain cultural and paradigm assumptions that must be identified, and strategies must be developed that overcome the barriers to team approaches to health care delivery. The organizational leadership must ensure the opportunity to evaluate the existing evidence regarding these barriers as well as establish care delivery metrics. This will result in improved patient and organizational outcomes (Pogue, 2007).

CONCLUSION

The nurse practitioner role in the tertiary medical system adds value to patient care. Patients report increased satisfaction with NPs, and they acknowledge improved communication with the care team. Nurses report improved communication when an NP provides the patients' medical decision making. One nursing survey conducted at the University of Maryland reported 95% of RNs preferred the NP to manage the patient and 95% reported confidence in the NPs' care. NPs provide patient-centered, culturally sensitive, evidence-based care in interdisciplinary teams. They are well suited, with continued system support and leadership, to lead the interprofessional collaborative team of the future. An effective leadership strategy is necessary to assure optimal performance of this critical provider group.

REFERENCES

Bahouth, M., Ackerman, M., Ellis, E., Fuchs, J., McComiskey, C., Stewart, E. et al. (2012). Centralized resources for nurse practitioners: Common early experiences among leaders of six large health systems. *Journal of the American Academy of Nurse Practitioners*, accepted for publication.

Committee on the Robert Wood Johnson Foundation Initiative on the Future of Nursing, at the Institute of Medicine. (2010). *The future of nursing: Leading change, advancing health*. Retrieved from http://www.nap.edu/catalog/12956.html

Hazy, J. K. (2006). Measuring leadership effectiveness in complex socio-technical systems. *E-CO, 8*(3), 58–77.

Institute of Medicine. (2003). *Health professions education: A bridge to quality*. Washington, DC: National Academy Press.

Lichtenstein, B. B., Uhi-Bien, M., Marion, R., Seers, A., Orton, J. D., & Schreiber, C. (2006). Complexity leadership theory: An interactive perspective on leading in complex adaptive systems. *E-CO, 8*(4), 2–12.

Morse, C. J., & Brown, M. (1999). Collaborative practice in the acute care setting. *Critical Care Nursing Quarterly, 21*(4), 31–36.

Newhouse, R. P., Stanik-Hutt, J., White, K., Johantgen, M., Bass, E. B., Zangaro, G., . . . Weiner, J. P. (2011). Advanced practice nursing outcomes 1990–2008: A systematic review. *Nursing Economics, 29*(5), 1–22.

Pogue, P. (2007). The nurse practitioner role: Into the future. *Nursing Leadership, 20*(2), 34–38.

Porter-O'Grady, T., & Malloch, K. (2007). *Quantum leadership a resource for health care innovation*. Sudbury, MA: Jones and Bartlett.

Reay, T., Golden-Biddle, K., & Germann, K. (2003). Challenges and leadership strategies for managers of nurse practitioners. *Journal of Nursing Management, 11,* 396–403.

Richmond, T. S., & Becker, D. (2005). Creating an advanced practice nurse-friendly culture: A marathon, not a sprint, *AACN Clinical Issues, 16*(1), 58–66.

Robles, L., Stogoff, M., Ladwig-Scott, E. L., Zank, D., Larson, M. K., Aranha, G., et al. (2011). The addition of a nurse practitioner to an inpatient surgical team results in improved use of resources. *Surgery, 150*(4), 711–717.

van Soeren, M. H., & Micevski, V. (2001). Success indicators and barriers to acute nurse practitioner role development in four Ontario hospitals. *AACN Clinical Issues: Advanced Practice in Acute & Critical Care, 12*(3), 424–437.

4

Centralizing Leadership for Advanced Practice: A Model Program

Michael Ackerman, Susan K. Bezek, and Anne Swantz

Health care systems across the United States are facing tremendous pressure to provide health care of high value. Translated, this means high-quality care at reduced costs. These demands are complicated by the increasing acuity of hospitalized patients, the reduction in residency work hours in teaching hospitals, as well as the need to provide seamless care from pre-admission to post-discharge. To meet these demands many organizations have made the decision to increase the number of advanced practice providers (APPs). The term APPs is used to describe nurse practitioners (NPs) and physician assistants (PAs) as a collective group. In the United States, the need for APPs is growing considerably.

This increasing demand for APPs relates not only to the aging population and the Patient Protection and Affordable Care Act, but also to the increasing age of the NP. The Administration on Aging states that there is a rapid increase in our aging population. In 2007, about 12.9 million persons age 65 and older were discharged from short-stay hospitals. This is a rate that is about 3 times the comparable rate for persons of all ages (Department of Health & Human Services, Administration on Aging, 2007). According to a 2009 article by Sipe, Fullerton, and Schulling (2009), the average age for an NP is 47.7. This is slightly less for a PA, where the median age is 38 according to the AAPA (American Academy of Physician Assistants, 2011). Finally, the demand will also be increasing with the Affordable Care Act, which when enacted will increase the number of patients with health insurance and result in an increased need for providers, most notably in the primary care areas. Academic medical centers are being directly impacted by resident care hours that are constantly being scrutinized. As the resident work week is shortened (ACGME, 2011), the void is often filled with APPs.

To meet the needs of an increasing number of APPs, organizations have moved toward creating structural systems to provide appropriate support for this growing number of providers. Many organizations have created centers or departments of advanced practice. At the

University of Rochester Medical Center (URMC), there is a long history about NPs. Dating back to the 1960s when Dean Loretta Ford developed the first NP program in the United States, there has been continued growth regarding NPs both in primary care as well as in acute care. Some of the pioneers in the field of NPs, both in the field of acute care practice as well as in educational preparation of NPs, had their roots at the University of Rochester Medical Center (Ackerman, Mick, & Witzel, 2010; Davitt & Jensen, 1981; King & Ackerman, 1995). Additionally, as the demand for more APPs has intensified over the last 10 years there has also been an increase in the number of PAs who have been employed in hospital settings.

The University of Rochester was an early leader in developing a center of advanced practice leadership. Described is our early experience in creating this program and the key elements that have contributed to our continued success.

CREATION OF THE SOVIE CENTER OF ADVANCED PRACTICE

The decision to create the Margaret D. Sovie Center of Advanced Practice at the URMC was driven by the need to provide centralized support with respect to advocacy for the role, communication, accountability, problem resolution, and professional development of APPs. At the time, there was limited representation for APPs at the organizational level.

At the time of creation of the Center in 2005, there were approximately 350 NPs and 50 PAs. In 2012, the number of NPs has expanded to approximately 400, while the number of PAs has also increased to approximately 100 providers. The goals in developing the Center were to centralize key administrative functions (hiring practices, salaries, credentialing), improve communication with the APP group, increase accountability, optimize APP organizational contributions, and provide advocacy.

Prior to the creation of the Center, the Chief Nursing Officer conducted an extensive assessment of the structure of nursing practice. This assessment included input from NPs and nursing associate directors as well as from nurse managers. It was clear from numerous interviews and assessment that centralized support was required. This was driven by both the hospital administration as well as by the APPs themselves. The Chief Nurse's assessment was shared with and buy-in was provided by the Chief Medical Officer and Chief Operating Officer.

Strong leadership of the APP group is critical. The individual selected to lead the APP group must be either an NP or a PA, depending on the composition of the group, and must be experienced in strategic planning, program management, and clinical practice. There are models in the United States where this leadership is shared by both an NP and a PA.

The decision at our organization was to hire an NP, as the position was funded out of nursing practice. The director of the Sovie Center is a doctorally prepared NP. A key element of success of the leadership person is that there is line authority over the APP group. The director of the Sovie Center has a wide range of authority that is shared with an assistant director.

Critical to the successful creation of system-wide central support for APPs is the decision as to where this support sits in the organization and who funds it. There are many different models across the United States, but most centers sit organizationally within nursing practice. The Sovie Center is within nursing practice; however, there is a need to form a matrix with both operational leadership within the Medical Center as well as with medical leadership. This has been especially true as the Sovie Center has assumed more responsibility for central support of PAs. The funding of the Center is provided through nursing practice. This funding provides salary support for a full-time director, and half-time assistant director, as well as an administrative assistant and secretarial support. Additionally, the Center has an operating budget to support items such as office supplies, copying, and employee recognition.

BUDGETARY CONSIDERATIONS FOR CENTRALIZED SUPPORT

The scope of support and the number of APPs will determine the budgetary support necessary. Salary support for the APP director position may require funding for a complete full-time equivalent (FTE) workload or a percentage depending on the responsibilities of the position. Typically the director is a more experienced APP, thus the salary will be on the high end of the pay scale. Additional support that needs to be considered is office staff, including administrative and secretarial staff, as well as the office itself. It is important to have designated space where the Center or office is located. Resources are also required to run the office, including supplies, furniture, copier and fax machines, as well as the maintenance for the equipment. If education is a core function of the APP support, consideration should also be given to funding of education programs and retreats.

Nursing practice within the University of Rochester Medical Center provides almost all the support for the Sovie Center. This support includes 1 FTE of director salary as well as 0.7 of an assistant director. There are 2.5 FTE of administrative assistants funded, as well as a secretary to support both the director and assistant director. There is also an office budget to support the day-to-day operations. Additional funding is provided by a generous donation from a "Friend of Nursing Practice." This additional support helps to fund an annual lecture as well as a leadership retreat for the Sovie Center.

CORE FUNCTIONS OF THE SOVIE CENTER OF ADVANCED PRACTICE

One of the first steps in the Center development was the establishment of the core functions to support the mission of the Center. These core functions included education, coaching and mentoring, regulation and credentialing, advocacy and, innovative practice design and implementation. Each core function evolved over a period of time.

Education

There is a need for centralized educational programs for APPs. A variety of programs offered through medical departments may be available, but there also needs to be curriculum developed that is specifically targeted for APPs. An annual needs assessment of the APP group, in addition to changes in clinical practice recommendations, provides the foundation for developing yearlong educational offerings in an APP grand rounds forum and Pharmacology Updates forum. The clinical topics in these forums are determined annually and then are repeated quarterly to allow for advanced planning for attendance. It is important to recognize not only the imperative for ongoing professional development but also to facilitate meeting the requirements for APP staff to satisfy thresholds for annual continuing education, so educational offerings should include contact hours.

Additionally, a Sovie Center Colloquium Lecture is offered annually for the community, where a national speaker is featured in celebration of NPs in the greater Rochester area. The pediatric and psychiatric NP also provides specialty-specific grand rounds on a regular basis.

Recently an Education Committee was formed to plan and organize the educational agenda for the Sovie Center. The committee is composed of various NPs and clinical nurse specialists from all areas of practice. This committee has oversight of the topics and format for the formal educational programs of the Center. The committee has also been charged with establishing a strategic plan for the Center around the education agenda.

Coaching and Mentoring

One of the critical areas identified with the introduction of the Sovie Center was the need for more formal coaching and mentoring besides traditional orientation. The Sovie Center has established a formal mentoring program where individuals entering a new APP position can self-select or be assigned a mentor in addition to their preceptor. The mentor is intended to be someone outside their clinical area. Additionally, through a database of mentors, any APP who has a particular professional need can search for a mentor through the system. The system will match the APPs needs with the skill set of the mentor.

The director and assistant director of the Sovie Center each provide a significant amount of coaching and mentoring to others. This can range from crucial conversation tips to rules on billing and coding. The coaching and mentoring role have a direct impact on the professional growth and development of the APP group.

Regulation and Credentialing

It is important that each APP discipline retain authority for regulatory requirements and credentialing. A centralized approach to this helps to assure that appropriate standards are met across the organization. Individual state legislature governs the scope of practice, prescriptive authority, and requirement of physician collaboration, if any, for NPs and PAs. The practice issues that come under state legislation are requirements for licensure; scope of practice; prescriptive authority; requirement of collaboration or supervision; basis for license suspension, revocation, or nonrenewal; reimbursement under Medicaid; reimbursement by indemnity insurers; requirements of educational programs; and standards of practice (Buppert, 2012). In addition to state regulations, the 2007 Joint Commission standards for provider privileging and credentialing require institutions to utilize an evidence-based process (Freedman, 2007). Each individual provider group (e.g., physicians, NPs, PAs, psychologists, and dentists) has the autonomy to develop its own process to fulfill this requirement.

The process of identifying how the APPs would be privileged and credentialed for procedures in our institution included all of the following:

- Review of the current Delineation of Privilege (DOP) forms specific to NPs
- Ensuring that the DOP forms accurately capture all special procedures NPs were currently performing
- Stratification of procedures into low, medium, and high risk, based on the risk of the procedure to the patient, as well as the risk of litigation relative to the procedures potential complications
- Identification of required thresholds for each stratification level for new providers, under direct supervision, and before privileging would occur for the specific procedure
- Identification of the required annual threshold for each stratification to maintain privileging for the procedure
- Identification of the process for how privileging would be handled if an APP provider did not meet the required annual threshold for a procedure.

The component parts of the new Joint Commission standards also require that a process exist for both Focused Professional Practice Evaluation (FPPE) and Ongoing Professional Practice Evaluation (OPPE). The underlying tenet is to ensure that institutions perform ongoing assessments that substantiate the clinical performance of the provider.

The FPPE is intended to be diagnostic in nature (Joint Commission, 2007). Triggers for FPPE include any of the following: review of any new provider within 6 months of granting full privileges, a significant patient event involving the provider, a critical patient complaint, or the request of a practice site based on ongoing practice concerns (Joint Commission, 2011).

The interval for OPPE is not prescribed but must be more frequent than annually, as annually would be considered a periodic assessment. OPPE in our institution includes all of the following: submission of documentation that one met the required threshold per year for special procedures, quarterly chart reviews by collaborating MD, information obtained from the quality assurance person for the practice group regarding any issues for the provider, participation in morbidity and mortality rounds for the practice group as appropriate, and a peer-review process that provides meaningful feedback about the provider's practice, as well as about interpersonal relationships within the practice group.

Innovative Practice Design and Implementation

This core function involves working with individual APPs or practice groups in regards to practice related activities. This includes projects involving productivity, innovations, new revenue, billing opportunities and workload, as well as issues around culture and teamwork. At the request of a department or individual, the Sovie Center will make assessments and recommendations based on the needs of the practice. The Center will also assist at assessing what is the right skill mix for a particular practice based on the goals and objectives on the practice.

Advocacy

This function involves ensuring APP representation on all key clinical and administrative committees within the institution. At URMC, APPs serve on various councils and committees. The director and assistant director of the Sovie Center also sit on the Medical Center credentialing committee as voting members. Decisions that affect providers in any way need input from the APP group. Assuring membership on key committees facilitates this and strengthens collaboration with hospital administrators, medical leadership, and nursing colleagues.

STRUCTURAL DEVELOPMENT OF THE APP LEADERSHIP MODEL

The increase in numbers of APPs within an organization necessitates the creation of a structure that allows for enhanced communication and accountability. Typically, breaking down the larger group into more manageable subgroups helps to assist in the achievement of these goals. To serve this purpose within URMC, a large percentage of the APPs were placed into "clusters." The clusters serve as a functional unit typically around specialty or service lines—for example, heart failure, neurosurgery, hospital medicine, and so on. Each cluster contains different numbers of APPs, depending on the size of the service. Figure 4.1 contains a model of the cluster structure. Within each cluster there is a designated "cluster leader." The cluster leader acts as the lead member of the cluster, serving as the conduit for communication as well as the advocate for the group. The amount of time committed to the leadership role varies based on cluster size; however, typically it is not more that 4 to 8 hr/wk. Exhibit 4.1 outlines key responsibilities of the cluster Leader.

The cluster leaders as a group make up the APP leadership team. This team is critical to the operations of the Sovie Center as much of the decision making, program development, and communication occurs through this group. This group meets monthly, and each cluster leader meets with the Sovie Center director or assistant director regularly. The cluster leaders are required to function as the liaison between the Sovie Center leadership group and the APPs in the clusters. The individual clusters meet regularly with their cluster leader and periodically together with the Sovie Center director or assistant director. This structure has led to a greater sense of

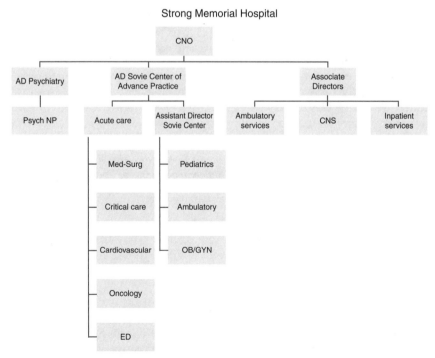

FIGURE 4.1 Sovie Center within the Organizational Model of Nursing Practice.

EXHIBIT 4.1   Advanced Practice Practitioner Cluster Leaders

KEY RESPONSIBILITIES

Summary

The cluster leader serves as the administrator for a group of Advanced Practice Practitioners (APP) with whom one works while maintaining expertise in the clinical arena. (A cluster is defined as a group of APPs who work together in a given service area.)

Qualifications

Senior Nurse Practitioner (level VI) or the most senior Nurse Practitioner (Level V) or Physician Assistant for a group of APPs.

Responsibilities

1. Oversees or develops a work schedule for the cluster to ensure that patient care needs are met
2. Oversees the quality of care and productivity of the cluster
3. Promotes education of the cluster members by facilitating participation in educational programs
4. Performs Annual Performance Appraisals for the cluster
5. Evaluates the cluster member's progress toward goals at midyear and offers suggestions to help meet these goals
6. Meets regularly with the cluster to evaluate needs for change in practice and to discuss issues within the group
7. Attends monthly Advisory Group Meetings with the director of the Sovie Center and disseminates information to the group
8. Submits quarterly reports of cluster productivity to the director of the Sovie Center
9. Schedules cluster meetings with the director of the Sovie Center no less than three times per year
10. Participates in hospital committees and work groups as requested
11. Facilitates cluster member participation in committees and work groups

---

engagement for APPs within the organization. The structure has also enhanced the degree of shared governance within the APP group.

CREATING AN APP CULTURE

Creating the culture for APPs can be a challenge within an organization. Centralizing support for APPs can have a very positive influence on the culture. With strong leadership, the APP has the potential to drive a variety of initiatives within the organization. Some of the activities that can have a major impact include: patient-centered and family-centered care initiatives, incorporating outcome-specific data into the evaluation process, formal mentoring programs, as well as clinical and programmatic leadership. With health care reform comes a sense of urgency to provide a seamless system of care from pre-admission until post-discharge. APPs are in a perfect position to do this. At URMC, the APP evaluation has been completely redesigned to focus on outcomes in addition to competencies. This change in culture has challenged the APPs to better understand the business/systems side of health care. With central oversight and support, this has been a very successful transition.

APPs are also in a great position to develop, manage, and evaluate programs based on the systems savvy of the group. Providing central resources for the APPs to accomplish goals related to programmatic initiatives is critical to the APPs success. Examples of this include support for the Sexual Assault Nurse Examiner Program, advanced trauma life support, as well as a centralized orientation and education committee.

APPs are also well positioned to influence patient and family-centered care initiatives since typically patients have more contact with the APP than with physician providers. It will be important as public reporting of the patient experience becomes more widespread that the influence of the APP group is truly appreciated. Most commercial patient satisfaction surveys have the ability to incorporate questions designed specifically to address patient satisfaction with APP practice.

CONCLUSION

The landscape of health care is changing. As the acuity of hospitalized patients increases, and the requirement to provide high-quality care at a lower cost becomes paramount, health care organizations must develop highly effective teams. It has become more and more evident that APPs must be members of the team. As the workforce of APPs grows, organizations will need to develop strategies and methods to support this provider group. This can be a challenge in that APPs are typically positioned in a variety of places within organizations, depending on the structure. This chapter has described key elements found critical to the success of a highly effective APP leadership model, which may provide guidance to others beginning to embark on this process.

REFERENCES

Accreditation Council for Graduate Medical Education. (2011) *Resident duty hours in the learning and working environment*. Available at: http://www.acgme.org/acWebsite/dutyHours/dh-ComparisonTable2003v2011.pdf

Ackerman, M. H., Mick, D., & Witzel, P. (2010). Creating an organizational model to support advanced practice. *Journal of Nursing Administration, 40*(2), 63–68.

American Academy of Physician Assistants. (2011). *Physician Assistants Census Report: Results from the 2010 AAPA census.* Available at: http://www.aapa.org/uploadedFiles/content/Research/2010%20Census%20Report%20Natio nal%20_Final.pdf

Buppert, C. (2012). *Nurse practitioner's business practice and legal guide* (4th ed.). MA: Jones and Bartlett.

Davitt, P., & Jensen, L. (1981). The role of the acute care nurse practitioner in cardiac surgery. *Nursing Administration Quarterly, 6*(1), 16–20.

Department of Health & Human Services, Administration on Aging. (2007). Available at: http://www.aoa.gov/AoARoot/Aging_Statistics/index.aspx.

Freedman, S. (2007). *New Joint Commission medical staff standards.* Physicians News Digest Website. http://www.physiciansnews.com/business/1007freedman.html. Accessed May 13, 2008.

Joint Commission. (2007). Credentialing and privileging conference call [transcript]. April 30, 2007.

Joint Commission. (2011). *Standards boosterpak for focused professional practice evaluation/ongoing professional practice evaluation.* Oakbrook Terrace, IL: The Joint Commission. Retrieved from http://2011.july.qualityandsafetynetwork.com. Accessed July 31, 2011.

King, K. B., & Ackerman, M. H. (1995). An educational model for the acute care nurse practitioner. *Critical Care Nursing Clinics of North America, 7*(1), 1–8.

Sipe, T., Fullerton, J., & Schulling, K. (2009). Demographic profiles of certified nurse midwives, certified registered nurse anesthetists, and nurse practitioners: Reflections on implications for uniform education and regulation. *Journal of Professional Nursing, 25*(3), 178–185.

5

A Practical Approach to NP Recruiting and Onboarding

Mona N. Bahouth

> *Success depends upon previous preparation, and without*
> *such preparation there is sure to be failure.*
> CONFUCIUS

As your institution begins to gain momentum toward the hiring of a new group of NPs, there are several factors that will positively or negatively influence the experience for these providers. Identifying the right NP for the position can be a difficult and time-consuming process. Once hired, efforts are directed to assuring that the new NPs will have success in their position. Team readiness has an impact on a number of issues that lead to early turnover (Aberdeen Group, 2006; Nozdrovicky et al., 2007). This chapter provides the hospital administrator and other NP leaders with a step-by-step approach to the hiring and onboarding process, including creating an NP job description, establishing a system for efficient NP recruitment, devising a strategy for salary setting for the new provider, and implementing a process for onboarding. We will review the development of efficient recruitment systems, position descriptions, salary structures, and processes for preparing the NP manager for the role. If you are an NP interviewing for a hospital-based position, utilize this chapter as a compass to guide you as you explore the readiness of the institution at which you are considering employment.

BACKGROUND

The cost burden for replacing experienced staff is enormous and can be calculated using numerous online estimators (e.g., Fazzi turnover calculator). More importantly, the emotional toll on unit morale due to staff turnover is significant. Therefore, the recruitment process for hiring NPs effectively is the first step to creating and maintaining a group of expert NPs at your institution (see Figure 5.1). Kleinpell and colleagues (1999) identified

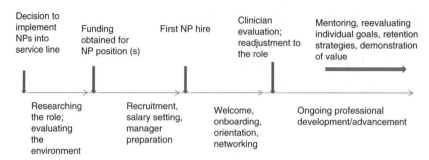

FIGURE 5.1   An overview of the process of creating and maintaining a group of expert NPs.

several reasons that board certified NPs were not working in the hospital setting—not realizing the full potential of the NP role, job dissatisfaction, and excessive work-load. This suggests an at-risk population of employed NPs and an untapped reservoir from which to recruit.

Preparing for the hire of any new employee comes with a lot of fore-thought and preparation. By now your institution has considered the need for this expanded role, evaluated the match between service needs and pro-vider capabilities, and determined that the clinical service would benefit from the addition of a nurse practitioner. As you prepare to hire your first NP provider, it is helpful to pause to reconfirm that the desired role of the provider and the skill set of the NP are well matched. This is a good time for the manager to double-check that the role will not only meet the needs of the patients and clinical service line, but also align with the professional scope of practice of the NP. If the responsibilities have changed or are better suited for other types of personnel (e.g., RN coordinator, research assistant) then this discrepancy should be rectified before the recruitment process begins. There will be little chance of success if the responsibilities are outside of the scope of NP practice, impossible for a single individual to attain, or more consistent with the skill set of a different provider (Bahouth, Esposito-Herr, & Babineau, 2007), therefore it is important to clearly define the NP role prior to the initiation of the recruitment process.

ROLE DEFINITION

The NP position description is one of several critical documents needed at the time of employment. This document serves as a checkpoint that all are in agreement about the duties of the role. The NPs will use this description to frame their practice, understand their purpose within the current organiz-ational culture, and allow for reflection related to the achievement of their professional goals. Many organizations have fallen into a "develop as you go" mentality in terms of creation of a formal NP job description. Undoubtedly the position description will be revised over time as the NP evolves and the organizational needs change. However, having a clear initial description of the components of the NP role will reduce frustrations for the new NPs who are attempting to fully understand their responsibilities and will reduce the chance of the NPs' developing unrealistic expectations.

When drafting the position description, begin by envisioning all of the potential functions of the NP within your institution. This may include direct patient care, research, staff education, and administrative responsibilities. Afterwards, a generic position description template can be drafted that speaks to all of those responsibilities, providing one common document that can be adapted to each individual practice area. The template can then be modified in each specialty area in order to describe the specific NP duties in the individual clinical area. See Appendix A for sample documents. The NP and manager can eventually use this document to frame the direction of the position—removing parts that are not applicable and emphasizing areas of priority. A formal meeting focused on the job description during the orientation period also allows the organizational leader and the NP to understand each other's common goals in order to achieve the best possible outcomes. During the first 6 to 12 months of employment, this document can be considered a draft document, with the expectation that it will be redefined and modified to meet both the NP's goals and institutional goals. Creating a tailored position description is critical to identifying the unique responsibilities of the role; it provides clarity and initiates a critical dialogue for the NP and manager during the interview, orientation, and performance review processes.

SALARY SETTING

Once the role and responsibilities of the NP are clarified, it is time to set the salary commensurate with the duties of that role. Many times this can be a multistep process best managed with the support of human resource personnel who are experienced in this activity.

There are three broad steps to determine the appropriate salary offer for a new NP:

1. Ensuring the job is in the correct salary grade: This is done by reviewing the market annually for the job in question. Market analysis is a complex process of surveying regional institutions similar in size and acuity for comparison of salary models. Most hospitals target either the average or 50% of the market data. This data point is then used to compare to the closest internal salary midpoint. The grade is changed as this data point indicates.
2. Once the grade is determined to be competitive in the market, the applicant's salary is determined based on internal equity. The applicant is compared to current employees in the same job title, using several

individualized variables: the applicant's years of total experience; years of specialty experience when applicable; type/scope/level of experience; and any other skill, knowledge or ability that the organization has determined should be considered. To determine a base salary for the individual NP, count the total number of years experience in nursing, giving additional weight to those years employed as a nurse practitioner or within the specialty service line.

3. Last, final salary adjustment is made based on position specific factors such as "risk" and hours of duty. In prior years, a nurse practitioner working within the intensive care unit (ICU) environment might have had a higher salary adjustment, based on risk and on the acuity of the patient population. This approach is becoming outmoded as institutions realize that care of the hospital patient occurs along a continuum, and no section is more important or risk-free than an other. Regardless, there is still financial compensation for those who have on-call duties or a percent adjustment for those who work less-desired hours such as nights or weekends. This rate of compensation will be variable, depending on the details of that call (in house, home call). Without these compensations, recruitment to those positions scheduled for the "off hours" has been exceedingly difficult.

The partnership between the hiring manager and the HR representative is critical to assure that compensation programs are administered on a fair and equitable basis. Salary is set with clear expectations of the NP duties in the hospital setting with remuneration based on responsibilities, prior experience, and regional salary levels.

A note to the NP applying for a hospital based position: Take the time to compare several of the online salary estimators to best understand the salary trends in the region where you are seeking employment. It is expected that there will be some negotiation of salary and benefits at the time of a position offer. This is your time to learn about both the position responsibilities and the compensation that you deserve for providing this unique expertise. If the salary range is nonnegotiable, consider the adjustment of other variables that could impact your salary needs (relocation expenses, parking, professional fees, continuing education, and vacation time) to offset a lower than estimated salary.

RECRUITMENT

Next comes the important step of finding the right NP to fill these vacant positions. The demand for nurse practitioners for the care of the patients in the hospital setting continues to expand at a rapid pace. Experienced and graduating NPs have a wide variety of opportunities from which to choose. Recruiters therefore must be skilled and efficient in the process of identifying and hiring the best and the brightest NPs to their institution in order to keep up with patient and service demands. Establishing a robust system for efficient recruitment requires some effort and system development. Teamwork and communication are essential. Recruiters must be prepared for this specific type of recruitment, and managers must be responsive to recruiter inquiries in a timely manner. Establishing a process and standards provides expectations for the recruitment team, thus facilitating a more efficient system.

Several common factors have been identified as potential causes of inefficient NP recruitment:

1. Poor communication between clinical managers and recruitment specialists
2. Advertisements written by individuals not familiar with the NP role that were worded ineffectively
3. Incorrect assumptions that positions were posted and were actively being recruited for
4. Inadequate recruiter understanding of the role of the NP
5. Multiple recruiters hiring NPs to different clinical areas
6. Varying recruiter approaches to the recruitment for the NP (interview agenda, travel reimbursement, hotel accommodations, etc.)
7. Confusion about state regulations regarding appropriate licensure for the variety of positions in the medical center

Any of these issues may lead to a lengthy turnaround time for identifying and hiring the NP. These delays may lead to multiple consequences, including loss of highly qualified applicants to other institutions and frustration within the hiring service as a clinical need is going unmet. Managers are often forced into more expensive coverage schemes in these situations, which adds to the urgency for a smooth hiring process.

Exhibit 5.1 suggests a 6 step process for enhancing NP recruitment at your institution. When surveying your current system, several specific strategies could yield positive results and should be considered: (1) develop a multidisciplinary committee charged with improving the NP recruitment process; (2) evaluate all currently vacant NP positions; (3) write all advertisements for nurse practitioner positions, (4) utilize the knowledge of a

---

EXHIBIT 5.1   Basic Steps to Standardize NP Recruitment

Step 1:   Identify stakeholders in the process and develop a work group
Step 2:   Educate recruiter about the NP role
Step 3:   Identify a process leader
Step 4:   Communicate available positions broadly
Step 5:   Organize the interview day and standardize the process
Step 6:   Set expectations of all involved for an expedited process
Step 7:   Provide timely feedback to the candidate

lead NP to review each applicant resume; (5) add an NP interviewer to each applicant's interview day; (6) develop guidelines and matrices for anticipated flow of the pre-interview to hire process; (7) develop an objective evaluation form for use by each interviewer in order to objectively score each applicant's strengths; (8) develop a tracking grid for trending activity related to applicant flow for each position. Critical aspects of these strategies will be discussed in the following sections.

Establish Vehicles for Communication

As you begin to create or enhance your recruitment system, it is important to recognize that there are multiple participants invested in the process. It will be important to bring all of those individuals to the table in order to understand individual priorities. Representation from human resources, the advertising agency, the hiring manager, the collaborating MD or medical director and a senior NP/ lead NP should be invited to a preliminary brainstorming session about the current process for NP recruitment at your facility. Consider establishing a standing meeting including the above individuals to enhance patterns of communication. Initially, meetings should be considered weekly until a smooth process is established. These meetings become the cornerstone for optimizing communication regarding NP recruitment and reduce the recruiter's sense of isolation from the clinical team. Clinicians will begin to learn the language of the recruitment process and have the opportunity to underscore essential components or identify problem areas. Meeting-agenda items may include review of all current vacancies, discussion of all applicants for each position, any difficulties or challenges encountered. Once per month, the focus should shift to review of advertising strategies, which may include verifying accuracy of postings, evaluating posting effectiveness, and identifying new opportunities for advertising NP positions. This process provides a system of checks and balances to assure that the recruitment process is optimized.

Identifying a Process Leader: Accountability

Integral to the success of recruitment is the human resource specialist in charge of the process of NP recruitment. Independent of the size of your institution, we recommend identifying a single recruiter responsible for this task. If the recruiter is new to NP recruitment, education should be provided, delineating some of the subtle differences in the NP role as compared with their more familiar roles (MD or RN). As the recruiter becomes more comfortable with the role, he or she will be able to communicate more effectively with applicants. Additionally, recurrent interactions with this single individual will reduce the recruiter's sense of isolation, provide resources to the recruiter, simplify communication, and result in a more rapid turnaround time for hiring. Finally it will improve applicants satisfaction, as their encounters are with one consistent individual well versed in the role of the NP and unique opportunities that this role brings.

Realistically, there will be times that this individual is unavailable, requiring cross-coverage. Therefore, the initial education series should be delivered more broadly to the entire group of recruiters who may in the future provide cross-coverage for the lead recruiter. Sessions may consist of both didactic presentations about the NP role and interactive case study specific to the hiring process. This time investment at the start of NP recruitment will yield more efficient results later and less frustration for all involved parties. Most importantly, this education will assure that all personnel encountering the NP applicant are delivering a consistent message about the role of the hospital-based NP within your institution.

Finding the Best NPs: Advertising

Notoriously, hospital postings have been the primary mechanism for advertising vacant clinical positions within the hospital. It is essential that these postings speak directly to the NP with wording that displays the institution's philosophy of practice, with the NP as a key member of the team. Assure that you are using consistent and NP-directed language.

Next, consider the location of the advertisement. Will you utilize a purely online marketing scheme? Is there a need for print advertisement? Both the NP recruiter and the hiring clinicians will have different feelings about options and locations that may be appropriate for publicizing your vacancy. Come to a consensus about the highest yield, cost-effective options via frequent discussions. Niche journals and websites can be identified by your expert committee members for ad placement based on the specific position. Some may choose to formally recruit at national meetings. The right approach will depend on the type of institution and the NP that you are recruiting. Exhibit 5.2 summarizes several additional creative strategies that can be considered to enhance visibility of your hospital-based positions and enhance recruitment.

Online professional networking sites are great forums for identifying applicants. Recruiters review sites such as LinkedIn for resumes that are

---

EXHIBIT 5.2 Creative Marketing Strategies: Brainstorming

- Attend national conferences—booth and distributed materials
- Send letters to deans of Schools of Nursing
- Encourage current NPs to contact their alma mater for direct recruiting
- Establish an annual education conference
- Develop a postgraduate NP fellowship
- Journal postings
- Develop a website
- Send e-mail blasts through Board of Nursing mailing lists
- Use social media

posted for good candidates, as do many companies, who also post on these sites. Many NPs will post their CV online for networking purposes, and this may be a good resource for potential candidate identification. Additionally, many human resource representatives review a variety of social network-ing sites and their content to get a feel for the type of applicant prior to inter-view day. For the interviewing NP, remember that an embarrassing post could give the wrong impression to a recruitment team conducting prelimi-nary review.

Experience has demonstrated that NPs are the best recruiters of NPs. Assure that the NPs employed with your institution are aware of current vacancies and encourage them to reach out to potential applicants as they travel to their various professional activities. Having updated material in writing may also be helpful to be sure that the potential applicants have contact information for the recruiter. These print items may include a business card specific for NP recruitment or a brochure that describes NP life at your specific institution. An NP-specific website will bring pre-viously unidentified traffic to the institution, helpful as you begin the recruitment of large numbers of NPs. Most institutions have a web devel-oper to assist you with the creation of this site. Also consider placing adver-tisements for specific NP roles within professional organization websites.

Finally, it will be important for you to develop an alliance with local schools of nursing and members of the acute care program. These students will have a variety of employment options upon graduation and will be seeking out the best practice environment. An ongoing relationship with these students exposes them to your practice culture and encourages them to apply to your institution if they feel that there is support for the newly graduating NP. Invite the students to rotate through your clinical areas in both formal and informal capacities. Teach them about life in the first year as a hospital-based NP to assure that their expectations are realis-tic. Provide professional support and networking opportunities as they envision their first interview and position. Invite students to NP-specific meetings and educational opportunities on your campus. Through all of these activities, you will develop key relationships with the students, estab-lish your institution's position as a professionally supportive practice environment and ultimately will enhance recruitment to your institution.

Standardizing the Process and Setting Expectations

It is important to delineate expectations of each team member of the recruit-ment team in order to keep your process efficient. Set realistic goals about your timeline through the application and hiring process. Your system should allow for rapid response once the NP application has been sub-mitted. All members of your recruitment team will have competing priori-ties and therefore establishing consensus guidelines and clear expectations of each member will avoid unnecessary delays and will underscore the importance of their contributions to the process.

The Interview Day

Structure and organization of the interview day is critical to the NP candidate. It gives the candidates confidence in the work environment that they are considering for employment. Therefore, attempt to streamline and reduce variability in this process.

All travel arrangements are coordinated by the NP recruiter and reimbursement is often but not always provided to out of town candidates. This assures that all questions and travel needs are addressed in a consistent and timely fashion. The interview itinerary is designed to give a comprehensive look at the team recruiting the NP and ranges from one-half day to 2 days in duration. Most itineraries begin with a chance to observe the clinical team on rounds, followed by formal interview sessions with the recruiter, medical director, NP manager, peer NPs, and other essential colleagues. This itinerary is provided to the NP candidates electronically prior to their interview day to allow for preparation.

Providing Feedback in a Timely Manner Is Critical

Once NPs have interviewed for the position, they will be eager to hear about an offer. Many acute care NPs will be considering several offers simultaneously so rapid turnaround from your group will assure that a well-qualified NP is not lost to another institution. A standardized and user friendly form can hasten the process of collecting feedback about each NP candidate from each interviewer. This type of feedback mechanism also provides an objective means to rate the strengths of the applicant and compare several applicants. Each interviewer rates the candidate independently of the evaluation by others. Early notification and feedback to the candidate is a priority and each institution should estimate their target response time for a hiring decision and convey that to the applicant at the time of interview.

OPPORTUNITIES FOR NEW GRADUATES: FELLOWSHIP

Hiring large groups of newly graduated NPs to a single service can be a challenge. The trajectory toward full and independent practice for the new graduate is lengthier when compared to that of a newly hired NP with prior experience. Most new NP professionals describe common feelings when transitioning into new positions or experiences: worry, isolation, feelings of being unprepared. In the majority of professional disciplines, there is a prescribed period of mentorship to adjust to both the technical and psychosocial experiences of the transition into full practice (ex-apprenticeship, residency, etc.). This is not always the case for the newly graduated NP. Many hospitals are establishing orientation programs for their new NPs (see Chapter 6). But what if preparation for this time of transition could begin prior to hire?

An NP fellowship designed to provide specialty clinical education to the new NP uses this time between graduation and full certification. Additional postgraduate clinical development can bridge this gap and benefit the new NP and the hiring institution if education targets clinical knowledge development, skill acquisition, and confidence enhancement.

The goal of such fellowships is to increase the knowledge base and clinical skill set of the new NP graduates prior to being placed into their formalized roles. There are secondary gains for the institution, including the ability to identify strong clinicians for hire in a nonthreatening, observational environment. These clinical experiences allow you to market the strengths of your NP-focused practice environment.

One pilot program conducted at a large academic center graduated five NP fellows from a variety of 3-month specialty programs. NP fellowship candidates were identified via an application process and were selected by the lead NP within the institution. Written goals were created by the applicant and face to face sessions with the senior NP solidified clinical areas of need and interests. Each 3-month fellowship was designed individually; the unique components targeted meeting the specific learning needs of the NP. These rotations took advantage of the expertise of the institution and existing resources to augment the newly graduated NP's foundational educational preparation. Many rotations incorporated a series of didactic and specialty clinical experiences—some rotated through anatomy labs, some performed procedures in the simulation center, others worked with pathologists. Upon completion of these rotations, the NP fellows verbalized enhanced clinical knowledge, improved basic invasive skills relevant to their desired practice area, and overall had more confidence in their role. Three of five NPs who completed this pilot fellowship were hired by the specialty group once they completed their fellowship and obtained national certification. Funding for such a program is critical to its sustainability. Several institutions are currently formalizing such programs. Much work is needed in this area in order to develop such programs and evaluate their impact on the NP transition into practice.

MANAGER READINESS

Now the new NP has been hired and we are approaching Day 1 of employment. A large part of the successful transition of this selected individual will depend on the readiness of the manager. These managers are outstanding clinicians who have been identified as leaders or administrators demonstrating prior success in the direction of other types of staff members. However, the NP manager may be new to the leadership role or inexperienced in working with NPs. Keep in mind that each manager comes with a unique education, background, and skills. Therefore, not all will plan to prepare for the arrival of the new NP in the same way. This can be a stressful time for the manager, whose goal is to successfully integrate this new staff member to their team. To this end it is helpful to standardize the onboarding process so that managers have the tools that they need to assist their NP staff as they begin this chapter of their career. A standardized process will make important information more accessible to the NP leader. Further, it equips the managers with an understanding of the potential obstacles to the NP's success so that they can devise a strategy for dealing with these potential issues before they become problematic. The goal is to provide the managers with the easiest system in which they can get to know the NP role and foster its growth in their unique practice setting.

Creating Resources for the Manager

Initially, the new manager should focus efforts on a system for more efficient onboarding as summarized in Table 5.1. The accumulation of resources combined with a brief educational series by an NP who is expert in the process will be of great benefit. The educational sessions can provide foundational information about the role of the NP and later can be used as a forum for managers to dialogue about NP specific issues as they arise. The tool box (likely electronic or web-based) should contain all of the documents and resources needed for the new NPs as they try to get practice up and

TABLE 5.1   Planning for Your Responsibilities in the NP Onboarding Process: A Snapshot

	THE RECRUITER	THE MANAGER	THE MEDICAL DIRECTOR	THE PRECEPTOR
Developing advertising material	X	X		
Organizing the interview day	X	X		
Recruiting NPs	X	X	X	X
Determining pay scale	X	X		
Drafting the position description		X		
Developing the orientation plan		X		
Preparing the preceptor		X		XX
Introducing the NP to key personnel		X	X	X
Evaluating NP successes through the orientation process		X	X	X
Encouraging the NP attendance at institution-wide meetings		X	X	X

Note: As the NP being hired, you will play an active role in these activities.

TABLE 5.2 Manager Toolbox; Checklist of Items to Prepare Prior to Day 1

PRACTICAL		PSYCHOLOGICAL		CLINICAL
1) Key licensure secured	1)	How will the NP be introduced: −staff meeting −newsletter	a)	Are there reading materials assembled?
2) Credentialing process defined, started or ideally completed prior to start	2)	Business cards should be ready	b)	Is the orientation schedule devised and tentatively printed?
3) Access to computer systems (radiology, electronic records, scheduling)	3)	Desk or office should be prepared and labeled	c)	Review of job description within 2 weeks
4) Lab coats handy				
5) Pager/cell phone assigned and working				
6) Prepare a workspace that is functional for the duties of the provider (private for patient related telephone interviews, dictations, etc.)				

running. Table 5.2 provides a checklist to use prior to the new NP start date. As you review this table, many of the items seem basic, but are often overlooked as the start date for the NP rapidly approaches.

Formal Introduction

The manager should plan and schedule time during formal meetings for the introduction of the new NPs and their role. This will allow for critical dialogue about the introduction of the new personnel and will resolve any preconceived notions about the role. One on one introductions around the clinical unit, group introductions at meetings, and written introductions via newsletters and website announcements also enhance team building. For the managers new to the leadership of an NP, consider reviewing written announcements with colleagues familiar to the role to assure that the language is accurate and reflective of the true NP scope of practice.

Finally, there are many platforms for the new NPs to shine in their role and these settings should be sought after first in order to include the NPs in locations where they can have the most immediate impact. Nothing serves as a better introduction than having the NPs solve an important clinical issue or system problem for a patient to announce their arrival to the team. As an example, encouraging early NP participation in multidisciplinary patient rounds may give immediate exposure to the NPs' skill base and underscore the depth of their patient care experience and system awareness.

Informal Introduction

It is also important for the NPs to prepare for their personalized introduction of the role. There will be many opportunities for the new NPs to speak about their role in both formal and informal capacities, and preparing the new NPs for these encounters is critical. The manager should encourage every new NP to think about this concept and how their role is different from other more commonly understood positions. Many successful leaders have challenged the new NPs to develop two versions of their introductory speech, ready for use when asked "So what do you do?"—a common question to the newly hired NP within a clinical service. Some instinctively know how to answer it well, however most don't and need to give it previous thought. The problem for most NPs is that the path to this particular role may be long and complicated, and it is hard to know what is most important to discuss during a brief or spontaneous conversation. The most effective introduction is brief but filled with goal directed information. These sentences demonstrate a strong vision for their role as well as a strong basis on which to have a longer conversation at a future date.

A note to the new NP: We encourage all new NPs to have several versions of their introductory speech. One should prepare "an elevator speech;" a 1-minute summary of the role to use when a colleague approaches the new NP without any knowledge of the role. There is no single way to describe who you are and what you do in a short answer of several sentences. For the newly graduated NP, this may be a difficult task since it is hard to cover up the self-doubt common to the first NP role. It is an accomplishment to figure out how to work around that doubt. Having a pre-prepared, semi-rehearsed speech is one way to reduce anxiety and develop confidence about your role and future contributions. The key is to tailor your answer to your audience. The way to know which answer is best for which audience is to envision all personnel who you will encounter in the hospital setting: patient, bedside RN, collaborating physician, and administrator. Then, you can choose your one-sentence summary from the list of elevator speeches that you have prepared. A sample elevator speech is noted in Exhibit 5.3. This exercise may seem trivial to you as the new NP or new

---

EXHIBIT 5.3   Sample Elevator Speech

Sample elevator introduction: "What is a nurse practitioner anyway?"

A nurse practitioner is a nurse with advanced education to diagnose and treat patients within a subspecialty population. As the nurse practitioner to the ____ service I will be collaborating with the team to directly manage the patient's care and provide continuity within the system to assure that all patient care needs are met efficiently.

manager, but in the busy hospital setting, this may be the only opportunity for you to enlighten a colleague about your important contributions as an NP with the service.

Preparing the Preceptor

The role of the clinical preceptor will be discussed in Chapter 6. There are several considerations for the manager when organizing the preceptors for their role in new NP orientation (see Exhibit 5.4). As many units are hiring several NPs simultaneously, it is likely that a relatively novice NP will be asked to serve as a preceptor for a new nurse practitioner. This can place unexpected pressure on the precepting NP, leading to an entirely new phase of self-doubt at a time when the NP was beginning to acquire some confidence in the role. This being said, it can be a tremendous experience for the precepting NP and can provide a sense of acknowledgment for the NP's abilities and importance on the team when conducted in a thoughtful manner. This again takes some preparation with a senior NP, manager, or collaborating physician in order to be accomplished smoothly.

Creating a Rich Practice Environment

As manager, your ongoing involvement and commitment to the success of the process will play a large role in assuring that the practice culture for the NP is as obstacle free as possible. If this is the first time that a new nurse practitioner will be incorporated into the team, you can expect a variety of feelings to surface from the existent staff. As the manager, you must find ways to support the NP through these issues and during the transition.

Encouraging the new NP to behave in a consistent and professional way is essential to positively incorporating this role into the existent practice team. There are several ways to assist the new NPs as they establish their credibility with all team members. Richmond and colleagues established 10 points for new NPs to consider as they establish their role (2005). See Exhibit 5.5. Review these principles with the new NPs and remind them that they will be asked to reflect on professional behavior

---

EXHIBIT 5.4   General Tips to Help the Preceptor

- Network with other units who have had prior success
- Involve a senior educator/education department
- Reassess the schedule of the precepting NP to assure time for mental preparation prior to the arrival of the new NP
- Provide background about the preparation of the new NP so that the precepting NP tailors the orientation plan
- Create opportunities for the precepting NP to discuss his or her role in the orientation process

---

EXHIBIT 5.5   Establishing the Credible NP Role and Creating an NP-Friendly Environment

1) Demonstrate confidence and expertise in your specialty
2) Function as a dependable team member
3) Encourage and incorporate input from all team members
4) Keep the patient central to all decision making
5) Explain the rationale for management decisions based on literature and current guidelines
6) Establish a solid foundation of clinical decision making
7) Recognize limitations and seek consultation
8) Maintain a no-blame environment
9) Be accountable for your decisions
10) Be generous with compliments and gracious in accepting kudos

Source: Adapted from Richmond (2005).

---

during future performance reviews. Additionally, the new NPs should anticipate completion of a "self-evaluation" that includes reflection on their professional behavior during this transition time. See Chapter 7 for additional information.

Success within the first year cannot occur in isolation. The manager and collaborating team members will have a major impact on the NPs in their new roles, but NPs should also seek networking opportunities outside of their unit. Creating a forum for interaction with other advanced practice nurses is an essential part of developing a culture of inclusion and camaraderie. Often when nurses enter advanced practice in an organization, they describe feelings of being socially disconnected. The sense of isolation is even more prominent when the NP is the only advanced practice nurse with the service. Social networking is an important factor in nurse retention and therefore should be considered specifically as the NPs transition into their new role.

The need for social bonding in the workplace can be addressed by developing forums to discuss the professional issues of the NP. Monthly NP meetings can be established for the purpose of NP networking but also serve as a forum for communication of key institutional agendas and provide NP-specific education (e.g., journal clubs, professional development speakers, NP-specific grand rounds). This time can also be utilized to identify and foster the development of future NP leaders (see Chapter 13 for more about succession planning). It is likely that NP membership will be broad and will span a variety of clinical areas, so it is important to keep topics for review and presentation general, but applicable to all NPs. Larger organizations can create forums for specialty-specific advanced practice nurses, thus allowing for presentation of specialty-specific topics, including case studies and clinical grand rounds. Regardless of how it is done, finding a mechanism to aid advanced practice nurse social support and camaraderie is critical for success.

If your institution is hiring larger groups of NPs to a variety of services, consider the addition of a meeting focused on issues of the new NP. A forum for these NPs, within their first 2 years of practice, provides the opportunity for additional group mentorship and allows for protected time to explore their unique challenges. Networking with others in a similar position in their professional development avoids feelings of isolation and confirms that they are on track with their professional development. This group interaction additionally provides leadership, camaraderie, and access to hospital-wide role development opportunities for the new NP. The success of the group will depend on the energy of the leader and the creation of a safe and confidential environment for open discussions of true feelings about the transition process. Managers should encourage their new NPs to attend this type of meeting, even when busy clinical services attempt to derail their efforts to participate.

CONCLUSION

Preparing for the arrival of the NP into the clinical service takes time, planning, and interdepartmental collaboration. The effort put forward will yield great rewards for years to come. A well thought out approach to the hiring and implementation of the new NP is essential. This chapter summarizes some basic concepts for drafting a position description, recruitment, preparing managers, and enhancing the NP practice community. The majority of discussion in this chapter is based on common sense but underscores the need for preparation and teamwork in order to optimize your onboarding system. Attention to detail with the recruitment and onboarding process will lead to higher probability of success and increased retention of NP staff beyond 1 year—a major cost-saving measure and key to excellent patient care in your clinical area.

REFERENCES

Aberdeen Group. (2006). *The onboarding benchmark report.* Aberdeen Group, Inc; 1–26. Retrieved from http://www.hreonline.com/pdfs/10022007Extra_AberdeenReport.pdf

Bahouth, M. N., Esposito-Herr, M. B., & Babineau, T. J. (2007). The expanding role of the nurse practitioner in an academic medical center and its impact on graduate medical education. *Journal of Surgical Education, 64*(5), 282–288.

Fazzi Calculator. Retrieved from www.fazzi.com/tl_files/pages/research-and-resources/QWL08.pdf

Kleinpell, R. M. (1999). Longitudinal survey of nurse practitioner practice: year 1. *AACN Clinical Issues, 10*(4), 515–520.

Nozdrovicky, M., Vezina, M., Quinn Griffin, M., & Fitzpatrick, J. J. (2007). Empowerment among nurse practitioners in an acute care setting. *American Journal for Nurse Practitioners, 11*, 34–41.

BIBLIOGRAPHY

Background

Druss, B. G., Marcus, S., Olfson, M., Tanielian, T., & Pincus, H. A. (2003). Trends in care by non-physician clinicians in the United States. *New England Journal of Medicine, 328,* 130–137.

Fairman, J. A., Rowe, J. W., Hassmiller, S., & Shalala, D. E. (2011). Broadening the scope of nursing practice. *New England Journal of Medicine, 364,* 193–196.

Fry, M. (2011). Literature review of the impact of NPs in critical care services. *Nurse Critical Care, 16*(2), 58–66.

Gerchufsky, M. (2011). Nurse practitioners: A timeline. *Advance for NPs and PAs, 2*(11), 66.

Gershengorn, H. B., Wunsch, H., Wahab, R., Leaf, D., Brodie, D., Li, G., & Factor, P. (2011). Impact of nonphysician staffing on outcomes in the medical ICU. *Chest, 139*(6), 1347–1353.

Hill, W. T. (2002). Expanded use of nurse practitioners. *American Journal of Managed Care, 8*(2), 130–133.

Larson, E. H., Palazzo, L. Berkowitt B., Pirani, M. J., & Hart, L. G. (2003). The contribution or nurse practitioners and physician assistants to generalist care in Washington State. *Health Service Research, 38*(4), 1033–1050.

Laurant, M. G., Hermens, R. P., Braspenning, J. C., Sibbald, B., & Grol, R. P. (2004). Impact of nurse practitioners on workload of general practitioners: Randomized controlled trial. *British Medical Journal, 328*(Supp.), 1–6.

Role Definition

Boyle, D. A. (2011). Are you a midlevel provider, a physician extender, or a nurse. *Oncology Nurse Forum, 38*(5), 497.

Furlon, E., & Smith, R. (2005). Advanced nursing practice: Policy, education and role development. *Journal of Clinical Nursing, 14,* 1059–1066.

Gershengorn, H. B., Johnson, M. P., & Factor, P. (2011). The use of nonphysician providers in adult intensive care units. *American Journal of Respiratory Critical Care Medicine,* published ahead of print; Retrieved from http://ajrccm.atsjournals.org/content/early/2010/12/31/rccm.201107-1261CP.full.pdf+html

Hoffman, L. A., Happ, M. B., Scarfenberg, C., DiVirgilio-Thomas, D., & Tasota, F. J. (2004). Perceptions of physicians, nurses, and respiratory therapists about the role of acute care nurse practitioners. *American Journal of Critical Care, 13*(6), 480–488.

Howie, J. N., & Erickson, M. (2002). Acute care nurse practitioners: Creating and implementing a model of care for an inpatient medical service. *American Journal of Critical Care, 11*(5), 448–458.

Howton, T. (2009). The scope of acute care practice: Hammering out the details. *Advance for Nurse Practitioners and Physician Assistants, 17*(2), 40.

Kleinpell, R. M. (2005). Acute care nurse practitioner practice: Results of a 5-year longitudinal study. *American Journal of Critical Care, 14*(3), 211–219.

Kleinpell, R. M, Hudspeth, R, Scordo, K. A., & Magdic, K. (2012). Defining NP scope of practice and associated regulations: Focus on acute care. *Journal of the American Academy of Nurse Practitioners, 24*(1), 11–18.

McCabe, S., & Burman, M. E. (2006). A tale of two APNs; Addressing blurred practice boundaries in APN practice. *Perspectives in Psychiatric Care, 42*(1), 3–12.

Phillips, S. J. (2012). APRN consensus model implementation and planning. *The Nurse Practitioner, 37*(1), 22–45.

Tilford, A. K., Jones, D., Keesing, H., & Sheehan, A. (2012). A description of nurse practitioner practice: Results of a NAPNAP membership survey. *Journal of Pediatric Health Care, 26*(1), 69–74.

VanSoeren, M., Hurlock-Chorostecki, C., & Reeves, S. (2011). The role of nurse practitioners in hospital settings: Implications for interprofessional practice. *Journal of Interprofessional Care, 25*(4), 245–251.

Salary Setting

AANP National NP Compensation Survey. (2011). *American academy of nurse practitioners.* Retrieved from http://www.aanp.org/NR/rdonlyres/F7E4A2F4-7597-4BF7-8D0F   97C56BD7FC2D/0/2011AANPNationalNPCompensationSurveyPreliminary.pdf

Kleinpell, R. (2005). Acute care nurse practitioner practice: Results of a 5-year longitudinal study. *American Journal of Critical Care, 14,* 211–219.

Lowe, G., Plummer, V., O'Brien, A. P., & Boyd, L. (2012). Time to clarify—The value of advanced practice nursing roles in health care. *Journal of Advanced Nursing, 68*(3), 677–685.

Pronsati, M. P., & Gerchufsky, M. (2010). National salary report: Inching forward with mixed results. *Advances for NPs and PAs,* Retrieved from http://nurse-practitioners-and-physicianassistants.advanceweb.com/Features/Articles/National-Salary-Report-2010.aspx

Wiers, S. (2010). Incentive pay for nurse practitioners: What's it all about. *Advance for Nurse Practitioners and Physician Assistants, 18*(5), 17.

Recruitment

McLaughlin, R. (2007). Preparation for negotiating scope of practice for acute care nurse practitioners. *Journal of the American Academy of Nurse Practitioners, 19*(12), 627–633.

Moote, M., Krsek, C., Kleinpell, R., & Todd, B. (2011). Physician assistant and nurse practitioner utilization in academic medical centers. *American Journal of Medical Quality, 26*(6), 452–460.

Stewart, J. G., McNulty, R., Griffin, M. I., & Fitzpatrick, J. J. (2010). Psychological empowerment and structural empowerment among nurse practitioners. *Journal of the American Academy of Nurse Practitioners, 22*(1), 27–34.

NP Fellowship, Preceptorship, Mentoring

Barker, E. R., & Pitman, O. (2010). Becoming a super preceptor: A practical guide to preceptorship in today's clinical climate. *Journal of the American Academy of Nurse Practitioners, 22*(3), 144–149.

Carroll, K. (2004). Mentoring: A human becoming perspective. *Nursing Science Quarterly, 17*(4), 318–322.

Doerksen, K. (2010). What are the professional development and mentorship needs of advanced practice nurses? *Journal of Professional Nursing, 26*(3), 141–151.

Dracup, K., & Bryan-Brown, C. W. From novice to expert to mentor: Shaping the future. *American Journal of Critical Care, 13*(6), 448–450.

Flinter, M. (2011). From nurse practitioner to primary care provider: Bridging the transition through FQHC-based residency training. *Issues in Nursing, 17*(1), 6.

Goudreau, K. A., Ortman, M. I., Moore, J. D., Aldredge, L., Helland, M. K., Fernandes, L. A., & Gibson, S. (2011). A nurse practitioner residency pilot program: A journey of learning. *Journal of Nursing Administration, 41*(9), 32–387.

Harrington, S. (2011). Mentoring new nurse practitioners to accelerate their development as primary care providers: A literature review. *Journal of the American Academy of Nurse Practitioners, 23*(4), 168–174.

Hill, L. A., & Sawatzky, J. A. (2011). Transitioning into the NP role through mentorship. *Journal of the Professional Nurse, 27*(3), 161–167.

Kleinpell, R. M., Perez, D. F., & McLaughlin, R. (2005). Educational options for acute care nurse practitioner practice. *Journal of the American Academy of Nurse Practitioners, 11*, 460–471.

Parse, R. R. (2008). A human becoming mentoring model. *Nursing Science Quarterly, 21*(3), 195–198.

Perkins, K. (2011). Nurse practitioners and interprofessional collaboration. *Journal of Interprofessional Care, 25* (4), 243–244.

Wilkes, Z. (2006). The student–mentor relationship: A review of the literature. *Nursing Standard, 20*(37), 42–47.

Manager Readiness

Englert, E. J., & Berger, M. A. (2011). How to add a new midlevel provider to your practice. *Journal of Medical Practice Management, 26*(6), 371–373.

Nicoletti, B. (2006). How to bill for services performed by nonphysician practitioners. *Family Practice Management, 13*(5), 45–46, 48.

Richmond, T. S., & Becker, D. (2005). Creating an advanced practice nurse-friendly culture: A marathon, not a sprint. *AACN Clinical Issues, 16*(1), 58–66.

Steuer, J., & Kopan, K. (2011). Productivity tool serves as outcome measures for nurse practitioners in acute care practice. *The Nurse Practitioner, 36*(5), 6–7.

6

Nurse Practitioner Orientation: The Transition

Cheryl R. Duke, Shari Simone, and Mona N. Bahouth

Transition is a natural life process, which includes periods of self-renewal and psychological growth (Bridges, 2001). Global properties of transitions are that they occur over time and can include changes in identity, roles, relationships, abilities, and patterns of behavior. Meleis (1986) describes this process as "periods in which change takes place within the individual and/or the individual's environment" (p. 4).

All newly hired nurse practitioners (NPs) experience a variety of transitions as they move into their new practice role; however, most dramatic are the transitions experienced by new NP graduates. These novice NPs frequently struggle with balancing the competing demands of gaining specialty clinical acumen and meeting a variety of organizational priorities. This role transition is a challenging professional event; however, novice NPs can expect to achieve success with the guidance of a well-developed orientation plan and the support of their peers (NPs, physicians, and administrators). Understanding the transition experience of the newly hired NP graduates is important for not only the NPs, but for those responsible for mentoring the NPs during this phase of their career. Knowledge of the transition process is the basis for guiding the development of structured education and support strategies to meet the needs of the NPs during and beyond the orientation period and will assure that they are ultimately successful and effective members of the health care team.

This chapter will discuss the new NP graduates' transition into hospital-based practice and the critical factors impacting this transition, both positively and negatively. In addition, the essential components in designing an orientation program will be described to guide NPs, physicians, and nursing leadership in ensuring the successful transition of NPs into practice. Sample orientation tools are also included.

THE SIGNIFICANCE OF THE TRANSITION INTO PRACTICE

The hospital setting is a fast-paced, high acuity environment. Providers in this environment must have broad clinical knowledge, as well as the ability to manage rapidly changing clinical scenarios while utilizing advanced technologies. NPs are ideal for the provision of this type of acute care and are being integrated into the staffing models of many clinical-based service lines and intensive care units (ICUs) across the country to meet both patient and staffing demands with increasing frequency. NPs beginning clinical practice in this setting require a well-orchestrated orientation plan to improve their transition into the role, ensure excellence in patient care delivery, and to assure job satisfaction. Historically there has been little in the way of predeveloped orientation planning for these providers.

All newly certified NP graduates will experience role transition to some extent as they enter the domain of advanced practice. As of January 1, 2000, national certification from regulatory board(s), such as the state board of nursing, medicine, or pharmacy became a requirement for all new NP graduates in order to obtain approval to begin practice. Although having the credentials and certification are major accomplishments, these events may imply the NP is clinically prepared to manage a full complement of patients, despite not actually having practiced in this new advanced nurse role. In addition, the new NP graduate will need time to become fully socialized to the advanced practice role, including identifying with and developing the professional behaviors expected of the NP role. Not surprisingly, as with all new NPs, the role transition process from RN (registered nurse) to NP has proven to be highly stressful (Brown & Olshansky, 1998; Chang, Mu, & Tsay, 2006; Heitz, Steiner, & Burman, 2004).

Typically, for the hospital-based NP, it takes several months to successfully transit from RN to the NP role. This transition includes recognizing and working through a typical period of uncertainty and a degree of identity crisis to learn to think and behave like an NP. For the newly hired NP graduate, identifying with the values and norms of the advanced practice role and incorporating these into their daily practice requires gaining knowledge and skill development in a supportive learning environment. Although individual and institutional influences on the role transition experience vary, it is important to recognize that successful transition is critical for complete actualization of the NP role, and therefore it is imperative that strategies are developed to support the NP through this process.

Developing a comprehensive orientation program is critical to the success of the NP's integration into hospital-based practice and should address the expected role transitions of the new NP by including elements common to all newly hired NPs, elements unique to novice NPs, and strategies to gain skills and knowledge specific to the designated clinical area. Critical components of NP orientation include: (1) a structured onboarding process to complete required preemployment activities and the credentialing process; (2) system orientation to achieve knowledge and skills with processes and tools used in the work environment; (3) clinical training program with identified goals, time frame for achievement, and learning methods; (4) evaluation and goal-setting process which identifies frequency of review for meaningful feedback; and (5) socialization opportunities with other hospital-based NPs for networking and ongoing support (Bahouth & Esposito-Herr, 2009; Huffstutler & Varnell, 2006; Sorce, Simone, & Madden, 2010; Yeager, 2010). These elements will be further described later in this chapter.

THE BUILDING BLOCKS: DEVELOPMENTAL TRANSITIONS

Novice to Expert

The developmental transition experience of the new NP parallels Benner's highly cited (1982) novice to expert model of nursing clinical competence. Benner's stages of clinical competence include novice, advanced beginner, competent, proficient, and expert. As the new NP gains knowledge and skills in the practice environment, an incremental progression in the practitioner's clinical competence is observed. The trajectory in achieving this clinical expertise is influenced by a variety of factors including previous work experience; characteristics of the work environment; opportunities for relevant, repeated clinical experiences during the orientation period; skillful mentorship; and personal attributes of the NP. One of the unique challenges of the new NP graduate is the transition from expert bedside RN to novice NP. This role transition can cause significant emotional stress on the new NP as this experience typically instills a new uncertainty in clinical judgment and personal feelings of inadequacy, ultimately affecting performance. Designing the clinical training program in a supportive learning environment with opportunities to reflect and build on experiences is critical to ensure appropriate progression of the NP's skill and knowledge during the orientation phase.

Despite years of nursing expertise and NP academic educational preparation, the new NPs will likely experience feelings of uncertainty in their abilities especially in the first 12 to 18 months of practice (Brown & Olshansky, 1997; Cusson & Strange, 2008; Duke, 2010). In addition, returning to the same hospital or unit as an NP after having previously worked there as an RN may or may not be helpful. Duke (2010) found having prior work experience and familiarity in routines helpful in some instances;

however, she also noted examples of the new NP experiencing resentment and/or being challenged by former RN colleagues.

The Imposter Phenomenon

The transition from expert RN to novice NP can evoke an array of emotions and feelings of clinical incompetence, referred to as the imposter phenomenon (Brown & Olshansky, 1997, Clance & Imes, 1978; Huffstutler & Varnell, 2006). To some degree, all novice NPs will experience this phenomenon as they face new feelings of self-doubt and inadequacy. It is important for the NP and preceptor to acknowledge these feelings and the reality that it will take time and practice for the novice NP to gain expertise. The preceptor plays a key role in guiding the novice NP through this initial transition, providing encouragement and clinical experiences that give the NP repetitive exposure and practice to achieve fluid performance. Ensuring achievement in basic skills and tasks before introducing more difficult or integrated tasks can help to prevent the NP from feeling overwhelmed or frustrated by the inability to meet expected standards. However, it is also important for the preceptor to incrementally challenge the NPs to guide them through new situations that would typically cause anxiety. This may simply require reminders of the clinical resources available to the NP during new situations and the application of knowledge and skills learned from prior experiences.

In Duke's phenomenological study (2010), novice NPs described positive and negative feelings associated with their transition. Positive feelings associated with the new NP role included feelings of excitement and empowerment; negative descriptions related to the perceived workload and personal emotions experienced, including fear, anxiety, and feelings of being overwhelmed (Duke, 2010). Feeling overwhelmed with daily responsibilities was a common theme, even for new NPs beginning practice in the same hospital or clinical area where they previously worked as RNs. Learning to think, feel and behave like an NP takes several months. Duke (2010) found that the time needed to become comfortable in the NP role ranged from 6 to 18 months, with an average of 12 months. In this particular study, the NP participants were asked to share advice for new NP graduates beginning hospital-based practice. The overall consensus was the new NPs needed to give it time and not give up or judge their satisfaction with the role too quickly. A strategy identified for gaining confidence included being actively involved with an NP peer group or network. These meetings provide opportunities to develop relationships with other novice NPs navigating similar transitions and obtaining guidance from other experienced NPs. In addition, ongoing dialogue and feedback from the NP or physician mentor promotes the novice NP's development of self-awareness and allows opportunities to dialogue and discuss strategies to improve communication skills and relationships with others.

SITUATIONAL TRANSITIONS: ALIGNING SELF-CONFIDENCE AND PERCEIVED COMPETENCE

Novice NPs experience not only transitions in their role development but often simultaneously experience situational transitions that further influence their progress (Schumacher & Meleis, 1994). Brown and Olshansky (1997) found that new NPs frequently experienced stress associated with the responsibility of decision making as a health care provider. This anxiety was related to the perceived lack of confidence and competence that occurs when starting a new position and returning to a novice skill level. Self-confidence is developed over time when mentors and other significant role models, such as the collaborating physician, provide ongoing encouragement and constructive feedback (Kelly & Matthews, 2001; Maguire, Carr, & Beal, 1995). Perceived competence is closely linked to self-confidence and has a significant influence on role development for the NP (Brown & Olshansky, 1997). With a well-structured orientation plan, mentor, and setting realistic expectations through provision of ongoing feedback in a supportive, learning environment, the new NPs will experience improved feelings of competence and self-confidence in their clinical skills and decision-making.

While experiencing the RN to NP situational transition, the novice NP will confront unique obstacles and challenges. Identifying these obstacles and challenges early can help the new NP anticipate and prepare for a successful transition. Some of these challenges include learning the nuances of the new role, aligning role responsibilities and the expectations of others, adjusting to a new unit or service and hospital system where the NP role may be new to all of these areas; learning how to effectively function as a NP while simultaneously working to reestablish oneself as a proficient clinician with a newly expanded scope of practice; building key relationships with clinical staff, physicians, and other providers; and educating these individuals and groups about the NP role (Duke, 2010).

The relationships that NPs establish with others in the workplace will have a significant influence on their role development, particularly in the initial 6 months of practice. Progress during this time is dependent on how leadership, physicians, clinical staff, patients, and families accept and support the NP's role. In addition, their level of understanding of the NP's role will have a tremendous impact on how the NP transits. Examples of negative interactions impacting role development may include resistance when requesting assistance from a nurse, confrontational exchanges from colleagues, or patients that require the NPs to defend their role. When NPs work in an environment where they feel unsupported and routinely challenged by others, feelings of apprehension and self-doubt surface and can paralyze performance. Identifying the challenges and initiating early discussions with nursing leadership and/or collaborating physicians are important ways to receive support and identify potential solutions.

Mentorship

Mentorship is critical to the novice NP's successful transition and positively influences feelings of interconnectedness and role socialization. The mentor's teaching style, level of support, and effective role modeling are key components for the new NP's successful transition. Nurturing is an essential characteristic to help assure adequate role adjustment, job satisfaction, and role transition (Bosch, 2000; Kelly & Matthews, 2001).

The new NP may be required to be proactive and assume personal responsibility for finding a mentor if one was not designated or if the organization does not have the infrastructure to provide this support. Some important considerations in seeking a mentor include finding an individual who, if not an NP, is very familiar with the NP role, has frequent availability for dialogue and collaboration, is supportive, and is skillful in cultivating the clinical expertise and judgment needed to fully practice as an NP. Identifying a mentor is even more important if a formal orientation to the role is not provided.

The collaborative relationship between the physician and NP will have a significant influence on role development and transition for the NP. This relationship requires a mutual respect for the similarities and differences in knowledge, training, and competence. As the new hospital-based NP's role evolves, the validation of decision making and provision of constructive feedback is important for ongoing engagement and support of learning. Refer to Chapter 8 for more information on developing NP–physician collaboration.

Physicians have a significant opportunity to endorse and promote the NP role in the hospital setting. Fostering this working relationship is key for gaining support for the role as well as helping to assure the physician's commitment to investing sufficient time and effort in mentoring the new NP. Therefore, the NP should establish a meeting schedule with the collaborating physician and nursing leadership to promote ongoing dialogue. During the NP's orientation a standard meeting schedule should be enforced to ensure expected progress. Table 6.1 outlines a suggested meeting schedule and agenda items to assist the NP and/or collaborating physician and NP supervisor in meaningful dialogue that allows for continual assessment, evaluation, and refinement of the role.

TABLE 6.1 Meeting Schedule and Agenda with Collaborating Physician/Nursing Leadership

FIRST MEETING (FIRST WEEK OF EMPLOYMENT)	MONTHLY	QUARTERLY	ANNUALLY
1. Discuss physician & leadership expectations, lines of communication, etc.	1. Discuss orientation progress, challenges, opportunities, outcomes	1. Discuss issues regarding relationship building and collaboration with the multidisciplinary team	Formal evaluation based on position description
2. Review position description and if appropriate, Collaborative Practice Agreement	2. Review skill competencies & plan for achievement	2. Identify needs and opportunities to gain skills and knowledge	1. Evaluation of performance including skills, knowledge, professional behaviors
3. Identify mentor	3. Discuss and review required documentation (i.e., skill competencies, orientation objectives, education activities)	3. Review skill competency and needs assessment	2. Goal setting & action plan including opportunities for professional development
4. Review formal orientation plan	4. Review goals and action plans, make revisions as needed	4. Establish goals for NP role (i.e., financial & quality focused)	
5. Review work schedule and daily responsibilities		5. Discuss potential quality measures, outcomes, expectations with metric on how outcomes will be measured	
6. Discuss management model, level of autonomy, etc.		6. Identify areas for participation in process improvement	
7. Schedule time for MD to introduce NP to staff			
8. Plan follow-up meetings			

ORGANIZATIONAL TRANSITIONS: SYSTEM INTEGRATION

Organizational transitions can be a significant stressor for all new NPs especially if the process is haphazard and left to the NP to navigate through the system without appropriate guidance. Although the general hospital orientation provides necessary start-up information, there are many employment activities required of NPs that can be initiated prior to or on the first day of employment. Many of these start-up activities can be coordinated with the NP nurse recruiter or other representative from the human resource department. The reader is referred to Chapter 5 for more detailed information regarding this process. Critical processes to successful system start-up requirements and training are the onboarding process, system/unit orientation, and the clinical training program. (Bahouth, & Esposito-Herr, 2009; Goldschmidt, Rust, Torowicz, & Kolb, 2011).

Onboarding Process

The onboarding process refers to the start-up activities necessary to begin employment and include broad categories: preemployment, scope of practice, and system orientation activities. Appendix B outlines step-by-step instructions and key contacts to complete the typical start-up activities. Although this form was developed for a specific institution, it can easily be modified to meet individual state and hospital start-up requirements. Once completed, this form could be added to the employee file for documentation of completion. The broad onboarding categories are described below.

Preemployment Activities

The preemployment activities include completing state and hospital-required applications to practice and may include applying for licensure, NP certification, other certifications, such as ACLS or PALS, Drug Enforcement Application (DEA), Controlled Drug Substance Application (CDS) and credentialing application (see Appendix B). The most detailed of these applications is the credentialing and privileging application and is described below.

Credentialing process. The credentialing process is initiated as soon the NP has accepted the position, is licensed to practice in the state, and is certified to practice as a NP. The NP certification must also be appropriate for the position (i.e., acute care certification for hospital-based setting). The NP, collaborating physician(s), and supervisor must recognize and prepare for the credentialing process to take time, typically a minimum of 3 months, and know that the NP will not be able to function autonomously until the NP is granted privileges to practice within the identified scope.

The credentialing process typically requires completing an application that includes a criminal background check, verification of unrestricted licensure(s) to practice, obtaining written recommendation by peers, written verification of NP education program completion, and completion of regulatory paperwork as required by state Boards of Nursing. The momentum and efficiency of this process can be affected by hospital-related internal factors as well as by factors external to the hospital. In many hospitals, the NP begins supervised practice prior to having credentials and privileges granted. This can pose a negative impact on care because the NP may not have access to key resources needed for practice such as the electronic health record (EHR), dictation system, and so on. Failure to provide administrative support in completing the required start-up forms can result in significant dissatisfaction with the NP's onboarding experience and further delay the NP's ability to perform duties. Other factors that may contribute to delaying the completion of the credentialing process include waiting for verification of other required documents such as licensure from the state Nursing Licensure Board and the DEA.

At the University of Maryland Medical Center (UMMC), the completion of required paperwork was streamlined into a more visible and understandable process by providing each orientee with an electronic orientation manual. This manual provides a step-by-step list of required, administrative start-up activities and a timeline for expected completion. An advanced practice administrative assistant assists each NP in completing this process and has significantly reduced delays in completion and improved readiness to practice.

Scope of Practice

It is important to have a clear understanding of the role as it is reflected in the written job description (see Appendix A for a sample) and/or collaborative practice agreement. Having a formally written document that details job duties, scope of practice, and key responsibilities provides clarity to the role, allowing improved communication and work efficiency. As expectations vary from one physician to another in the practice setting, having a conversation up front with the collaborating physician to address these issues is recommended.

A collaborative agreement or attestation is required in most states to practice. This agreement will delineate how the NP and physician will work together in the clinical practice and the activities that can be performed autonomously and those that require physician collaboration.

Detailed daily responsibilities and work schedule must be outlined and reviewed with the NP. It is also important that this is communicated to the entire team so that there are clear expectations of the role from inter-disciplinary team members.

System Orientation

Regardless of prior familiarity with a hospital environment, NPs recognize and understand the need for a formal hospital orientation tailored to their new role. The new NPs should take the time to familiarize themselves with unit operations, standards of practice, methods of communication, and documentation guidelines. Additional system start-up activities required for daily clinical practice are outlined in Appendix B. Resources that will rapidly expose the new provider to many of these requirements have likely been previously developed for other members of the team. Providing a concise summary of these processes to the new NP may minimize time spent in this category of startup and allow time to focus on other aspects of the transition.

ORIENTATION PLAN

The generalized orientation plan consists of several components directed toward achieving cognitive and technical competency: skill acquisition, clinical knowledge expansion, and the development of systems for efficient practice. First, develop specific orientation goals to establish a foundation of core knowledge to build on. Second, define general content and a standardized plan that will achieve a level of basic competency. The process can then be individualized based on the NP's previous experiences and education and tailored to address gaps in knowledge and skill. Next, identify needed educational resources and anticipate the timeline needed for acquiring initial competencies (see Appendix of this book Appendix C for a sample orientation template). A well-formulated orientation plan allows for incremental expansion of duties and responsibilities over the first few months of practice and a pace of learning that will challenge the new NP.

All orientation activities are supervised by the preceptor or collaborating physician. At the start of the orientation process, the new NP should be introduced to the orientation plan and reminded that learning will be completed in a stepwise fashion but with opportunity for modification and reorganization as clinical opportunities present themselves. This schedule should be fluid yet flexible to take advantage of learning opportunities within the clinical service and meet individual NP learning needs. As the new NP progresses, more patients and responsibilities are added. By approximately the third month, it should be expected that the NP is increasing the number of patients that can be safely managed under continued but decreasing preceptor supervision, while continuing to develop invasive procedural skill competency.

The Preceptor

In addition to didactic and solid bedside clinical experiences, the preceptor is critical to the success of the orientation program. The preceptor should serve in four main roles. (1) Educator—develops critical thinking, teaches technical skills, and fosters the application of theoretical knowledge into practice. (2) Role Model—models professional and effective behaviors related to prioritization, time management, and communication with patients, families, and interdisciplinary staff. (3) Socializer—introduces the trainee to essential collaborators and team members. (4) Evaluator—maps progress, provides feedback on strengths and weaknesses and measures/documents competency.

Preceptors serve as resources during the completion of required paperwork and provide individualized attention to guide new NPs. In addition to functioning as the new NP's primary resource for navigating within the hospital, the preceptor will teach prioritization, time management, critical thinking, diagnostic reasoning, how to access clinical resources, how to handle emergencies, and clinical documentation. Other providers, including attending physicians, pharmacists, nutritionists, respiratory therapists, and fellows, are excellent resources for teaching advanced concepts and special procedures. The primary preceptor is accountable for tracking progress, affirming clinical decisions, and challenging the new NPs as they develop confidence in their role.

Didactic Education Content

Standardizing the educational content of hospital-based NP orientation can be a challenge. As a starting point, the Society of Critical Care Medicine's Adult and Pediatric Fundamentals of Critical Care Support Course (www.sccm.org/FCCS, 2008) is a way of solidifying and standardizing baseline understanding of critical care concepts important for any hospital-based NP.

Once the essential knowledge content is decided, the learning methods are determined. As an example, at one large academic center, to augment the NPs, cardiac surgery specialty knowledge, a two-conference system was designed to meet the goals for the orienting group—one NP-specific conference and one ICU-based conference which would allow for peer–peer networking as well as learning (Table 6.2). The NP conference covered a range of topics from the basics of how to present a patient to management of peri operative abdominal emergencies. The ICU conference covered more advanced topics including ventilator management and antibiotic use in the ICU. In addition to these regularly scheduled conferences, the NPs were encouraged to attend a weekly journal club, cardiac surgery morbidity and mortality, and hospital grand rounds. With the addition of ongoing educational opportunities, a cumulative, integrative,

TABLE 6.2 Sample Didactic Education for Cardiac Surgery ICU NPs

ACUTE CARE NP WEEKLY CONFERENCE TOPICS	CRITICAL CARE CONFERENCE TOPICS
• Presenting a patient • Calling a concise consult • Heart/Lung transplant basics • Antibiotic use in the ICU • Preoperative surgery workup • Inotropes and vasopressors • Prandial insulin management, transition from Insulin drip • Perioperative abdominal emergencies • Radiologic imaging of the chest • Radiologic imaging of the abdomen • Mortality-reducing medications • Operative procedures and related topics in cardiac surgery • Dictating a discharge summary • Acute kidney Injury • Extracorporeal membrane oxygenation • Perioperative neurologic emergencies • Anticoagulation/antiplatelet therapy in ventricular assist device patients	• Respiratory failure • Ventilator associated pneumonia and antibiotics/antifungals in the ICU • Ventilator management • Heparin induced thrombocytopenia with thrombosis • Challenge cases and jeopardy • Endocarditis • Lung transplants and immunosuppression • Arterial blood gas • Bronchoscopy • Infection in immunosuppressed patients • Challenge cases and jeopardy • Acute respiratory distress syndrome • Artificial Heart—Syncardia • Perioperative MI- Part 1 • Update on cardiac trauma • Statistics review • Robotic coronary revascularization • Aortic valve bypass • Perioperative MI-Part 2 • The Joint Commission preparation for prescribers • Fluid and electrolytes • Mechanics of continuous renal replacement therapy • Surgery in the HIV patient • Surviving sepsis campaign • Fluid, electrolytes and nutrition • Renal failure jeopardy • Hepatitis in the ICU

and multifaceted approach can be attained while creating an ideal setting to help these new practitioners master complex critical care concepts.

Technical Competence

Hospital-based practice often requires the development and maintenance of skills with invasive procedures. Determining a process for establishing technical competence may be challenging across a variety of practice settings and requires a plan for training in a way that is deliberate and intentional (Exhibit 6.1). Preplanning for this challenge can avoid "on the fly" learning that was found to be detrimental by Duke in her phenomenological study (2010). Evidence-based references such as acute care nurse practitioners (ACNP) competencies by the National Panel for Acute Care NP competencies (NONPF, 2004) should be incorporated into the NPs orientation. Time spent determining what invasive procedures will be performed by the NP and the method for determining initial competency

---

EXHIBIT 6.1   Credentialing of Nurse Practitioners for Invasive Procedures

Purpose: This document and accompanying forms clarifies the method by which Nurse Practitioners will be credentialed to independently perform invasive procedures. Prior to performing invasive procedures independently, approval from the medical staff office (Credentials Committee, Medical Advisory Committee, Board of Directors) and the Maryland Board of Nursing must be secured. The Maryland Board of Nursing New Procedure and Competency Checklist (Appendix I) may be submitted to both the medical staff office and the board of nursing.

Process:
1. Discuss plan to pursue competency of a new procedure with supervising NP and/or collaborating physician.
2. Obtain a Maryland Board of Nursing New Procedure and Competency Checklist. (Appendix I. Hereafter referred to as the competency checklist)
3. Review the education and supervision requirements for the procedure in which you wish to be credentialed. (Appendix II)
4. Complete required reading, tutorials, and/or practice using simulation. Document this under "education program" on the competency checklist.
5. Receive didactic face to face education by an approved instructor. (Check with your medical director or manager for a list of approved instructors). Document this under "workshop" on the competency checklist.
6. Complete supervised procedures and document evaluator signatures on the competency checklist.
   (a) Nurse Practitioners with procedure experience prior to UMMC employment may substitute documented, supervised procedures from past employment for up to 50% of the total number of supervised procedures required (i.e., 5 of 10); the balance of supervised procedures must be performed at UMMC.
7. Obtain signature from collaborating physician or supervising NP indicating adequate skill to perform the procedure independently.
8. Obtain final signature from the Physician-in-Chief of the Shock Trauma Center, by the Director of Critical Care, or by the Director of the Medical Intensive Care Unit.
9. Submit form to the Medical Staff Office and Maryland Board of Nursing for approval. Approval from both bodies must be received prior to performing procedures independently.
10. Ensure that the competency checklist and approval letters from the board of nursing and the medical staff office are placed in your employee file.
11. During employee annual evaluation, review procedures credentialed to perform independently. Document that competency is being maintained in these procedures.

(Continued)

EXHIBIT 6.1 *(Continued)*

UMMC Credentialing of Nurse Practitioners for Invasive Procedures: Appendix I

New Procedure and Competency Check List

*Nurse Practitioner Name:*_____

To obtain approval for procedures not previously approved. You may use this form to document any new procedure(s), and submit it to the Board. Do not include a procedure on the written agreemen t until competency has been obtained. Submission of this form will indicate that this procedure is to be added to the current agreement.

Title of Procedure: _____

Education Program: _____ *Dates* _____

Workshop: _____ *Dates* _____

Other: _____ *Dates* _____

Date	Observed	Performed	Evaluated By	Comments

(Use additional paper if necessary)

I *certify that* _____ *has performed the above procedure and is able to carry out the procedure* **competently and** *independently.*

_____

Signature of Collaborating physician or
supervising nurse practitioner indicating
competency to perform procedure independently   Print Name   Date

_____

Signature of the Physician-in-Chief of the Shock Trauma   Print Name   Date
Center, the Director of Critical Care, *or* by the Director
of the Medical Intensive Care Unit.

EXHIBIT 6.1	**Credentialing of Nurse Practitioners for Invasive Procedures (*continued*)**	

Education and Supervised Procedure Requirements for Credentialing Nurse Practitioners

PROCEDURE	EDUCATION PROGRAM	MINIMUM NUMBER OF SUPERVISED PROCEDURES PRIOR TO CREDENTIALING
Central Venous Catheters	Complete the online education pertaining to Central Venous Catheters found at http://safetycenter.umm.edu. To obtain access call 6-1859, or e-mail sseeb001@umaryland.edu.	5
Arterial Pressure Monitoring Catheters	Complete the online education found at http://content.nejm.org/cgi/content/video_preview/354/15/e13	5: Three in the radial artery, two in the femoral artery.
Pulmonary Artery Catheters	Complete the online education found at http://www.pacep.org/pages/start/ref.html?xin=sccm	5: Due to the nature of this procedure, regardless of credentialing status, an attending must always be geographically present in the ICU when this procedure is performed.
Open Thoaracostomy Tubes	Complete the online education pertaining to open thoracostomy tubes found at http://safetycenter.umm.edu. To obtain access call 6-1859, or e-mail sseeb001@umaryland.edu.	5
Seldinger (pig-tail) Thoracostomy tubes	Complete the online education pertaining to open thoracostomy tubes found at http://safetycenter.umm.edu. To obtain access call 6-1859, or e-mail sseeb001@umaryland.edu.	5: Chest CT or CXR must be reviewed with attending physician prior to Seldinger thoracostomy tube placement

(Continued)

EXHIBIT 6.1   Credentialing of Nurse Practitioners for Invasive Procedures (*continued*)

PROCEDURE	EDUCATION PROGRAM	MINIMUM NUMBER OF SUPERVISED PROCEDURES PRIOR TO CREDENTIALING
Thoracentesis	Complete the online education found at http://content.nejm.org/cgi/content/short/355/15/e16	5
Intra-Aortic Balloon Pump Removal	Education program: (searching)	3
Suturing-wound closure	Complete the online education found at http://content.nejm.org/cgi/content/short/355/17/e18	3
Lumbar Puncture	Complete the online education found at http://content.nejm.org/cgi/content/short/355/13/e12	5

**If a NP would like to become credentialed in a procedure not listed above, they must work with their supervising physician or nurse practitioner to develop an educational program, receive didactic education, and perform an agreed upon number of supervised procedures. As with any procedure, before being performed independently, the NP must obtain approval from the Maryland Board of Nursing and the Medical Staff Office.

---

will be well worth the effort (see Appendix E for a critical care example). Additionally, a schema for reviewing safety parameters and adherence to guidelines for maintaining competent status with each procedure will be required at the time of the annual performance review.

PSYCHOLOGICAL DEVELOPMENT: BEHAVIORAL COMPETENCE

Building Relationships

The level of understanding by hospital personnel, leadership, physicians, including patients and families regarding the NP role will have a distinct and specific influence on the initial role transition. Feelings of frustration may develop when the new NP feels misunderstood in the role. It is extremely important that the hospital leadership and collaborating physician(s) have an accurate and equivalent vision related to the purpose, goals, and scope of practice regarding the NP's role prior to incorporating the NP into any hospital-based model in order to minimize this source of frustration.

Physician level of understanding and acceptance of the NP role will have a significant impact on the transition experience for the new NP graduate. The physician's perception and behaviors regarding the NP role will have a powerful influence on the framework of this professional relationship as either collaborative or supervisory in nature. A single team member can impact the entire tone of the work environment if his or her skepticism about the role is not addressed. These feelings can manifest based on the physician's level of understanding of the role, involvement in the model development, or if any misperceptions of competition exist regarding the NP's role in the health care arena.

Additionally, the work environment will directly impact the NP–patient relationship. Patients and their families' level of understanding of the hospital-based NP role is variable. If conversations with other team members suggest that a hierarchy exists within the care team, the patient's ability to develop confidence in the NP will be inhibited. Introduction of the NP role with the team and scope of practice is key to establishing a solid NP–patient relationship.

Because the hospital-based NPs may be a new phenomenon for some organizations, administrators may not have a clear understanding of the NP role, the regulations guiding their practice, and their work-related needs. In many hospitals, administrators continue to learn in concert with the new NP about such issues. As a consequence, sharing information among NPs is at times fragmented, leading to frustration for the NP who is attempting to function within the philosophy of the hospital. An important aspect of the NP role is educating and informing others about the role and how it complements the interprofessional team.

Collaboration Is Key

Collaboration is a central concept for the hospital-based NP. Building relationships, particularly with hospital administrators, peer NPs, nursing staff, and the physician(s) with whom they will work will help assure a successful transition and strengthen the NP's professional growth. The rewards of a strong professional network cannot be realized without significant investment of time to build these relationships. For example, the support and positive influence of relationships with nursing staff and NP peers foster a partnership in patient care and are valuable clinical resources. In addition, investment of time to develop mutually respectful, collaborative relationships, including teaching and learning from each other, will result in a dynamic provider team. It will also make a significant difference with facilitation of a positive transition experience for the NP.

Ongoing Feedback and Support

Monthly meetings with the preceptor, new NP, their manager, and the collaborating physician should be arranged to provide regular feedback and to adjust the orientation process as needed. These meetings provide an opportunity to discuss the pace of orientation, concerns, and to encourage the new NPs in their progress. In addition, an assessment of the NP's progress in clinical practice competencies (knowledge acquisition and technical skill, clinical decision making, work efficiency), teamwork and communication, and professional behaviors is important to document progress, modify goals as needed, and identify next steps. Ongoing adjustments to the orientation plan enable a truly individualized approach. The manager can also obtain objective data about the orientation process in order to improve the plans for the next orientee. Table 6.3 includes a

TABLE 6.3 NP Orientation Evaluation Survey
Please rate your experiences specifically related to the orientation process in the CSICU on a scale from 0 (strongly disagree) to 10 (strongly agree).

1. My preceptor was helpful, knowledgeable and a good teacher.	0 1 2 3 4 5 6 7 8 9 10
2. Orientation consisted of a logical sequence of events.	0 1 2 3 4 5 6 7 8 9 10
3. The pace of orientation was	Too slow 0 1 2 3 4 5 6 7 8 9 10 Too fast
4. I feel prepared for autonomous practice	0 1 2 3 4 5 6 7 8 9 10
5. I feel supported by my preceptor	0 1 2 3 4 5 6 7 8 9 10
6. Realistic expectations were set for the orientation process	0 1 2 3 4 5 6 7 8 9 10
7. I felt understood by my preceptors and colleagues	0 1 2 3 4 5 6 7 8 9 10
8. My preceptors correctly assessed my baseline knowledge	0 1 2 3 4 5 6 7 8 9 10
9. I was able to develop the skills necessary for my role	0 1 2 3 4 5 6 7 8 9 10
10. Orientation helped me develop diagnostic reasoning skills	0 1 2 3 4 5 6 7 8 9 10
11. I am able to assimilate patient data into a plan of action.	0 1 2 3 4 5 6 7 8 9 10
12. I feel adequately equipped for working as an independent provider in the CSICU	0 1 2 3 4 5 6 7 8 9 10
13. The NP Conference/Critical Care Conference enhanced my overall orientation	0 1 2 3 4 5 6 7 8 9 10
14. Please describe aspects of orientation you thought were most beneficial	(this is an open-ended question)
15. Please provide suggestions for future orientation, which were not offered to you.	(this is an open-ended question)

survey used in the cardiac surgery ICU of a large academic hospital to solicit feedback and assess the overall experience. Open-ended questions should be also included to allow the NPs to offer suggestions for future orientation.

Socialization and Networking

It has become increasingly evident that the psychological health of the new NP is equally important to the skills development when considering an orientation process. Many of the above-described strategies and structures are helpful to foster confident practice in the new NP. The orientation process should also expand beyond the clinical development to nurture the NP. To assist with socialization and reduce feelings of isolation, the new NPs should be encouraged to participate in hospital-wide NP activities. This allows for a decreased sense of isolation and a feeling of belonging within the organization. If multiple new NPs exist in an organization, the development of a New NP Peer Group may be beneficial for all of the orienting providers. The purpose of this group is to explore challenges during the early years of NP practice and provide support via group mentorship. This group interaction additionally provides leadership, networking, and access to hospital-wide role development opportunities for the new NP. During the early months of development, NPs need encouragement to attend hospital wide monthly NP staff meetings for the opportunity to stay updated with regulatory changes and to network with peers across the institution. It is sometimes difficult for the new NPs to prioritize their time for such meetings within the course of often hectic clinical days, but they should be encouraged to attend, as these activities assist with confidence development, foster relationship building, and reduce chances for negative phenomena like imposter syndrome to derail the orientation process. Finally, participation in outside educational forums should be encouraged so NPs can take advantage of already existent educational opportunities and expand their knowledge base.

SUMMARY

The learning curve is steep and can be described as frustrating for the NP who is transitioning into a new role. It takes time, dedication, and perseverance on the part of the NP. Developing clinical expertise requires a concerted orientation plan incorporating formal and informal educational strategies as well as frequent evaluation of progress and achievement to successfully ensure the NP's ability to provide comprehensive, high-quality care for a complex patient population (Yeager, 2010). Understanding the transition experience of the new NP graduate into hospital-based practice will ultimately contribute to the evolution of successful, effective members of the health care team. As programs focus on developing and improving the NP transition to hospital-based practice, open discussion, and evaluation methods are critical to finding the right fit and improving the RN to NP transition.There are multiple challenges influencing the NP transition into practice: navigating the hospital system as an independent provider, gaining knowledge and skills as a NP while simultaneously promoting confidence in the NP role, and building key relationships with large interdisciplinary team members and patients. With this knowledge, key individuals will be equipped to garner the necessary support to develop a comprehensive orientation program and serve as champions of the process to assure that an ideal transition occurs for the new hospital-based NP.

REFERENCES

Bahouth, M. N., & Esposito-Herr, M. B. (2009). Orientation program for hospital-based nurse practitioners. *AACN Advanced Critical Care, 20*(1), 82–90.

Benner, P. (1982). From novice to expert. *American Journal of Nursing, 82*(3), 402–407.

Bosch, J. (2000). *Experience of military nurse practitioners during their first year of practice.* Master's thesis, Uniformed Services University of the Health. *UMI Microform 1399500.*

Bridges, W. (2001). *The way of transition: Embracing life's most difficult moments.* Cambridge, MA: Perseus.

Brown, M. A., & Olshansky, E. F. (1997). From limbo to legitimacy: A theoretical model of the transition to the primary care nurse practitioner. *Nursing Research, 46*, 46–51.

Brown, M. A., & Olshansky, E. F. (1998). Becoming a primary care nurse practitioner: Challenges of the initial year of practice. *The Nurse Practitioner, 23*, 46–66.

Chang, W. C., Mu, P., & Tsay, S. (2006). The experience of role transition in acute care nurse practitioners in Taiwan under the collaborative practice model. *Journal of Nursing Research, 14*, 83–91.

Clance, R. R., & Imes, S. A. (1978). The imposter phenomenon in high achieving women: Dynamics and therapeutic intervention. *Psychotherapy Theory Research and Practice, 15*, 241–247.

Cusson, R. M., & Strange, S. N. (2008). Neonatal nurse practitioner role transition: The process of reattaining expert status. *Journal of Perinatal Neonatal Nursing, 22*(4), 329–337.

Duke, C. (2010). *The lived experience of nurse practitioner graduates' transition to hospital-based practice.* ProQuest (UMI Dissertation Publishing No. 34119121).

Goldschmidt, K., Rust, D., Torowicz, D., & Kolb, S. (2011). Onboarding advanced practice nurses: Development of an orientation program in an cardiac center. *JONA, 41*, 36–40.

Heitz, L., Steiner, S., & Burman, M. (2004). RN to FNP: A qualitative study of role transition. *Journal of Nursing Education, 43*, 416–420.

Huffstuttler, S., & Varnell, G. (2006). The imposter phenomenon: New NPs: New nurse practitioner strategies for success. *Topics in Advanced Practice Nursing, 6,* 2.

Kelly, N., & Matthews, M. (2001). The transition to first position as nurse practitioner. *Journal of Nursing Education, 40,* 156–162.

Maguire, D., Carr, R., & Beal, J. (1995). Creating a successful environment for neonatal nurse practitioners. *The Journal of Perinatal and Neonatal Nursing, 9,* 53–61.

Meleis, A. (1986). Theory development and domain concepts. In P. Moccia (ed.), *New approaches to theory development* (pp. 3–21). New York: National League for Nursing.

National Organization of Nurse Practitioner Facilities (NONPF). (2004). *Acute care nurse practitioner competencies.* Washington, DC: National Panel for Acute Care Nurse Practitioner Competencies.

Schumacher, K., & Meleis, A. (1994). Transitions: A central concept in nursing. *IMAGE: Journal of Nursing Scholarship, 26,* 119–127.

Society for Critical Care Medicine. Critical care training program. Retrieved September 29, 2008, from http://www.sccm.org/FCCS

Sorce, L., Simone, S., & Madden, M. (2010). Educational preparation and postgraduate training curriculum for pediatric critical care nurse practitioners. *Pediatric Critical Care Medicine, 11*(2), 205–212.

Yeager, S. (2010). Detraumatizing nurse practitioner orientation. *Journal of Trauma Nursing, 17,* 85–101.

7

Measuring the Professional Growth of the NP

Shari Simone

Successful role integration for the nurse practitioner (NP) includes promoting professional advancement and growth to maximize the NP's organizational contributions and personal job satisfaction. The first year of any NP role is primarily devoted to achieving clinical competence. During this early stage, achieving targeted goals is largely dependent on having a structured orientation program, a mentor, a supportive learning environment, and ongoing evaluation and feedback.

Following the successful completion of this initial transition stage (described in Chapter 6) the journey begins toward achieving professional success in the role and contributing to the mission of the organization. Ongoing evaluation and measurement of the NP role to assure that the position meets organizational, service, and individual professional needs is critical to achieving success (Bryant-Lukosius & DiCenso, 2004). Best results are achieved when the evaluation process includes a combination of self-reflection on professional and personal contributions and frequent feedback and support from supervisors knowledgeable about the NP role.

This chapter will discuss several components to achieve successful professional advancement and describes measurements supporting NP organizational contributions. The development of a structured evaluation process and of elements to facilitate advancement of individual NPs is key to maximizing performance and promoting organizational value. Critical components that will be highlighted in this chapter include:

- Personal characteristics that enhance professional growth
- Performance evaluation process
- Performance and outcome measurements
- Performance documentation and competency maintenance
- Professional development plan
- Professional advancement models
- Barriers and facilitators to professional growth
- Strategies to achieve clinical mastery

This discussion will guide NPs and their supervisor in developing a professional trajectory course that matches the individual NP needs with the organizational expectations.

FOUNDATIONAL COMPETENCIES

Successful completion of the orientation process assures that the NP has met the basic competencies needed to begin entry-level practice; however, this transition is often a time of uncertainty for the NP and collaborating physicians. The NPs are typically anxious regarding their novice skill level and have feelings of "not measuring up" to their more senior NP peers. The collaborating physicians may also have unrealistic expectations of the novice NP as they trust and rely on the more senior NPs and often expect the novice NP to be more skillful.

In 2004, The National Organization of Nurse Practitioner Faculties (NONPF) developed entry-level competencies for acute care NPs graduating from master's and post-master's educational programs. These competencies were intended to be used together and build upon core competencies identified for both primary and acute care NPs. These core competencies have undergone considerable evolution to meet the changes in NP educational preparation and expanded practice. The most recent version (2012) integrates and builds upon existing Master's and Doctor of Nursing Practice core competencies to fully define essential behaviors of the NP as a licensed independent practitioner. These competencies lay the basic foundation for practice regardless of the population focus and are deemed necessary for NPs to function in the current complex health care environment and be armed with the skills to translate rapidly expanding knowledge into practice. These core competency domains are highlighted in Exhibit 7.1; the specific independent practice competencies are highlighted in Exhibit 7.2. The American Association of Critical Care Nurses (AACN)

EXHIBIT 7.1   NP Core Competency Categories

Scientific foundation competencies
Leadership competencies
Quality competencies
Practice inquiry competencies
Technology and information literacy competencies
Policy competencies
Health delivery system competencies
Ethics competencies
Independent practice competencies

Source: Adapted from National Organization of Nurse Practitioner Faculties (2012).

EXHIBIT 7.2   Specific Independent Practice Competencies

1. Function as a licensed independent practitioner
2. Demonstrate highest level of accountability for professional practice
3. Practice independently managing previously diagnosed and undiagnosed patients
   - Provides full spectrum of health care services: health promotion, disease prevention, health protection, anticipatory guidance, counseling, disease management, palliative, and end-of-life care
   - Uses advanced health assessment skills: differentiate between normal, variations of normal, and abnormal findings
   - Employs screening and diagnostic strategies in the development of diagnoses
   - Prescribes medications within scope of practice
   - Manages the health/illness status of patients and families over time
4. Provide patient-centered care recognizing cultural diversity and the patient or designee as a full partner in decision making
   - Establishes relationship built on mutual respect, empathy, and collaboration
   - Creates climate of patient-centered care
   - Incorporates the patient's cultural and spiritual preferences, values, and beliefs into health care
   - Preserves the patient's control over decision making

Source: Adapted from National Organization of Nurse Practitioner Faculties (2011).

---

further defined specific standards of clinical and professional practice for acute care NPs, which are outlined in Exhibits 7.3 and 7.4. Together these documents provide a basis for acute care NP competency development and evaluation; however, additional required competencies that are institutional and practice specific should be identified in the individual job descriptions.

IMPORTANCE OF SELF-AWARENESS AND REFLECTION

Knowledge and skill acquisition are a continuum that requires ongoing guidance and commitment following orientation to facilitate the development of the novice NP. Acknowledgment of the "beginning stage" of clinical competence by the individual NP, collaborating physicians, supervisor, and peers is important to ensure realistic expectations by all and allow time for the practitioner to become adept at meeting the needs of the complex health care system. Novice NPs must feel that they have ongoing access to information, support, and opportunities to learn and grow.

Benner's Novice to Expert Framework (1984) has been widely used to describe expected competencies and level of skill acquisition for staff

---

EXHIBIT 7.3   Clinical Standards of Practice for Acute Care NPs

Assessment
Critical assessment of acute, critical, and complex chronically ill patients
Diagnosis
Determination of diagnoses for the patient with acute, critical, and complex chronic illness
Identification of outcomes
Identification of expected outcomes individualized for the patient with acute, critical, and complex chronic illness
Planning
Development of a plan of care that identifies interventions to attain expected outcomes of the patient with acute, critical, and complex chronic illness
Implementation
Implements the interventions identified in the interdisciplinary plan of care for the patient with acute, critical, and complex chronic illness
Evaluation
Evaluates the patient's progress toward attainment of expected outcomes

Source: Adapted from AACN (2006).

EXHIBIT 7.4   Professional Standards of AACN for Acute Care NPs

Professional Practice
Evaluates clinical practice in relation to institutional guidelines, professional practice standards, and relevant statutes and regulations
Education
Acquires and maintains current knowledge in advanced nursing practice
Collaboration
Collaborates with the patient, family, and other health care providers in patient care
Ethics
Integrates ethical considerations into all areas of practice
Systems Management
Develops and participates in organizational systems and processes promoting optimal patient outcomes
Collegiality
Contributes to the professional development of peers, colleagues, and others
Resource Utilization
Considers factors related to safety, effectiveness, and cost in planning and delivering patient care
Leadership
Provides leadership in the practice setting and the profession
Quality of Practice
Systematically evaluates and enhances the quality and effectiveness of advanced nursing practice and care delivery across the continuum of acute care service

Source: Adapted from AACN (2006).

nurses, and evidence demonstrates its relevance and similarities in skill acquisition trajectory for advanced practice nurses (APNs) including nurse practitioners and clinical nurse specialists (Brykczynski, 1999; Fenton, 1985; Fenton & Brykczynski, 1993). Competence, defined as the "incremental development of clinical understanding, technical skill, organizational ability, and ability to anticipate events" (Benner, Tanner, & Chesla, 1996, p. 6), is successfully achieved with appropriate guidance and effective mentoring. During each developmental stage, the NP acquires new psychomotor, perceptual, and judgment skills as the focus from task prioritization and completion shifts to focusing on clinical conditions and management. When re-entering the workforce as a new NP, the NP struggles with transitioning once again from expert (bedside nurse) to novice (NP). The new NP then begins again to traverse the stages to move from novice NP to a more expert provider.

Benner's (1984) well described trajectory of nursing development requires passage through 5 stages before reaching expert status and acknowledges that nurses pass through the first three stages (novice, advanced beginner, competent) relatively quickly. Typically the NP can be expected to achieve competency by the end of the first year of practice; however, developmental progression from competent to expert takes several years and is largely dependent on the continued support and mentoring provided, as well as the personal attributes of the NP.

Early studies applying Benner's domains of expert practice to APNs demonstrated that APNs possess additional domains and competencies that are not achieved through experience alone (Brykczynski, 1999; Fenton, 1985; Fenton & Brykczynski, 1993). More recently, Gardner, Hase, Dunn, & Carryer (2008) sought to further understand the level of NP practice by exploring the concept of capability and its application to identifying attributes related to practice. The researchers postulated that the concept of competence does not adequately assess NP clinical skills and the potential for further development. The researchers suggest that the concept of capability and associated attributes—knows how to learn, works well with others, creative, high degree of self-efficacy, and effectively applies competencies to both novel and familiar situations—be used to evaluate and develop NP practice. The researchers argue that using competencies alone to assess skills limits the evaluation and development of practice. Competency refers to acquiring a certain level of skill. Assessment of this skill is based on what is essentially past knowledge and ability; whereas the attribute of capability, knowing how to learn, involves the ability to discover and deduce from previous experience, thus allowing for refinement of practice skills. Examples of all five capability attributes were articulated by NPs participating in the qualitative study. Working well with others was identified as a core value of capable individuals and interdisciplinary practice and teamwork as necessary for best outcomes of care. Examples of the attribute "applies competencies to both novel and familiar situations" were also well described. NPs have a level of skill that goes beyond competent as competency suggests skill in dealing with a predictable situation where as capability suggests ability to adapt, and to be flexible in responses to unpredictable circumstances. The findings from this study suggest that both competence and capability should be considered in understanding the multifaceted role of the NP.

There is clear evidence that expert staff nurses revert to the novice stage as entry-level NPs. Every NP experiences a unique pattern of role and life transitions concurrently that affects incremental growth and the journey to reattaining expert status (Brown & Olshansky, 1997; Cusson & Strange, 2008). In addition, the broad competencies required of hospital-based NPs, including direct patient management, organizational leadership, education, consultation and collaboration, and research are achieved in a unique pattern. Direct patient management, recognized as the core NP competency (Ackerman, Norsen, Martin, Wiedrich, & Kitzman, 1996; Calkin, 1984; Dunphy & Winland-Brown, 1998; Carryer, Gardner, Dunn, & Gardner, 2007; Hamric, 2009), encompasses a broad set of cognitive, technical, and judgment skills required to gain expertise. Although all of these required competencies are interwoven, early development of the novice NP is primarily devoted to gaining skill and knowledge in the core competency of clinical practice, as without it, the others cannot be fully developed. Skill in comprehensive assessment, diagnostic reasoning, clinical judgment, management, evaluation, and teaching requires substantial experiential learning in complex environments to gain autonomous and accountable NP practice. Examples of expected competencies and progression of developmental expertise are highlighted in Table 7.1.

ENHANCING PERFORMANCE WITH EMOTIONAL INTELLIGENCE

Several personal characteristics have been described as enhancing NP role development and include self-confidence, stamina, assertiveness, conflict resolution, and political astuteness (Jones, 2005). These characteristics make up some of the competencies best described as emotional intelligence. Goleman (1998, 2002) broadly defined emotional intelligence as representing a set of core competencies for identifying, processing, and managing emotions that enables NPs to adapt to the daily work demands in a knowledgeable, approachable, and supportive manner. Recent research illustrates the importance of emotional intelligence for promoting personal growth and professional competence development and it is a concept that has grown in popularity among nursing colleagues both at a social and professional level (Akerjordet & Severinsson, 2008). The five domains of emotional intelligence include self-awareness, self-regulation, self-motivation, social awareness, and social skills.

TABLE 7.1   Examples of Competencies and Progression of Developmental Expertise

COMPETENT	PROFICIENT	EXPERT
Consistently completes patient management activities— typically takes additional time with tasks	Demonstrates inreased skill in patient management and automony	Provides guidance and direction to others, contributes to staff development
Good working knowledge of area of practice and is routinely able to establish medical diagnoses for common medical problems	Increased depth of knowledge and understanding of area of practice	Actively role models highly effective skills and clinical judgment, and champions change and innovation
With complex, or unfamilar clinical experience uses deliberate analysis and planning	Improved recognition of expected pattern with clinical diagnoses and increased fluidity with management	Posesses and maintains in-depth skills required in work setting
Achieves most tasks using own clinical judgment, often needs supervision	Increased confidence in decision-making, indirect supervision more common	Recogzied leader of unit, organizational, and health care initiatives
Performs technical procedure, experiences performance anxiety	Demonstrates proficiency in advanced skills and teaching others	Exceptional problem solver for clinical and operational issues
Lacks confidence in ability to manage new clinical situations	Increasing ability to problem-solve complex clinical issues	Inuitive, comprehensive understanding of situation, rapid assessment of situations, provides direction for others
Limited ability to meet multiple priorities and complete duties	Able to adapt to competing priorities with increasing ease	Autonomous, skillful provider
Limited flexibility in problem solving clinical issues	Increasing ability to analyze familiar situations and identify solutions	Adept at understanding the complexities of novel and familiar situations & identifying innovative solutions

- Self-awareness is described as "knowing what we are feeling in the moment, and using those preferences to guide our decision making; having a realistic assessment of our own abilities and a well-grounded sense of self confidence" (Goleman, 1998, p. 318).
- Self-regulation is described as "handling our emotions so that they facilitate rather than interfere with the task at hand; being conscientious and delaying gratification to pursue goals; and recovering well from emotional distress" (Goleman, 1998, p. 318).
- Motivation is described as "using our deepest preferences to move and guide us toward our goals, to help us take initiative and strive to improve, and to persevere in the face of setbacks and frustrations" (Goleman, 1998, p. 318).
- Empathy is "sensing what people are feeling, being able to take their perspective, cultivating rapport and attunement with a broad diversity of people" (Goleman, 1998, p. 318).

- Social skills include "handling emotions in relationships well and accurately reading social situations and networks; interacting smoothly; using these skills to persuade and lead, negotiate and settle disputes, for cooperation and teamwork" (Goleman, 1998, p. 318).

The five domains all relate to understanding and managing ourselves and our emotions in the work environment, managing interprofessional relationships, and working in complex social systems. Examples of competencies and attributes of each emotional intelligence domain are illustrated in Table 7.2. This set of personal and social abilities is recognized as

TABLE 7.2 Emotional Intelligence Competencies

EMOTIONAL INTELLIGENCE DOMAINS	SELECTED COMPETENCIES	ATTRIBUTE EXAMPLES
Self-awareness		*NPs with this competence:*
	Emotional awareness: Recognize their emotions and their effects	Recognize how their feelings affect their performance
	Accurate self-assessment: know strengths and limits	Reflective, learning from experience
	Self-confidence: sure about their self-worth and capabilities	Able to make sound decisions despite uncertainties and stressful situations
Self-regulation		*NPs with this competence:*
	Self-control: Manage disruptive emotions and impulses	Calm demeanor even in crisis situations
	Trustworthiness	Adapt to change
	Conscientiousness	Maintain professional standards
		Hold themselves accountable for completing work
Self-motivation		*NP with this competence:*
	Achievement drive	Is results-oriented
	Commitment	Seeks opportunities to fulfill group's mission
	Initiative	Pursues goals beyond what is expected of them
	Optimism	Persists in seeking goals despite barriers
Social awareness		*NP with this competence:*
	Empathy	Promotes culturally sensitive patient-centered care
	Service orientation	Anticipates, recognizes, and meets patient/family needs
	Political awareness	Recognizes internal and external forces shaping perceptions of patients and families
Social skills		*NP with this competence:*
	Collaboration and cooperation	Collaborates, shares plans, information, and resources to achieve mutual goals
	Communication	Actively listens, seeks mutual understanding, and welcomes full sharing of information

increasingly important for effective work performance and team-based collaboration (McQueen, 2004). Developing these abilities requires thoughtful acknowledgment of one's emotions and how to manage emotions. Journaling and self-evaluation are two strategies that can be used to improve self-awareness and are most effective if done routinely. Candid, frequent dialogue with a mentor is also beneficial not only for improving self-awareness but for learning to manage emotions, as these conversations provide opportunities to dissect a challenging situation in a nonthreatening, nonjudgmental manner; explore options to handle the situation differently; and explore the same situation from another's perspective through role play.

THE INFLUENCE OF THE LEARNING ENVIRONMENT ON PROGRESS

Novice NPs typically gain significant skill and knowledge during their initial year of practice. However, during this time, they also experience multiple stressors that can be substantially reduced with a supportive work environment that values mentors and mentoring (Barker, 2006; Harrington, 2011; Stanley, 2005; Wolak, McCann, Queen, Madigan, & Letvak, 2009). Mentoring is a unique, voluntary relationship between a novice and expert with a primary intent of the expert's sharing knowledge and skills with the novice while creating a supportive environment to facilitate growth and development (Hayes, 2005). A study exploring the perceptions of a mentorship program in entry-level NPs revealed that in addition to being a valuable source of support and knowledge, mentors were considered integral to learning the culture of the organization and creating a sense of community (Wolak et al., 2009). This relationship is also beneficial for the mentor and the organization at large. Mentors grow professionally through the ample opportunities to teach and learn, and by remaining current with practice. Mentors also express a sense of pride in fostering the development of others (Myall, Levett-Jones, & Lathlean, 2008; Wolak et al., 2009). Health care organizations benefit from effective mentoring relationships as mentorship has been found to promote a work environment that encourages teamwork, learning, and improves employee satisfaction and retention (Kilcullen, 2007; Wolak et al., 2009).

An effective mentoring relationship requires commitment from both the mentee and mentor. The mentor must be willing to invest time and energy to facilitate growth and development of the mentee, and the mentee must be willing to learn and demonstrate an appreciation for the knowledge shared. A critical element of the mentoring relationship is effective communication involving respectful, open, and ongoing dialogue; sharing of knowledge; and constructive feedback. This relationship is most effective when selected by the individuals rather than appointed by a supervisor.

Informal and formal mentorship is a critical thread in all aspects and stages of professional development. A mentor may initially be selected to assist in development of clinical practice, but as knowledge and skills are achieved, the focus and mentor may change to meet needs in other areas of practice such as research or education. Doreksen (2010) recently explored professional development and mentorship needs of APNs and the benefit of mentorship in meeting those needs through a survey and focus groups. The findings strengthen the merits of mentorship for APNs and revealed three categories of supports needed for professional development: intellectual, administrative, and financial. As the NP role evolves, protected nonclinical time to develop other areas of practice and funding for projects and education were identified as important for professional development.

BENCHMARKING PROGRESS

Identifying and measuring personal goals is an important routine exercise to ensure ongoing professional growth and to ensure that this growth matches organizational expectations. Measuring professional progress is performed through a variety of processes. First, ongoing informal feedback from NP and physician mentors, peers, interdisciplinary team, and the NP's direct supervisor is one method for gauging skill achievement and provides an opportunity to discuss strategies for refinement. Second, the organizational performance review process is an opportunity to formally create a professional development plan. Third, the individual NP should engage in periodic self-evaluation to assess progress and to identify factors that may be impeding progress such as feelings of dissatisfaction or frustration, competing demands, workload, or other negative emotions or barriers.

A needs assessment is an activity that can be conducted by the organization, supervisor, or individual NP to determine and address needs or gaps between the NP's current and desired performance. It is also a method of identifying and documenting an accurate account of strengths and weaknesses. However, self-assessment and reflection are key to identifying individual learning needs to meet role expectations. Although this activity is part of the annual performance evaluation, NPs should be encouraged to perform ongoing personal and professional reflection to readily identify changing needs and resources to support professional improvement. Appendix D is an example of a self-assessment tool.

Performance Expectations

Minimum expectations for NP performance are defined by the scope of practice specifications, regulatory requirements, and the individual organization's job description for the particular role. In addition, professional organization standards specify clinical and professional performance expectations. Performance review is a process that evaluates the job-specific expectations, clinical practice, professional development, leadership responsibilities, and organizational competencies performed by the NP. This formal review of role performance should go beyond evaluation of specific competencies and ideally also evaluate the impact of the role on clinical quality indicators, and on the efficiency and effectiveness of system processes.

The annual performance review process includes methods that reflect a 360-degree evaluation of role performance. The process begins with a peer review system whereby the NP is evaluated by clinical and administrative team members and peers (Briggs, Heath, & Kelly, 2005). This feedback is an essential component for confirmation of practice according to standards. Again, self-assessment is an important part of the evaluation process as it provides information to identify differences in NP expectations about role performance and actual role performance. A sample tool that could be used as a peer review or self-assessment form is presented in Appendix D. Documentation of continued clinical competence, practice according to standards, and organizational expectations and professional contributions is incorporated into the assessment process.

The annual performance review is a time to acknowledge the practitioner's achievements over the previous year and establish goals to guide the next year's activities. This discussion involves transforming identified goals into measurable objectives, creating an action plan, and learning strategies to achieve goals, and establishing a time frame for achievement. Consensus between the NP and the supervisor regarding performance goals and projected achievement is documented and used for monitoring improvement or sustained high performance. Performance evaluation should ideally be an ongoing process with several self-assessments and formal assessments of performance and of achievement of individual and organizational goals throughout the year. Human resources (HR) departments can often be a good resource as you begin examining your evaluation process and tools; they can offer helpful advice in order to gain the most from this experience. Recent regulatory requirements related to provider evaluation have made this process a reality.

The Joint Commission, in 2010, mandated the use of on-going professional practice evaluation (OPPE) and focused professional practice evaluation (FPPE) for physicians and advanced practice providers. These reviews were created to provide a mechanism for organizations to evaluate practitioner's performance at specific intervals to determine whether the practitioner meets quality standards and if existing privileges should be maintained, revised, or revoked prior to or at the time of renewal. The OPPE process is conducted at a minimum of 6 month intervals, including but not limited to the annual evaluation, and during the recredentialing review process. The FPPE process is conducted for all new hires, typically at the end of the orientation or probation period, when the NP is seeking new skills and expanding privileges, and when an event occurs that raises concern regarding the practitioner's ability to provide safe, quality care. Core competencies identified by the Joint Commission to be evaluated include: patient care, medical knowledge, practice-based learning and improvement, interpersonal and communication skills, professionalism, and systems-based practice. The frequency of this review requires a structured process and sustained commitment by nursing and medical leadership that surpasses previous review processes. Hospitals are charged to create a model for centralized tracking and management of this evaluation process to enhance the quality of care and patient safety. Chapter 11 provides examples of organizational tools.

CREATING A PROFESSIONAL DEVELOPMENT PLAN

An individualized professional development plan is ideally initiated following completion of orientation and updated at a minimum on an annual basis. The intent of this activity is to develop goals, steps to reach goals, time frame to achieve, and criteria for measuring successful completion. Target goals and timelines must be realistic and should take into account the percent of work effort devoted to clinical practice. Goals are based on developmental needs and professional interests. Exhibit 7.5 outlines the general components of the development plan. As clinical practice is the core competency for NP practice, a primary component of this plan should include an assessment of the NP's current level of clinical competence and should identify areas for growth. In addition, an assessment of professional practice involvement including education, research, consultation, and leadership activities, areas of professional interest, and priorities of development should be incorporated. Also of importance is an evaluation of the NP's personal commitment to development, including willingness, interest, confidence, and motivation and strategies to promote growth if needed.

PROFESSIONAL ADVANCEMENT MODELS

Professional advancement models for NPs in hospital-based practice are gaining merit as efforts to advance NP practice through professional practice and leadership activities are needed. The existence of a professional advancement model for APNs within hospitals has important recruitment and retention implications. Career advancement through a clinical ladder program is well established for nursing advancement but has only recently been a focus for advanced practice nurses. Recent evidence describing role dissatisfaction among APNs has raised awareness among organizational leaders and has stimulated efforts to identify potential dissatisfiers within hospitals in order to develop innovative strategies and programs to retain NPs (DeMilt, Fitzpatrick, & McNulty, 2011; Faris, Douglas, Maples, Berg, & Thrailkill, 2010).

EXHIBIT 7.5 Professional Development Plan Components

Goal 1: _____

LEARNING ACTIVITIES	RESOURCES AND STRATEGIES	PROGRESS OR EVIDENCE OF ACTIVITY	TARGET DATES	PROGRESS REVIEW DATES

Goal 2: _____

LEARNING ACTIVITIES	RESOURCES AND STRATEGIES	PROGRESS OR EVIDENCE OF ACTIVITY	TARGET DATES	PROGRESS REVIEW DATES

Practitioner_____ Date_____

Supervisor_____ Date_____

Although NPs are considered to be practicing at the "highest nursing level" and may hold terminal nursing academic degrees (DNP or PhD), promoting lifelong learning and achievement recognition are important to sustaining engagement, interest, and organizational commitment. The goal of a promotional program is to advance the profession via education, science, and evidence-based practice changes. The individual NP chooses an advancement track or activities in areas such as clinical practice outcomes, scholarship (publications, presentations), research, leadership, and community service. Specific APN frameworks, such as the Strong Model (Ackerman et al., 1996), have been used to guide development of advancement models as have academic models such as the Boyer Model (Boyer, 1990). The Strong Model is a practice model that identifies the NP role as combining expert clinical practice with education, research, consultation, and leadership. Although this model demonstrates the breadth of the NP role, the challenge for most organizations is building the necessary structure (i.e., protected nonclinical time, mentorship) to support the NP's pursuit in developing these critical domains of practice. The Boyer Model is an academic model designed for recognizing and rewarding professors' scholarship achievements. The elements of this model include (1) traditional research or discovery, (2) integration of knowledge across disciplines, (3) application of research findings, and (4) the central element of teaching. Although this model was developed for academia, as more and more NPs hold joint academic and practice appointments, the desire to seek employment in organizations where scholarship achievements are acknowledged and supported will increase.

MEASURING QUALITY

Measuring the quality of our practice and of our contributions to achieving optimal outcomes has become increasingly important as the number of and perceived need for NPs in hospitals has increased substantially (Newhouse et al., 2011). However defining quality is difficult. The Institute of Medicine (IOM) developed one of the most widely accepted definitions of quality: the "degree to which health care services for individuals and populations increase the likelihood of desired health outcomes and are consistent with current professional knowledge" (Lohr & Schroeder, 1990, p. 8). This definition underscores the importance of multiple dimensions of quality impacting outcomes, including the importance of patient's values and preferences. Identifying the unique contributions of NPs in hospital-based practice, particularly academic centers, is a challenge as often the NP is not the sole provider of patient care, but rather, part of the collaborative health care team. An important but underreported dimension of quality is NP involvement in projects impacting the efficiency and effectiveness of the processes supporting patient care. This is a vast area where NPs can demonstrate the value-added emphasis of advanced practice nursing to patient care and health care systems.

Outcomes are a measure of health care quality, and the quality of health care is benchmarked and publicly reported, based on the expected and actual outcomes. Traditional outcome measures include length of stay, morbidity, mortality, complications, readmission rates; and costs of care; although important, these outcomes do not effectively measure the broader contributions of NP practice on patient care. Newhouse et al. (2011) recently conducted a systematic review to evaluate the effect of advanced practice nursing on safety, quality, and effectiveness of care. The heterogeneity of the individual study methods limited findings but NP patient outcomes in collaboration with physicians were found to be equivalent to those provided by physicians alone. This finding provides critical evidence to further substantiate NP clinical practice in hospital-based settings to physicians and hospital administrators. Our current charge is to identify and measure specific outcomes related to NP practice and report these findings. Outcomes that are a result of APN led initiatives including quality improvement initiatives, evidence-based practice protocols, clinical pathway development and implementation, best-practice initiatives, and research studies emphasizing NP impact on care are important outcome measurements (Kleinpell & Gawlinski, 2005; Gawlinski & McCloy, 2009). Mullinix and Bucholtz (2009) suggest that the debate regarding NP quality of care also stems from the assumption that the "art of care" is a specific strength of NPs; however, the unique contributions of NPs to the "art of care" have not been conceptualized and thus a major component of NP practice is not fully realized. The majority of NP outcomes research has focused on comparing the performance of NPs to physicians. Further research is needed on the quality of care received by NPs and on the impact of NP care on processes of care, to increase evidence demonstrating the value of the role.

As the NP community continues to grow, measuring our impact must also include productivity and cost containment measures. These measures include patient volume, procedures, management practices, and complications. Electronic tracking of procedures performed and outcomes should be maintained by all individual NPs to demonstrate competency as well as productivity. Evaluating unique ordering practices and management of in-hospital end-of-life issues will be critical to determine the true impact of an NP within the hospital setting. In addition, NP billing mechanisms, which link the NP provider to patient care, are necessary to identify productivity and cost containment data and will be described in Chapter 10.

It is important to recognize that choosing specific NP outcomes to measure differs between specialty practices and individual hospital settings. An outcome assessment should be performed to ensure feasibility and ease of measurement (Kleinpell, 2007). Exhibits 7.6 and 7.7 outline

---

EXHIBIT 7.6   Outcome Assessment

What are the components of the NP role that may impact outcomes?
How easily can the outcome be measured?
Can a relationship be established between NP care and the outcome?

EXHIBIT 7.7   Examples of NP Outcomes

Care delivery centered outcomes:
Adherence to or effectiveness of assessment protocols: falls, withdrawal syndrome, pain, failure to rescue, restraint utilization
Adherence to or effectiveness of prevention protocols: i.e. hospital-acquired infections, hand hygiene adherence, central insertion protocols, community acquired urinary tract infection (CAUTI), venous thromboembolism (VTE) prophylaxis, ventilator-associated pneumonia (VAP) protocol, etc.
Provider handoffs
Patient centered outcomes:
Physiologic: pain control, blood pressure control, hemoglobin A1C levels, blood sugar levels
Education: patient/family education related to surgical pain management, discharge planning
Satisfaction: patient and family satisfaction with overall care, pain management
Adverse events: accidental extubations
Provider performance
Procedural complication rates
Economic outcomes
Costs of care
Readmission rates
Length of stay

EXHIBIT 7.8   Outcome Assessment Steps

1. Identify outcome variables that the APN can affect
2. Organize a team and clarify current knowledge of the practice issue to be improved
3. Select practices and strategies for improvement
4. Develop plan and implement identified interventions
5. Check/analyze/review data and results
6. Institute improvement and evaluate effectiveness

---

critical assessment questions in determining outcome measurement and give examples of measurable outcomes. Kleinpell and Gawlinski (2005) describe the steps to outcome assessment, which are summarized in Exhibit 7.8.

EVALUATION OF THE NP ROLE WITHIN THE ORGANIZATION

Evaluation of new and established NP roles is necessary to ensure that the positions serve the needs of patients, interdisciplinary team, and the organization. Evaluation should occur formally and informally with review of structure, processes, and outcomes related to the NP role. The PEPPA (Participatory, Evidence-Based, Patient-Focused Process for Advanced Practice Nursing Role Development, Implementation, and Evaluation) Framework is a tool that can be used to evaluate the NP role; it is depicted in Figure 7.1.

The PEPPA framework involves a nine-step process, developed to provide advanced practice nurses, health care providers, administrators, and policy makers with a guide to promoting optimal development and implementation of APN roles such as the NP role. One important feature of this framework is that strategies to support meaningful outcome evaluations of the new role are incorporated throughout role planning and implementation. This framework is further described in Chapter 3 in the discussion regarding introduction and implementation of the NP role within the organization. The final steps of this framework pertain to the short- and long-term evaluations of the new role and model of care to assess progress and sustainability in achieving predetermined goals and outcomes. Step 8 involves the short-term evaluation of the NP role and new model of care. In this step, assessing the NP role structure and processes is extremely important to identify role barriers and facilitators and determine additional support needs to further role enhancement. Step 9 emphasizes the importance of the continuous monitoring of the role and model of care to ensure sustainability, effectiveness, and common vision

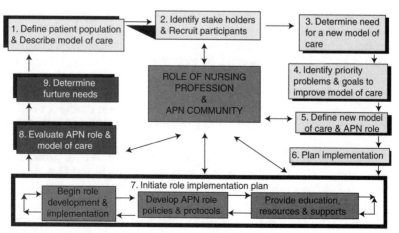

FIGURE 7.1 The PEPPA framework.
Source: From Bryant-Lukosius, & DiCenso (2004).

for the role within the organization. A critical part of this assessment involves determining the following:

- How are NP roles effective?
- For what patient populations, under what conditions, and in which models of care delivery are NP roles most effective?

BARRIERS AND FACILITATORS TO GROWTH

Lloyd-Jones (2005) conducted a systematic review to identify barriers and facilitators to role development and effective practice for advanced practice nursing roles in hospital-based practice. Fourteen studies were identified; most originated in the United Kingdom and thus differences in education, regulations, and NP practice exist. However, the findings confirm generally recognized influences of role development and are important considerations in designing support processes for NP professional development.

The most common personal characteristic identified as facilitating role development was confidence. This finding supports the importance of a mentor for effective development of skills and knowledge that in turn fosters interpersonal professional skills of the novice NP. Novice NPs typically underestimate the magnitude of feelings of self-doubt, and the lack of confidence in their ability fuels anxiety, which ultimately impacts performance. An effective mentorship ensures that the NP is receiving the support and guidance needed when learning new skills while it fosters independence and autonomy as competency is achieved.

Important educational issues that promote role development included mentorship, feedback from other health care professionals, performance measurement, and reflective practice. However, factors most commonly identified as important to successful role development were relationships with key personnel, role definitions, and expectations. Effective interprofessional relationships recognize the contributions of each member, are supportive, respectful, and promote effective work processes and role development. The very nature of the NP role embraces collaboration and coordination with other members of the interdisciplinary health care team.

This analysis revealed negative attitudes of health care professionals were common with integration of new roles and included lack of understanding of advanced practice nursing, fear of NPs encroaching on medical practice, and concerns of limiting resident staff skill. In addition, resistance or opposition from staff members occurred when changes in role boundaries lead to uncertainty in relation to professional identity. Without dialogue with key team members regarding role and clarification of responsibilities, job stress and negative attitudes can lead to unproductive behaviors.

Organizational culture was identified as extremely important in facilitating or limiting successful role implementation. Role ambiguity and incompatibility were identified as primary barriers and indicate the need for thoughtful planning before initiation of a new NP role. NP leaders must define role responsibilities, boundaries, and expectations to ensure successful role integration and must dialogue with collaborating physicians to ensure consensus before initiation of the NP role. Introducing the new NP role to key health care team members is important to provide opportunities for discussion regarding changes to the care delivery model. Lack of role clarity regarding scope of practice, responsibilities, and anticipated outcomes of NP practice may result in unrealistic expectations, work overload, and may limit role autonomy. Excessive workload was also described as affecting the NP's ability to develop other components of the role and as impacting job satisfaction. Finally, lack of resources including office space and supplies, administrative support, mentor, education, and research impacts role development and work productivity. Projecting resource needs is an important component of the business plan and is discussed in Chapter 2. Without sufficient resources, NPs cannot maximize their full potential.

ACHIEVING CLINICAL MASTERY

As health care becomes increasingly more complex, achieving clinical mastery, although a challenge, is critical for NPs to continue to demonstrate the clinical leadership and critical thinking skills so valued by the health care team and administration. Our value-added approach to patient care—the holistic perspective, engagement in patient/family partnership, commitment to individualized management guided by current evidence, leadership in managing and coordinating complex situations, and reflective practice, combined with critical thinking, knowledge, and skillful performance—complements the skills of physicians. A critical strategy during orientation that sets the stage for developing clinical mastery includes identifying the breadth and depth of cognitive and technical knowledge required for the specific role and education plan. Sample pages from the pediatric intermediate care orientation manual developed at the University of Maryland Medical Center are presented in Appendix E. A variety of learning methods should be provided to meet individual learning styles and needs such as attending courses, lectures, simulation exercises, clinical precepted time, case reviews, self-learning exercises, and role-playing. However, the NPs must take responsibility for critically evaluating their practice by identifying knowledge gaps, potential learning opportunities, and resources needed to meet gaps on a regular basis.

When does an NP achieve clinical mastery and how is it maintained? Clinical mastery clearly takes time, commitment, and perseverance as confidence and skill are developed. The first year of practice is devoted to achieving clinical competency and proficiency in skills and behaviors expected of the NP. Clinical mastery, on the other hand, requires repetitive exposure and management of common and uncommon clinical situations and typically takes a few to several years to achieve. This trajectory is primarily dependent on the individual NP's commitment to learning. Expert practice and clinical mastery successfully combine effective and simultaneous interactions, blending and execution of knowledge, skills, judgment, and personal attributes in a highly dynamic and complex health care system. Some examples of achievement include: consistent, comprehensive management of a full caseload; skillful performance in emergencies and highly complex, stressful situations; being viewed by others as a resource; actively participating in developing others; and physician colleagues trust the NP's judgment and encourage autonomous clinical decision making. Maintaining this high clinical skill level also requires an ongoing commitment to remaining current with practice standards. Certification and hospital credentialing regulations mandate minimum continuing education and clinical practice requirements, but the organization should promote a culture that encourages and supports NP involvement in professional development opportunities while expecting NPs to be accountable for improving their practice.

ACTUALIZATION OF THE APN ROLE

Reaching one's full potential requires a personal commitment to professional development, but it cannot be realized without thoughtful development, implementation, evaluation, and refinement of the role. The organization must demonstrate support for NP practice that is visibly appreciated by the NPs. Organizational leaders in nursing and medicine will then assume responsibility for identifying and removing barriers to practice as well as monitoring the effectiveness of the NP role and model of care. In addition, promoting role satisfaction and retention requires an appreciation for ensuring that NPs are able to use and develop their strengths and talents. NPs who receive ongoing support and guidance to fully develop their practice will be positioned to demonstrate quality work. Demonstrating quality and the value-added contributions of the NP role through measurement and documentation of outcomes provides meaning to our work—to ourselves, our patients, and the organization at large.

SUMMARY

Successful NP role integration requires a commitment to professional advancement by the NP, supervisor, collaborating physicians, and administration. The NP who embraces reflective practice will remain aware of strengths, limitations, learning needs, and be mindful of the need for effective interpersonal skills. The NP together with his or her supervisor is responsible for developing a plan for professional growth that is modified and updated with performance achievements and needs. Collaborating physicians and NP peers play an important role in fostering the development of novice NPs and ongoing advancement of seasoned NPs. Recognizing their contribution to ensuring effective implementation of the NP role is critical to strengthening this collaborative relationship and commitment. Finally, organizational and administrative support of the NP role is also important to maximize the NP's contributions and personal job satisfaction and demonstrates the value the role brings to the organization.

REFERENCES

Ackerman, M. H., Norsen, L., Martin, B., Wiedrich, J., & Kitzman, H. J. (1996). Development of a model of advanced practice. *American Journal of Critical Care, 5*, 68–73.

Akerjordet, K., & Severinsson, E. (2008). Emotionally intelligent nurse leadership: A literature review study. *Journal of Nursing Management, 16*, 565–577.

American Association of Critical Care Nurses. (2006). *Scope and standards of practice for the acute care nurse practitioner.* Aliso Viejo, Calif: American Association of Critical-Care Nurses.

Barker, E. R. (2006). Mentoring: A complex relationship. *Journal of the American Academy of Nurse Practitioners, 18*, 56–61.

Benner, P. (1984). *From novice to expert.* California: Addison-Wesley.

Benner, P., Tanner, C., & Chesla, C. (1996). *Expertise in nursing practice: Caring, clinical judgment and ethics.* New York: Springer.

Boyer, E. (1990). *Scholarship reconsidered: Priorities for the professoriate.* Princeton, NJ: The Carnegie Foundation.

Briggs, L. A., Heath, J., & Kelly, J. (2005). Peer review for advanced practice nurses. What does it really mean? *AACN Clinical Issues, 16*(1), 3–15.

Brown, M. A., & Olshansky, E. F. (1997). From limbo to legitimacy: A theoretical model of the transition to the primary care nurse practitioner role. *Nursing Research, 46*, 46–51.

Bryant-Lukosius, D., & DiCenso, A. (2004). A framework for the introduction and evaluation of advanced practice nursing roles. *Journal of Advanced Nursing, 48*(5), 530–540.

Brykczynski, K. A. (1999). An interpretative study describing the clinical judgment of nurse practitioners. *Scholarly Inquiry for Nursing Practice: An International Journal, 13*, 141–166.

Calkin, J. D. (1984). A model for advanced nursing practice. *Journal of Nursing Administration, 14*, 24–30.

Carryer, J., Gardner, G., Dunn, S., & Gardner, A. (2007). The core role of the nurse practitioner: Practice, professionalism and clinical leadership. *Journal of Clinical Nursing, 16*(10), 1818–1825.

Cusson, R. M., & Strange, S. N. (2008). Neonatal nurse practitioner role transition: The process of reattaining expert status. *Journal of Perinatal Neonatal Nursing, 22*(4), 329–337.

DeMilt, D. G., Fitzpatrick, J. J., & McNulty, R. (2011). Nurse practitioners' job satisfaction and intent to leave current positions, the nursing profession, and the nurse practitioner role as a direct care provider. *Journal of the American Academy of Nurse Practitioners, 23*, 42–50.

Doreksen, K. (2010). What are the professional development and mentorship needs of advanced practice nurses? *Journal of Professional Nursing, 26*(3), 141–151.

Dunphy, L. M., & Winland-Brown, J. E. (1998). The circle of caring: A transformative model of advanced practice nursing. *Clinical Excellence for Nurse Practitioners, 2*, 241–247.

Faris, J. A., Douglas, M. K, Maples, D. C., Berg, L. R., & Thrailkill, A. (2010). Job satisfaction of advanced practice nurses in the Veterans Health Administration. *Journal of the American Academy of Nurse Practitioners, 22*, 35–40.

Fenton, M. V. (1985). Identifying competencies of clinical nurse specialists. *Journal of Nursing Administration, 15*, 31–37.

Fenton, M. V., & Brykczynski, K. A. (1993). Qualitative distinctions and similarities in the practice of clinical nurse specialists and nurse practitioners. *Journal of Professional Nursing, 9*, 313–326.

Gardner, A., Hase, S., Gardner, G., Dunn, S. V., & Carryer, J. (2008). From competence to capability: A study of nurse practitioners in clinical practice. *Journal of Clinical Nursing, 17*, 250–258.

Gawlinski, A., & McCloy, K. (2009). Measuring outcomes in cardiovascular APN practice. In R. Kleinpell (Ed.)., *Outcome assessment in advanced practice nursing* (2nd ed., pp. 139–186). New York, NY: Springer.

Goleman, G. (1998). *Working with emotional intelligence*. New York, NY: Bantam Books.

Goleman, G. (2002). *Primal leadership. Realizing the power of emotional intelligence.* Boston, MA: Harvard Business School Press.

Hamric, A. B. (2009). A definition of advanced practice nursing. In A. B. Hamric, J. A. Spross, & C. M. Hanson (Eds.), *Advanced practice nursing: An integrative approach* (4th ed., pp. 75–94). St. Louis: Saunders Elsevier.

Harrington, S. (2011). Mentoring new nurse practitioners to accelerate their development as primary care providers: A literature review. *Journal of the American Academy of Nurse Practitioners, 23*, 168–174.

Hayes, E. F. (2005). Approaches to mentoring: How to mentor and be mentored. *Journal of the American Academy of Nurse Practitioners, 17*, 442–445.

Jones, M. F. (2005). Role development and effective practice in specialist and advanced practice roles in acute hospital settings: Systematic review and meta-analysis. *Journal of Advanced Nursing, 49*(2), 191–209.

Joint Commission. (2010). *The joint commission edition.* Retrieved from http://amp.jcinc.com/Standard.aspx?S=14085&M=1

Kilcullen, N. M. (2007). The impact of mentorship on clinical learning. *Nursing Forum, 42,* 95–104.

Kleinpell, R. (2007). APNs Invisible champions? *Nursing Management.* http://www.nursingmanagement.com

Kleinpell, R., & Gawlinski, A. (2005). Assessing outcomes in advanced practice nursing practice. The use of quality indicators and evidence-based practice. *AACN Clinical Issues, 16*(1), 43–57.

Lloyd-Jones, M. (2005). Role development and effective practice in specialist and advanced practice roles in acute hospital settings: Systematic review and meta- analysis. *Journal of Advanced Nursing, 49*(2), 191–209.

Lohr, K. N., & Schroeder, S. A. (1990). A strategy for quality assurance in medicare. *New England Journal of Medicine, 322,* 707–712.

McQueen, A. C. H. (2004). Emotional intelligence in nursing work. *Journal of Advanced Nurses, 47*(1), 101–108.

Mullinix, C., & Bucholtz, D. P. (2009). Role and quality of NP practice: A policy issue. *Nursing Outlook, 57*(2), 93–98.

Myall, M., Levett-Jones, T., & Lathlean, J. (2008). Mentorship in contemporary practice: The experiences of nursing students and practice mentors. *Journal of Clinical Nursing, 17,* 1834–1842.

Newhouse, R. P., Stanik-Hutt, J., White, K. M., Johantgen, M., Bass, E. B., Zangaro, G., ... Weiner, J. P. (2011). Advanced practice nurse outcomes 1990–2008: A systematic review. *Nursing Economics, 29*(5), 1–21.

National Organization of Nurse Practitioner Faculties. (2011). *Nurse practitioner core competencies.* Washington, DC: The National Organization of Nurse Practitioner Faculties.

National Organization of Nurse Practitioner Faculties. (2012). *Nurse practitioner core competencies.* Washington, DC: The National Organization of Nurse Practitioner Faculties.

Stanley, M. J. (2005). A nurse practitioner model of care in maintenance dialysis: A personal and professional reflective journal (part B). *Renal Society of Australiasia Journal, 1,* 40–47.

Wolak, E., McCann, M., Queen, S., Madigan, C., & Letvak, S. (2009). Perceptions within a mentorship program. *Clinical Nurse Specialist, 23*(2), 61–67.

8

Nurse Practitioner–Physician Collaboration: Strategies for Success

Alice D. Ackerman

"Collaboration" has become a buzzword as the medical world moves (or attempts to) from a model in which providers (generally physicians) engage in highly autonomous and individualized care of patients to a more team-oriented approach. "Collaboration" is not only expected, but in many states required between nurse practitioners (NPs) and physicians. It is the purpose of this chapter to (1) define the meaning of collaboration within a medical system; (2) review the essential components of a successful collaboration between NPs and physicians; and (3) identify the most common barriers to optimal collaboration and potential methods to overcome them.

AUTHOR BIASES

At the outset this author should disclose personal biases, so the reader can put this chapter into perspective.

Background

I am a trained pediatrician and a pediatric intensive care physician. I have worked with NPs since the early days of my general pediatric residency. I was lucky enough to do my training (3 decades ago) in a system that was at the forefront of collaborative practice models. My training in general pediatrics included one session a week in "continuity clinic." I was on the Green Team. We had a group of attending physicians, residents, and an NP that truly functioned as a team in providing collaborative, coordinated interdisciplinary care to the patients in our clinic group. Because I was only able to be physically present one afternoon a week, when one of my patients required a visit during the rest of the week, the patient was seen by either a Green Team attending physician *or by* the NP. We shared among all of us communication about new or chronic issues in these patients, and I learned at least as much from the NP in my clinic group as I did from the senior residents and attendings. I thought this was the way everyone did it.

As my career progressed, I was shocked that some physicians were unfamiliar with the benefits NPs could bring to a practice, and that some were even defensive, thinking NPs wanted to usurp the physician's autonomy and authority in directing care of patients in the practice or acute care setting. I found that other pediatric residency programs did not pay as much attention to ensuring continuity of care for the patients of pediatric residents. When the resident was unavailable, patients were often sent to the emergency department, or were seen by another doctor in the system, who did not necessarily have any knowledge of that particular patient's needs. I was faced with dumb stares when I asked questions about why these other systems did not include NPs as part of the team. What team? Doctors are independent practitioners. They do not need help, partnership, or someone with whom to discuss patients. That would be a sign of weakness. Oh my.

Evolution

When I began my tenure as a faculty member in pediatric critical care, charged with developing a pediatric intensive care unit (PICU) and a division of Pediatric Critical Care, I was determined to include NPs. I detest working in a vacuum. I appreciate being able to discuss ideas and thoughts; not only about specific patients, but about how things should work; how the system should evolve. And so continued what has turned out to be a professional lifelong relationship with a number of individual NPs who have significantly enriched my life and enhanced the care provided to patients in a variety of inpatient venues. I believe that my relationships with these practitioners have been highly collaborative, but there is always a chance that my impression varies from that of the NPs with whom I have worked (Wauben et al., 2011).

COLLABORATION DEFINED

Merriam-Webster online dictionary (2012) lists three definitions for the intransitive verb collaborate: (1) "To work jointly with others or together especially in an intellectual endeavor;" (2) "To cooperate with or willingly assist an *enemy* of one's country and especially an occupying force;" (3) "To cooperate with an agency or instumentality with which one is not immediately connected." Wikipedia (2012) defines collaboration as "a recursive process in which two or more people or organizations work together to realize shared goals." The remainder of this chapter focuses only on how individuals (predominantly NPs and physicians) approach working with each other over time to reach a common goal.

Most states have a requirement for a "collaborative agreement" between the NP and the physician or group of physicians with whom one works. By reading the content of some of these agreements one might conclude that collaboration *implies* supervision. While supervision is NOT the sole purpose of these agreements, it clearly plays some role in the relationship between NPs and physicians in those states in which NPs cannot legally practice independently. The legal aspects helping to define the role are covered in Chapter 4 and will not be considered here.

We may learn much about collaboration from watching children at play. Although sometimes competitive, there seems to be an intrinsic tendency toward working together to gain a single objective, such as when preschool children try to solve a problem, or try to move an object too big for any one of them to manage. Collaboration implies that each party to the relationship brings specific skills to the table that *enhance the ability of the team* to reach a common goal.

FEATURES OF A SUCCESSFUL COLLABORATIVE RELATIONSHIP

Collaboration requires *cooperation* and *communication*. Clear communication about roles, responsibilities, and patient care is essential for a working collaborative relationship between the NP and any other health care provider, especially the physician. Without clear and frequent communication, the NP cannot add value to the health care equation. Collaboration also implies that all parties are of *equal or equivalent* stature in the relationship. That means that each *respects* the professional standing of the other and is willing to infuse *trust* into the relationship.

DEVELOPING THE RELATIONSHIP

A relationship built on collaboration with clear communication, trust, mutual respect, and cooperation that leads to a system in which all parties work together to achieve a common goal doesn't just "happen." It takes commitment, understanding of the obstacles, understanding of the respective roles and responsibilities, patience, and hard work. It is a bit like a marriage, only more difficult because as you enter the relationship it is likely you both have much to learn about each other.

So let us assume you have recently started or are about to start in a new position as an NP in a hospital setting. What will you do to help ensure this new relationship is collaborative?

Preparation

Working to secure success in the role starts long before the first day on the job. Theoretically, the physician or physicians with whom the NP will work were intimately involved in the recruitment process. Theoretically, they were involved in the description of the role and welcomed it as an addition to the existing team. However, this is not always the case, and therefore the NP, as a candidate for a new NP position, needs to explore the culture of the organization (what examples already exist of interprofessional collaboration between physicians and other members of the health care team?). One will need to understand the *organizations's goals* in adding NPs. Is it solely to allow the physicians to work fewer hours? Is it to enhance education of other members of the team (residents, students, bedside nurses)? Is it being done because it is the "in" thing to do these days? It is most helpful to be certain that there are *clear expectations* on the part of the employer/organization before the first day on the job. It is also critically important that the NP has clearly defined goals as to the role or roles that he or she envisions as leading to satisfaction and to add value for the patient. If the goals of the organization are not congruent with the NP's goals at the outset, this author would urge caution in entering the position. More issues related to finding the optimal position are covered in Chapter 5.

Assuming both the NP and the organization's adminstration and physicians have completed the appropriate preparation, the specific components of the collaborative relationship are ready to be developed. Although many NPs in an outpatient role will have a collaborative relationship with a single physician, it is more typical for an NP with a hospital-based practice to work with several different physicians and be "service" or "unit" based. This may make the process of development of the collaborative relationship more difficult. Multiple individuals bring multiple personalities to the table, which need to be considered as the practice develops.

It is essential that the administration of a hospital or unit not initate or introduce an NP practice without the full buy-in of the physician leaders and staff members. It is also important that all parties understand the role the administration envisions for the NP within the practice. This author has witnessed many NP/physician collaborative relationships evolve appropriately, only to be sabotaged by potentially unrealistic although generally unspoken administrative goals.

Evaluation of Current Culture

Without an evaluation of the current state of acceptance of a collaborative NP practice, it will be hard to achieve a positive working relationship, regardless of the attention to other issues in getting the relationship off the ground. Culture significantly impacts the perception of nurses and physicians of how their unit functions and how well different groups are able to work together (Malloy et al., 2009). The culture of the unit in which the NP will work may reflect the culture of the entire organization, or it may be idiosyncratic within the organization. For example, pediatric units are often seen as more cohesive and patient-centered than many of the adult units in the same hospital.

Evaluation of the current culture will allow the NP to understand the potential barriers within this work environment that must be addressed by both the NPs and the physicians in developing their relationship. A unit in which a prior NP was deemed to have failed in the role would be important to identify and address in advance.

Understanding Individual Roles

For a successful team dynamic to evolve in the inpatient arena, it is essential that each member of the health care team have a clearly defined role in patient care, policy development, and staff education. Physicians often report a lack of understanding of an NP's scope of practice and specific role in the health care system, whereas NPs tend to have a better understanding of the role of the physician (Clarin, 2007). This provides an *opportunity for the nurse practitioner to educate the physician* about the specific education and training the NP has had thus far, and to engage the physician in a discussion on how the NP's expertise may be best utilized in enhancing the care of patients in the specific team or unit. Interprofessional education (IPE) is becoming more common in medical schools, so newly trained physicians may have a better intrinsic understanding of the background and perspective of various health care team members (Blue, Mitcham, Smith, Raymond, & Greenberg, 2010; Liston, Fischer, Way, Torre, & Papp, 2011). They are learning that interprofessional collaboration can reduce preventable errors and improve patient outcomes. They may therefore be more motivated to work in a collaborative fashion with NPs than physicians who were trained in prior decades. Medical students who have learned from educators within other professions accept those teachers as part of the educational milleu of the field of medicine.

In a multigenerational inpatient situation, where multiple physicians are working with NPs, discussing roles and establishing guidelines for expectations is even more essential. Different physicians, bringing varying prior experiences with multiprofessional collaboration, may have very diverse expectations of the NPs with whom they work.

Communication

In health care as well as in most other work or personal settings, communication is a key driver of success (Curtis, Tzannes, & Rudge, 2011; Robinson, Gorman, Slimmer, & Yudkowsky, 2010). Mind-reading is not a skill learned in any of our professional schools. To be understood, one must communicate one's thoughts, needs, goals, issues, and concerns on a regular basis. NPs must encourage others with whom they work to do the same. In this author's opinion, *the ability to have open communication in the NP/physician relationship is the single most important factor contributing to optimal collaboration and success of the NP role.*

Communication to Define Individual Areas of Expertise

Every individual brings to the job the sum total of prior experiences. Course work and clinical rotations add to prior knowledge and skills. Yet, despite clear curriculum goals, no two NPs will finish their training or come into a new role with the same set of skills or specific interests. Two NPs completing their certification as acute care NPs may be very different. One might be specifically interested in and competent in the recognition and prevention of child abuse; the second may have more experience in identification of adults at high risk of coronary artery disease. Specific areas of interest and knowledge may lead the NP to seek a position in a particular unit (pediatric emergency department or cardiac care unit, respectively), but even within those patient care areas, different individuals have specific interests. It is important for the NP to explore interests and areas of special knowledge and investigate ways in which to remain active in those areas, using any specialized knowledge to the benefit of the unit, as well as of the patients and their families. It is important for a new NP to avoid appearing to be setting up a competetive environment regarding special interests, but rather to offer to share knowledge while simultaneously learning from others.

If the NP will be expected to perform specific procedures, it is imperative to understand those expectations at the onset of building the collaborative practice. Within the hospital setting, NPs will be required to obtain privileges to perform these procedures, and may need to demonstrate proof of competency, or supply a list of the number of procedures that have been accomplished successfully during training. Alternately, the particular hospital medical staff may require certain high-risk procedures be performed under direct observation by another provider (physician or NP) who is already credentialed in such a way. Even if a provider enters the hospital setting with demonstrated competency that was acceptable in another institution, some hospitals require first-hand observation by another member of the medical staff. It is essential to understand which of the NP's physician partners, other NPs, or physician assistants are willing and able to provide such mentoring and oversight, so the NP is able to function independently as soon as possible.

Defining Bidirectional Expectations

This author has heard many times from colleagues in pediatric intensive care units, as they were starting to incorporate NPs into their teams, that it "just didn't work." When asked to define how and why it "didn't work" those same colleagues were often incapable of describing what they were expecting, so it was impossible to assess why the attempt to bring the NPs into the team did not meet those expectations. When I would ask whether the expectations had been made clear to the NP at the start, or whether the entire group of pediatric intensivists had met to discuss how they envisioned the role working within their unit, I would more often than not be met with blank stares and looks of incredulity.

Clinical Expectations

In a collaborative practice, the discussion about expectations should go both ways (or multiple ways, if we include administration in the conversation). The NP has a right, and in fact a duty to herself and to the patients, to understand what she can expect from the other members of the team. How much autonomy is expected? Does every new patient have to be discussed immediately with the attending physician? How will the NP interact with residents, fellows, medical, and nursing students? Is there an expectation to assume typical nursing duties when the unit is short-staffed? Who does the NP call first when there are questions about patient care? An NP who spent a decade as a bedside nurse in a critical care unit before pursuing his NP degree may be considerably more experienced at identifying critical illness and taking immediate action than a first-year medical resident. The NP has a right to know what to expect when there are conflicts between the NP and others on the team. Generally, since the official collaborative agreement is made between the NP and attending physicians, it is from the established MD, not from a physician in training, that the NP should take guidance when this is necessary. However, there may be occasions when someone with specialized knowledge, such as a critical care fellow, may be competent to direct the care of patients in an area. This must be established at the outset so that the service provided to the patients can be smooth and coordinated. There is great opportunity for NPs to enhance the team function in the hospital setting. This can only be accomplished if the *expectations of all parties are identified at the outset*, and maintained through the longer term.

Nonclinical and Professional Expectations

Other areas in which expectations must be addressed revolve around the nonpatient care aspects of the NP role. If the NP is appointed as a faculty member in the School of Medicine or Nursing, is there an expectation to engage in scholarly activities? Is professional development supported? Can the NP expect to receive support and mentoring in her or his career goals by the physician partners, the nursing administration, or both? How much time is allocated for scholarly activities if such is expected as part of the role?

Many NPs also participate in the committee structure within a hospital and/or at the professional schools in which they are appointed.

Understanding the time commitment for such activities and whether or not such activities are considered part of the NP's scheduled hours is important. There are many ways in which to address such issues. The point is that they must be discussed at the outset so that every one understands the ground rules and the road map for long-term success of the individual NP, as well as the NP role within the unit or hospital.

Introduction to the Team

When a new NP enters a practice, all team members need to become familiar with the role he or she will play in the care of patients and the development of the unit; therefore, the new NP needs to be introduced to the other members of the team. It is appropriate for the lead physician to make that introduction to the other physicians, and to instruct the fellows, residents and medical students on the NP role, so there are no misunderstandings. It is also necessary for the NP to be introduced to the nursing and ancillary health care staff, with similar delineation of the role and expectations. Sometimes nursing staff members find it difficult to "take orders" from someone who until recently was one of them. This must be handled with some sensitivity. However, in most situations, the bedside nurses are ready to welcome the NP once they fully understand the role and visualize how patient care may be improved by the addition of such a role to their team. NPs are in a unique position to help both physicans and nurses to understand the other's point of view. They are also uniquely positioned to become stuck in the middle of a no-win situation if communication about their own role has not been handled well.

Ongoing Communication

Routine Communication

Effective communication is not a one-time event. It must be an ongoing priority of the NP/physician team if true collaboration is going to exist. It may be helpful to arrange a time to touch base weekly in the beginning, even if it seems as if all is going well. As every one settles more comfortably into their roles, standing communication times can be less frequent. However, having an opportunity to speak with each other before a crisis occurs can often avert that crisis. Setting aside time in advance makes it less intimidating to discuss small issues. Concerns can be addressed as a matter of course and not seem more critical than they are. If all is going well, eventually routine communication can occur monthly, or quarterly. Depending upon the institution, it may be useful to review process improvement activities, revenue, expenses, and patient care parameters at these meetings if that data is available. Short-term objectives related to patient care will be a focus of these meetings; but some attention needs to also be paid to the further development of the NP role, as well as career evolution of the NP. Again, depending upon the system and the structure, mentoring in the role and in an individual's career may be provided by a senior level NP. This is one of the foci of the relatively new degree of Doctor of Nursing Practice (DNP).

Communication Around Emergencies

Regardless of the level of preplanning, patient care emergencies happen with some frequency in the inpatient setting. While many can be addressed by the NP without consultation, there is still a need to communcate the change in patient status to the physician of record. It is useful to discuss in advance with the collaborating physician(s) how to best accomplish this emergency communication. The immediacy of communication will likely diminish with increasing experience and expertise of the NP, and growth of trust between the physician(s) and the NP(s). Regardless of the standards or protocol for emergency communciation established, the NP should ALWAYS communicate with the physican if a patient is not responding appropriately to care delivered by the NP, if the NP has limited experience with the current situation, or if the NP is not certain what treatment to initiate. The NP is likely to be given more autonomy more rapidly if the physician is secure that the NP can recognize his or her own limitations of knowledge or skill set.

For emergent patient care issues, it may be useful to adopt a scheme for communication that is clear and succinct. Many hospitals and practices have adapted the SBAR (situation, background, assessment, and recommendation) mnemonic for consistency and brevity (Vardaman et al., 2012). SBAR has been shown to enhance safe communication around patients in surgical residencies (Telem, Buch, Ellis, Coakley, & Divino, 2011) and in morbidity and mortality conferences (Mitchell et al., 2012), demonstrating it is a technique not limited to nurse–physician communication.

Communicating to Resolve Conflicts

Conflict will occur as the practice develops. These conflicts may be within the NP's team or between your team and others in the same or other institutions, units, or services (Azoulay et al., 2009). Conflict may be a necessary part of the change process, and therefore cannot be avoided, although it can be ameliorated by communicating clearly and in advance around any issue likley to be controversial. Confusion and competition can breed conflict (Gardner, 2010). There are many individuals in any institution or on any service who will be threatened by the introduction of an NP, especially if this is a new role for that particular area. Conflict left unaddressed will fester and become worse over time. There is never reason to ignore it, although many of us are loath to deal with it directly.

Success of the NP role requires a willingness to address conflict as or before it develops, and to work with the collaborating physician(s) to understand it and address it. Conflict between the NP and collaborating physician(s) may require mediation by a trained counseler from HR or the professional affairs or medical staff office of the hospital. Conflict between the NP and other physicians can be addressed in concert with the collaborating physician(s). Conflict must always be handled respectfully, and by addressing knowledge gaps that may be there regarding the NP role. Conflicts between the NP and the unit-based nursing staff may be handled jointly by the physician, NP, and the nursing manager or a representative from HR. The collaborating physician(s) can help to prevent conflicts by explaining the NP role to prospective patients, to physicians on other services, and to bedside nurses. This author, who often accepts patients in transfer from other doctors or hospitals, tries to inform the patient and family before they arrive that they will be seen and examined by the NP on arrival, so that they are not expecting to see me right away. I explain to physicians on other services that if they receive a call from the NP on my service they are to treat it as if it were a call directly from me. I send the bedside nurses back to the NP if there are questions about an order she wrote, and do the same if a family member has a concern related to the NP's practice area.

POTENTIAL OBSTACLES TO COLLABORATION

At every juncture in the development of the inpatient NP practice, obstacles may occur that have the potential to derail the process. If attention is not paid to the areas described above, a successful practice may not be possible over the long term.

Competition Versus Collaboration

Despite the best efforts of the hospital administration and nursing leaders in the institution, and despite a voiced willingness or even interest on the part of the physician(s), there is a significant risk that physicians will view the NP as a competitor rather than a partner. This may be related to the long-standing conflict between many state medical societies and their related NP associations or state boards of nursing practice relating to independent NP practice. It may also be related to a real or perceived risk that the NP's role may take patient encounters or billable hours away from the collaborating physician(s), resulting in a potential decrease in physician compensation. Hopefully, there were discussions about compensation during the preparation for the NP's entry into the role. But if not, that discussion needs to occur as soon as possible once the NP has started in the role. There are many compensation arrangements in which NP productivity can add to the physician(s)'s accrued productivity, while not diminishing the opportunity for the NP to generate quantifiable revenue (see Chapter 10 for additional information about NP compensation plans and how salaries are set). In academic settings, collaboration among faculty remains an often unrealized goal (Carr, Pololi, Knight, & Conrad, 2009), so if the NP has an appointment in the relevant school of medicine, perceived competition regarding advancement of rank may also be a problem interfering with collaboration.

Lack of Understanding of NP Role and Scope of Practice

Clarification of the NP role as well as scope of practice is crucial to establishing a truly collaborative practice. Lack of regulatory uniformity between states and lack of standardization among NP graduate training programs makes understanding the role difficult (Clarin, 2007). In addition, as the specific practice is being established, NP roles and responsibilities often overlap those of other members of the team. This causes confusion for the physician(s), the NP, the nursing staff, and any associated medical residents, students, and allied health professionals. *Confusion regarding the role is sure to lead to the perception that the NP has not met goals.* Over time, this can erode not only that particular practice, but the perception of physicians and administration with regard to ALL NP practice.

Autonomy Versus Supervision

The opening sections of this chapter mentioned that the physician's interpretation of collaboration is often very different from that of the NP. Many physicians view the NP as functioning in a dependent fashion that requires direct supervision, whereas most NPs view collaboration as occurring in the framework of an independent practice that allows for consultation with the physican when the NP believes it to be necessary (Cairo, 1996). It is not hard to imagine how conflict can develop when these perceptions are ingrained in each of the participants. How can two individuals collaborate when they do not agree on the need for consultation and supervision?

Physician Attitudes

Poor physician attitude is sometimes mentioned as a potential barrier to collaboration. While this may be the case, this author prefers to look at the reasons underlying that attitude. Generally it is more effective to consider the cause, such as prior work experience, lack of understanding of the role, worry about competition, impact on compensation, and so on, rather than poor attitude per se. While there are some perpetually irascible physicians, they are in the minority. The majority of physicians welcome

NPs into their hospital-based practice, once they understand fully the role and scope of practice.

Hierarchical Practices

The American hospital and health care system remains hierarchical (Carr et al., 2009; Conrad et al., 2010), with the physician generally taking the role of leader of the health care team. In community hospitals, physicians are generally accustomed to giving orders and having those orders obeyed without question. In academic medical centers, attending physicians expect to direct the team of residents, medical students, nurses, and allied health professionals, and have generally had no other provider vying for that leadership role. It is not always clear where the NP fits within this hierarchical structure, which does not traditionally revolve around collaboration. The earliest adopters of collaborative, team-based multidisciplinary teams within hospitals have been those intensive care units that are highly patient-centered, evidence-based, and egalitarian. The Society of Critical Care Medicine invigorates and supports the collaborative work between all members of the health care team and can be a wonderful place for an NP to experience collaboration.

Attempts to Place the NP Into More Familiar Roles of Resident or Fellow

Owing to the evolution of medical training programs, and to residency work hour restrictions, some hospitals are hiring NPs to compensate for lost manpower hours previously and traditionally filled by residents. It is tempting and easy for physicians, nurses, and hospital administrators to assume the NPs hired will fulfill residents' roles and responsibilities. This becomes problematic for a number of reasons. Not only does this practice or assumption interfere with collaboration between the NP and the attending physician(s), but it makes role clarity difficult with regard to residents, medical students, fellows, bedside nurses, and others, not to mention the patient and their family. Junior residents require supervision by senior level residents, fellows, and/or attending physicians. Others may assume that the NP therefore requires the same level of supervision. The attending physician may also make that assumption. If supervision is assumed to be the norm, collaboration will be harder to achieve.

Bedside Nurse, Care Coordinator, Case Manager, Clinical Nurse Specialist

Nurses and physicians may make an assumption that because the NP posesses an RN that he or she can still perform the duties of the bedside nurse, especially if staffing is limited. While this may be technically correct, and it can be done in an emergency situation, the NP needs to be careful not to fall into the comfortable role of bedside nursing. Because NPs generally take a holistic and patient- and family-centered approach to patient care and discharge planning, some on the team or in the hospital may presuppose that having an NP on the team precludes the need for a nurse coordinator or case manager role. Strong ties to the community and an understanding of how best to move patients back from the hospital setting to their medical home can be very useful skills of the NP. But care must be exercised or the NP risks becoming the owner of team discharges, and risks not being able to work up to her potential. Other advanced practice nursing roles, such as that of the clinical nurse specialist (CNS), may overlap with those of the NP. Programs, degrees, and licensure vary considerably. While in some situations an NP may be able to perform both a clinical (NP) and a predominantly teaching/practice development (CNS) role, the two are not interchangable, and may even be seen as competitive (McNamara, Lepage, & Boileau, 2011).

The NP's Potential Contribution to Overcoming Collaboration Barriers

Developing a new role for herself, or starting in a role that is new for the hospital or unit in which she will work, the NP has a significant part to play in making collaboration happen. If the NP does not have a clear vision of his potential value to the institution and the patient, he will not be able to develop a collaborative relationship with the physician and the rest of the health care team. The individual NP must develop a vision of the future, have clear professional and behavioral standards, and must know what is acceptable and what is not. The NP must have a strong sense of self, utilize reflection and cooperation in analyzing problems, and come to the table as an equal to the physician, if the physician is going to respect the NP and trust his skills and knowledge. That does not mean to be egotistical or condesending. But acknowledging where one wants to go, having a vision of how to get there, and being open and transparent about knowledge and skill deficits will enable optimal collaboration to occur.

SUMMARY: STRATEGIES TO OVERCOME POTENTIAL BARRIERS AND ENHANCE NP-PHYSICIAN COLLABORATION

It should be clear that establishing a collaborative practice in the hospital setting may not be simple, straightforward, or rapid. However, the rewards are great if the barriers can be overcome. The following list summarizes the early parts of this chapter and may be used as a guideline for yearly, quarterly, monthly, weekly, and daily activities that may enhance and sustain the collaborative relationship.

NPs Entering Hospital-Based Practice Should

1. Prepare for the new role by learning everything possible about the institution, unit, practice, and physicians
2. Be clear about the envisioned role, scope of practice, and expectations for their own professional development
3. Be prepared to educate others about their role and scope of practice
4. Communicate, communicate, communicate
5. Address areas of real and potential conflict early
6. Not allow themselves to assume the responsibilities traditionally assigned to other members of the health care team unless they intend for it to become their role permanently
7. Do all they can to understand the culture of the environment in which they will practice
8. Be aware of their own needs, be introspective. Reflect on what has gone well and what would benefit from improvement and work on it!
9. Seek mentoring and advice from others—a lead NP in their institution, a trusted physician, a former mentor or professor who has been in the trenches
10. Admit what they do not know and never try to practice beyond their competency or comfort level.

REFERENCES

Azoulay, E., Timsit, J. F., Sprung, C. L., Soares, M., Rusinova, K., Lafabrie, A. , . . . for the Ethics Section of the European Society of Intensive Care, M. (2009). Prevalence and factors of intensive care unit conflicts: the conflicus study. *American Journal of Respiratory Critical Care Medicine, 180*(9), 853–860.

Blue, A. V., Mitcham, M., Smith, T., Raymond, J., & Greenberg, R. (2010). Changing the future of health professions: Embedding interprofessional education within an academic health center. [Comparative Study]. *Academy of Medicine, 85*(8), 1290–1295.

Cairo, M. J. (1996). Emergency physicians' attitudes toward the emergency nurse practitioner role: Validation versus rejection. *Journal of the American Academy of Nurse Practice, 8*(9), 411–417.

Carr, P. L., Pololi, L., Knight, S., & Conrad, P. (2009). Collaboration in academic medicine: Reflections on gender and advancement. *Academy of Medicine, 84*(10), 1447–1453.

Clarin, O. A. (2007). Stategies to overcome barriers to effective nurse practitioner and physician collaboration. *Journal of Nursing Practice*, 538–548.

Collaborate. (2012). Merriam-Webster.com. Retrieved January 12, 2012, from http://www.merriam-webster.com/dictionary/collaboration.

Collaborate. (2012). Wikipedia.org. Retrieved January 14, 2012, from http://en.wiki pedia.org/wiki/Collaborate

Conrad, P., Carr, P., Knight, S., Renfrew, M. R., Dunn, M. B., & Pololi, L. (2010). Hierarchy as a barrier to advancement for women in academic medicine. *Journal of Womens Health (Larchmt), 19*(4), 799–805.

Curtis, K., Tzannes, A., & Rudge, T. (2011). How to talk to doctors—A guide for effective communication. [Review]. *International Journal of Nursing Reviews, 58*(1), 13–20.

Gardner, D. (2010). Expanding scope of practice: Inter-professional collaboration or conflict? *Nursing Economics, 28*(4), 264–266.

Liston, B. W., Fischer, M. A., Way, D. P., Torre, D., & Papp, K. K. (2011). Interprofessional education in the internal medicine clerkship: Results from a national survey. *Academy of Medicine, 86*(7), 872–876.

Malloy, D. C., Hadjistavropoulos, T., McCarthy, E. F., Evans, R. J., Zakus, D. H., Park, I., ... Williams, J. (2009). Culture and organizational climate: Nurses' insights into their relationship with physicians. *Nursing Ethics, 16*(6), 719–733.

McNamara, S., Lepage, K., & Boileau, J. (2011). Bridging the gap: Interprofessional collaboration between nurse practitioner and clinical nurse specialist. *Clinical Nurse Specialist, 25*(1), 33–40.

Mitchell, E. L., Lee, D. Y., Arora, S., Kwong, K. L., Liem, T. K., Landry, G. L., ... Sevdalis, N. (2012). SBAR M&M: A feasible, reliable, and valid tool to assess the quality of, surgical morbidity and mortality conference presentations. *American Journal of Surgery, 203*(1), 26–31.

Robinson, F. P., Gorman, G., Slimmer, L. W., & Yudkowsky, R. (2010). Perceptions of effective and ineffective nurse–physician communication in hospitals. *Nursing Forum, 45*(3), 206–216.

Telem, D. A., Buch, K. E., Ellis, S., Coakley, B., & Divino, C. M. (2011). Integration of a formalized handoff system into the surgical curriculum: Resident perspectives and early results. *Archives of Surgery, 146*(1), 89–93.

Vardaman, J. M., Cornell, P., Gondo, M. B., Amis, J. M., Townsend-Gervis, M., & Thetford, C. (2012). Beyond communication: The role of standardized protocols in a changing health care environment. *Health Care Management Reviews, 37*(1), 88–97.

Wauben, L. S., Dekker-van Doorn, C. M., van Wijngaarden, J. D., Goossens, R. H., Huijsman, R., Klein, J. et al. (2011). Discrepant perceptions of communication, teamwork and situation awareness among surgical team members. *International Journal of Qualitative Health Care, 23*(2), 159–166.

9

Building the Practice Community

Tim Porter-O'Grady

As the nursing profession matures, it is appropriate to consider the configuration of the profession and consider how a professional community behaves. It is critical to consider the life of the profession if its activities are to be sustained for a long term. Clearly, professions represent a unique gathering of individuals with a particular mandate and a specific milieu that characterizes their membership. Because of the unique considerations related to professional bodies, special consideration of their foundations, characteristics, and interactions is critical to both the full understanding of the nature of professions and the support needs necessary to sustain them (American Association of Grant Professionals. Research and Authority Committee, 2006).

COMMUNITY AS THE FOUNDATION OF PROFESSIONALISM

Professions are communities. They are membership communities and distinct communities of practice. What gives professions life and meaning is their relationship to each other and their collective relationship to the broader community to which they are specifically directed to serve. Without the notion of community, there is no active life and the work of the individual becomes simply functional, iterative, and process driven. Missing in this set of conditions for the professional are the values, social obligations, ethics, collective consciousness, and the purposefulness that frames both meaning and action (Figure 9.1).

Advanced practice nurses especially demonstrate both the characteristics and obligations of a profession as the foundation for the full expression of their role. Because they must exercise independent judgment and act interdependently, they most represent the unique characteristics of the nursing profession within the capacity of their role to coordinate, integrate, and facilitate clinical decision-making and specific clinical action. Furthermore, they serve as the exemplar of the fullness of practice and of excellence both to members of their own profession and to members of those other professions and patients with whom they intimately interact to advance both care and health. Advanced practice nurses demonstrate

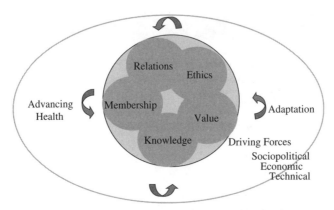

FIGURE 9.1   Building the professional community.

the deepest character of their profession in their individual performance and their collective relationship to each other as practitioners, for the profession and for the larger communities they serve.

The Profession's Social Foundations

Professions have been historically defined by sociologists as the establishment by an effective interest group of control over a particular area of expertise with a socially constructed method of exercising the power of that expertise in society (Bergquist et al., 2010). A more contemporary allusion to that definition would be more clearly described in the context of professions as a socially sanctioned mandate. The traditional and contemporary view of professions emphasizes their role in acting as expert agents in the best interests of society in a way that advances benefit for both the individual and community.

The more traditionally recognized professions associated with religion, law, medicine have a long tradition of social benefit and position representing a history of esteem over the past centuries of organized human communities (Rivington, 1879). These three professions represent a more historic and traditional view of professions and characterize social images most often associated with professions. From the beginning of the Victorian age and throughout the industrial age, the notion of membership professions has expanded to a larger group to generally include scientists, architects, engineers, academics, and accountants (Cody, 2003). Nurses came late to this table although there has been a general indication that they have lived in the reflective company of the medical profession (Ashley, 1976).

Professionalization of nursing has essentially been a work in progress for the past 100 years (Oermann, 1991; Porter-O'Grady, 2001a; Spalding, 1954; Tanner, 2006). While nursing has a history as long as the human species, its formal movement into the professional infrastructure has been relatively historically short. It's really only since the passing of Florence Nightingale's formalization of the professional structure that nursing has been undertaken in earnest. Efforts at professionalization such as developing a specified body of knowledge, learning/academic frame, practice foundations, an ethical framework, professional structures, and a formal professional identity have been the primary work of the profession during the whole of the 20th century (Chaska, 2001).

While these formalization activities have been occurring, social and political realities of the predominant medical model health system have had a strong influence on the rate of progress of the nursing profession within the practice and applications milieu. Because of the particular gender and role characteristics of the profession, significant historical limitations played out strongly in creating both context and content for building a professional structure. Historic female gender limitations have intensified the difficulty related to finding a legitimate place for the profession of nursing within the larger professional communities. Also, during this time the nursing profession was establishing its own internal rubrics, standards, practices, and social infrastructure. Since most of this was unfolding within an employee frame with all the attendant issues related to employment, the challenges of creating a professional identity were significantly multiplied. During nursing's primary development in the 20th century, its predominant role unfolded in an employment context, thus creating a social milieu that sustained social and gender-related concerns and added to them issues of subsequence, subordination, and institutional control (Long, 2010). This ran counter to the normative professional delineations for other more male-dominated disciplines reflected in role primacy, collateral relationships, practice independence, and organizational interdependence; therefore much of the development of the nursing professional community paralleled that of teachers rather than that of physicians, to whom nurses were more directly related. Interestingly enough, both teaching and nursing professions began predominantly as women's pursuits as nursing remains today (Collard & Reynolds, 2005). In teaching and to a limited extent in nursing, the trajectory to equity and professional influence has been primarily through collective bargaining action rather than through legislated control and privileging (Waltenburg, 2002). As a result, the character of community formed by nursing more represents its historic journey rather than prevailing notions of right, privilege, and legally ascendant practice such as that evidenced by lawyers, physicians, architects, and accountants, and so on.

Nursing as a Social Mandate

In the first decade of the 21st century, much has coalesced to create the conditions for building a professional script for nursing. Certainly, one of the fundamental characteristics of a professional community is its recognition of professional expectations and behavior representative of them. The struggle here is to create the internal dynamics and behaviors that exhibit to the world the self-understanding and characterization of a professional community. For nursing this means not only a verbal representation of nursing as a profession, but also a lived exemplar demonstrating a pattern of behavior that fulfills established norms of professionalization.

Shared Governance: The Structure of the Professional Community

The first requisites of established professional communities are represented in the governance structure of the profession and how it manages and controls its practice. For the past 25 years, the profession of nursing in a wide variety of organizations has been slowly constructing a professional shared governance infrastructure, which painstakingly and carefully transitions ownership for decisions about the work of the profession and its practice framework to those who actually undertake its practice (Porter-O'Grady, 2009). This is historically important since much of the direction and control for nursing practice came from those whose primary role was organizational management rather than clinical practice. The resulting behaviors created a rather passive sense of ownership of clinical decisions embedded in the staff and gave an overactive control of practice into the hands of nursing organizational leadership. In practice professions, the single clearest sign of professionalism is the full and engaged ownership of decisions about practice by practitioners (Pinkerton, 2008). Building an accountable community delineating distributed decision making has been and continues to be serious work in building an infrastructure for the governance and sustenance of the professional nursing community.

Second, important to the further understanding of professional characterization is the delineation of the nursing profession as a social mandate rather than as a job category. Nursing has been a licensed profession for some time in the United States. While that ostensibly creates for nursing an air of legitimacy, it has not itself translated its meaning into the minds and hearts of most who practice the profession. A social mandate becomes a condition of personhood rather than simply a functional attribute. When one becomes a licensed registered nurse, one does not simply enter a job category. The person, instead, becomes a nurse with the full social expectation that she or he will act in the best interests of society 24-7 wherever and whenever a critical need for that may arise (Porter-O'Grady, 2001b). The advanced practice nurse has additional obligations to exemplify the foundations of the social mandate, and indeed is required to evidence the fullness of the expression of the mandate simply because he or she characterizes the full range of practice incorporated within the nursing frame of reference. For the advanced practice nurse, all of the evidence of value-driven practice must be exemplified in the

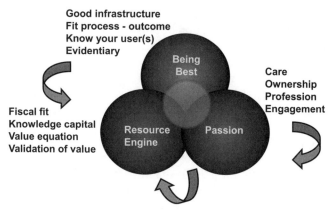

Good infrastructure
Fit process - outcome
Know your user(s)
Evidentiary

Being Best

Care
Ownership
Profession
Engagement

Fiscal fit
Knowledge capital
Value equation
Validation of value

Resource Engine

Passion

FIGURE 9.2   Value-driven practice.

role since for both the profession and the patient, the fullness of the value and application of nursing is invested in that person (Figure 9.2).

One of the unique notions of the professional life is this understanding of the person as professional such that individuals perceive themselves and the role as one and their identity becomes fused with the role. As a professional nurse, I act out of the "I am" rather than "I do" such that everything that I do represents who I am. Indeed, I don't do nursing; I am a nurse therefore everything that I do exemplifies my person as a nurse. As a profession therefore, nursing is not a job, it is instead, a social contract, a commitment to society indicating that I am its agent and will always advance its best interests within the purview of my social role as a nurse and through the scope of practice that represents.

This understanding of nursing as a condition of being rather than a function of action is a critical foundation for building a professional nursing community. As a professional nurse I hold membership in the profession and it is this membership in aggregation that empowers me to practice, informs my practice, and determines whether my practice has been appropriate and has achieved the values and outcomes for which it was purposed (Bednarski, 2009).

Every professional registered nurse from beginning practitioner to the most experienced advanced practice nurse represents the same basic obligations of the professional community. Once they are licensed, they are certified for membership not simply to do the work of practice but instead to make a difference in the world through the vehicle of practice. Value in the professional membership community is not embedded so much in the action of the nurse as it is in the impact. For the professional, the work is not so much to do something as it is to make a difference. Indeed, the work is actually purposed by value such that the work essentially has no value if it does not fulfill its purpose. The role of the professional is not simply to take action but instead it is to make sure that there is a defined relationship between action and impact (Malloch, 2010). The professional acts with the intent to make a difference, to change something. It is this change that is the enumerator of value for the professional. For nurses, this has been a difficult translation to visualize, evidenced by a historically almost slavish commitment to rituals and routines that may only tangentially evidence value, meaning, or impact. The value of the professional membership community is more clearly enumerated by what it has changed than in what it has done. For the health professions, including nursing, the yardstick of measure is the impact of their work in advancing social health and the quality of life. In the final analysis, a profession's work is measured by its significance rather by than the volume of its actions.

Requisites of the Nursing Professional Community

Nursing is unique among the professions. If only because its membership is 96% female, an adequate case could be made for nursing's uniqueness (Institute of Medicine, 2010). The historic trajectory of nursing's professional development follows fairly clearly enumerated gender differences. No one will debate the female associations and images created simply through the use of the word "nurse." And because the long history of women is a testament to oppression and subsequence, there are clear reflections of this pattern in the role and development of the nursing community. One could almost parallel nursing's struggle for parity with women's struggle for equity (Scully et al., 2010). While not seeking to dwell on this reality, it would be grossly negligent not to note, at least momentarily, gender implications and their effect in differentiating the developmental maturation of the nursing professional community.

In reflecting on the characteristics of community for the nursing profession there are special considerations that must be incorporated in any clearly delineated effort to establish and strengthen it. Some of the specific content of this reflection contains the following considerations.

- The characteristics and elements of the nursing professional community reflect different relational and interactional dynamics than is evidenced in predominantly masculine professional frames.
- The structure of the work role establishes a different set of parameters for the infrastructure of the nursing community when compared to other professional disciplines.
- The predominant employment-structured role paradigm for nursing establishes a different power construct for nurses, affecting issues of locus of control, role independence, functional interdependence, and professional power.

- The management-driven frame for nursing establishes organizational preeminence in power expression and decision-making, permitting the exercise of control affecting practice decision-making by laypersons unfamiliar with and uncommitted to the impact those decisions have on specific nursing clinical decision-making.
- The conflict between expectations of professional autonomy and accountability for nurses and the institutional, hierarchical locus of control for power creates in the nurse a nihilistic condition resulting in behaviors of passivity, functionalism, "jobism," noninvestment, reactivity, and oppressed group syndrome.

These considerations require an essential focus from nursing leadership if a sustainable and viable nursing professional practice community is to be built. Regardless of the role the nurse may play, from beginning practice through advanced practice, including nursing leadership, one or more of these conditional circumstances operates to influence effective construction of the nursing community. Building community inherently affects the power and relational equation within disciplines, between disciplines, and with the larger constituencies with which they interact. The ability to impact and make a difference depends on both perceived and actual conditions of balance among these variables, establishing a sort of even table around which stakeholders can be equitably engaged to the extent of their particular contribution to the decisions and work that flow from that table (Kritek, 2002).

Interestingly enough, social research, especially that related to social advocacy, demonstrates that the obligation for making space, establishing presence, and shifting the power equation comes from those who are most disenfranchised by existing disequilibrium (Erickson et al., 2003). Evidence suggests quite clearly that those most advantaged by power disequilibrium have no incentive to change it. Indeed, the evidence suggests that those advantaged by the disproportionate distribution of power do much to maintain their advantage (Schuman and International Association of Facilitators, 2006).

The implications for building an effective advanced practice community remain essentially the same as that for any other category of nursing practice. While advanced practice nurses represent a broader expression of both role and practice, the functional circumstances out of which these nurses have developed creates a contextual framework that transitions into the role, behavioral, and relational sets of nurses in advanced practice settings (Exhibit 9.1). Because of long experience in the historic, well honed and familiar mental models, advanced practice nurses bring with them into the advanced practice clinical work setting much of the practice arrangements, expectations, and performance configurations of existing organizational, structural, and behavioral frames that drive nurses in other employment settings. In most, if not all states, nurse practitioners (NPs)

> ### EXHIBIT 9.1 Obligations of the Advanced Practice Nurse in the Nursing Community
>
> - Full range (scope) of practice
> - Educating peers
> - Mentoring for growth (APN)
> - Interfacing with interdisciplinary networks
> - Exemplifying practice excellence

are predominantly employed in institutional structures subject to the same management infrastructure as was present in other nursing clinical settings. Furthermore, in most of these environments advanced practice nurses are frequently delineated as "mid-level practitioners," which simply and linguistically identifies them and places them in subsequent and subordinate roles, serving as a reflection of whoever occupies "first level" practice roles (generally reserved for physicians) where these more primary clinical decision roles (Arnold, 2002), by inference, control and direct the roles of those at the "mid-level." Here again, rather than carve out a broader context for equity in a larger clinical decision-making capacity, what has essentially occurred is the replication of historic role characteristics for nursing, resulting in the same subordinating, passive, and oppressed group behavior, only operating at a higher level of functional capacity.

What is important for the NP and for the advanced practice nursing community as a whole is the fundamental recognition that they have a defined scope of practice for which they are appropriately educated. In many states the current legal parameters are essentially restrictive because of preexisting notions of what those parameters should be, determined predominantly by their restrictive and dependent relationship to the medical profession. This does not mean that they do not have the right to act within the full scope of their competence. It does mean that they are legally limited with regard to the expression of this right by the parameters and restrictions placed on its expression through legislative and regulatory constriction. In states where this is the case, it is both the legal and ethical obligation of the advanced practice nursing community to strongly and sustainably advocate for legal protection and support for the capacity to practice to the full scope of advanced nursing practice competence. This mandate is a part of their social obligation to fully express the capacity they have to the patients they serve. Because they are nurses and their scope of practice is driven by their nursing values and commitment, this advocacy is not an attempt to limit or traverse the practice opportunities or obligations of another discipline. Instead, advanced nursing practice simply demonstrates the impact of the full expression of that practice and its competence. The value of the role is not its dependence on the approval and supervision of another discipline. Instead, it is a reflection of the extent of impact and outcome for the patient when the partnership between the disciplines clearly demonstrates its power to make a difference in the lives of others. This can only occur if their collective effort is integrated and interfaced. The net aggregated impact on care and service of this mutual partnership, where both partners are practicing to the fullest extent of their competence, is the best demonstration of more definitive and sustainable outcomes than any subordinating or subsequent relationship could ever achieve. It is the obligation of the nursing community to reach for this equity and advocate for the removal of any legislative or regulatory restriction that fails to promulgate the capacity of nurses to fully practice, to partner equitably with others, and to achieve the full impact evidence has already demonstrated is possible (Naylor & Kurtzman, 2010; Pohl et al., 2010).

Effective Construction of the Nursing Practice Community

It is clear that realities impacting the role of the nurse within health system infrastructures works strongly against creating both the structure and framework for the development of a truly sustainable professional nursing community (Porter-O'Grady, 2001a). However, doing so is not impossible. As has been strongly evidenced in the significant successes of the Magnet Recognition Program, the nursing profession can make significant structural changes (Balogh & Cook, 2006). Through those changes, there are many sources of evidence of success in building the structure of a sustainable professional nursing community in those health care systems recognized by the Magnet Program. Tremendously powerful and effective shared governance structures have emerged to create a structural frame within which truly professional behaviors can emerge, be supported by the system, and transform the relation, role, and equity of the profession within the clinical system (Bednarski 2009; Pinkerton, 2008; Styer, 2007).

Certainly, clarity regarding essential structure and the membership community character of the professions must be firmly embedded in the principal foundations underpinning construction of the nursing professional practice community. Ignoring these structural implications results in a prevailing infrastructure or contextual framework within which particular patterns of behavior representative of professional delineations never become codified into the cultural and relational expectations of membership. It is important to recall here that professional practice communities are essentially membership communities. As with all membership communities, terms of engagement, membership expectations, participation obligations, conditions for sustaining membership, and rules for expulsion need to be unambiguously articulated as they form the foundation for members (Porter-O'Grady, 2009). In addition, an essentially professionally derived locus of control and authority for these delineations rests with the profession, not with the institution. In relationships with professional communities, institutions have a right to expect that the professional community maintains its control over practice and practitioner and through its internal mechanisms works to assure the highest quality of professional decision-making, performance, and impact.

Therefore, the structural expectations that underpin the successful formation of a sustainable professional nursing community are:

- Behavior cannot be changed by addressing the behavior alone. Structure is the essential frame for behavior and creates the vessel within which behavioral definition and expectations take form. Without beginning construction of the professional community through the auspices of structure, creating behavioral expectations for the community will fail. It is this absence of professional community structure that most works against sustaining essential professional communities of practice.
- All professions reserve to themselves accountability for control over practice, quality, and competence (including knowledge creation, research, and evidentiary dynamics). These three fundamental accountabilities are reserved to the role of the profession and professional; they do not transfer to the control of institutions or laypersons. When control for these practice accountabilities shifts to institutions, they move to a position of an illegitimate locus of control, which guarantees a loss of legitimacy in the profession's locus of control with the resulting behaviors of non-investment, non-ownership, nonengagement, and the continuing diminishing economies of scale with regard to clinical impact, outcome, and value.
- Professionals will not sustain the commitment to excellence in practice through mechanisms of external incentives. Professionals advance only through internal motivators, demonstrated through mechanisms of engagement, ownership, investment, and a high level of peer involvement. Professionals are motivated predominantly through peer approval and do not consistently value, as a primary source of motivation, management-derived approval mechanisms.
- The professional community must be grounded in practice. In professions, the power of the profession is inherently embedded in its practice. If power is not embedded in the practice of the profession, the profession has no power.
- In the professional community, the purpose of structure is to build an operating frame for practice decision making. In professional structures, the format is designed around decisions, not around positions. The legitimate locus of control for practice decisions is practitioners; all other roles in the clinical system are support to this central decisional capacity.
- In the nursing professional community, the advanced practice nurse is delineated as the expert practitioner and must be located in the practice system in a way that reflects that perspective. Advanced practice nurses are not mid-level practitioners; they are, instead, practice experts at the apex of nursing practice. Being at the apex of nursing practice does not position them at the mid-level of practice relationships with other

disciplines. Advanced practice nursing is not mid-level medical practice. Nursing is not medicine and medicine is not nursing. If this distinction cannot be articulated and clarified, there are no legitimate grounds for building a context or constructing the frame for a professional nursing practice community.

- All professions are essentially self-governing. The infrastructure for a professional practice community is grounded on the premise of professional self-determination. While nursing practice is essentially and functionally interdisciplinary, it must be grounded in its own delineations of competence, its self-declaration of contribution, and its own knowledge-driven body of evidence that validates its unique professional identity.

- Governance of the nursing community must reflect the appropriate structural framework identified in purpose, bylaws, membership obligations, rights, privileges, and expectations for participation, competency determination and demonstration, requisites for individual role expression, codes of ethics, standards of behavior, and conditions of removal. These codes of professional delineation and conduct provide a structural framework within which the behavioral expectations and performance factors unfold. Through the demonstration of these factors, the professional expression of the exemplars of these practices gives witness, both internal and external, to the delineation, characterization, expression, and performance consistent with the normative parameters informing the action of professionals. Without these, the normative rules of employeeism, management hierarchy, and institutional mandate become the only frame within which work practices are legitimized.

In constructing a professional nursing practice community and creating the conditions of sustainability, the above principles are established as foundational requisites. In the absence of appropriate professional structure, organizations and health care leadership have no option but to assume routine employee–employer frames of reference for defining and managing the work of the operating construct. It is the obligation of the discipline to create the frame of reference within which it works and from that position to advocate and justify a differing relationship with the organization, other disciplines, and the system in a way that represents a more accurate and potentially effective set of interactions that mutually advantage all stakeholders.

Specific Functional Characteristics for Advanced Practice Nurses in Shared Governance

NPs and other advanced practice nurses play a critical role in professional governance activities in hospitals and other settings. First, of course, advanced practice nurses must realize that they are members of the nursing profession, not subsets of another profession. They are grounded in nursing, they are members of the nursing profession, and they are licensed by nursing bodies. There can be no stronger or clearer a level of clarity than that they are fully and completely nurses and therefore need to play a part in the nursing governance structure. There are two critical areas where their role is essential: credentialing and exemplifying the highest standards of nursing practice.

NPs and other advanced practice nurses must be involved in the credentialing process that incorporates the related activities of both the nursing and medically related professions. In an ideal structural setting, the hospital, service, or institutional credentialing body should be composed of the related disciplines who, together, credential all included disciplines with whom they collectively relate. Instead of simply having a medical credentials committee, an institutional credential committee, which represents all of the credentialed professions, provides a mutual approval process representing the hospital, service, or agency. For those places where law and bylaw mandate, individual discipline review processes can be the first stage of credentials review with the integrated interdisciplinary credentials review enumerated as the final stage of approval for all practice disciplines. Clearly, the first step for all nurses, including advanced practice nurses, is review and approval of all nursing credentials within the nursing community and subsequent referral of that to the interdisciplinary credentials review process (Figure 9.3). Many professional nursing shared governance models have a credentialing process that makes it easy to incorporate this level of credentials review and approval into existing nursing professional shared governance structures.

The second critical developmental area for advanced practice nurses is the formation in the hospital, service, or agency setting of the Advanced Practice Nursing Council. This Council is a standards setting,

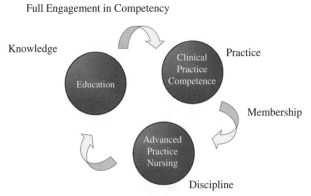

Full Engagement in Competency

Knowledge

Practice

Membership

Discipline

FIGURE 9.3 Elements of professional credentialing.

decision-making council that drives decisions and actions related to the role in relationship with advanced practice nurses in the clinical setting. The Advanced Nursing Practice Council fulfills the following requirements:

- Provides a locus for advanced practice nurses to establish standards related to credentialing, role, performance, decision-making, and contribution to the nursing profession in the system.
- Delineates the role characteristics and the particular contribution in mentoring and modeling exemplary standards of nursing practice, creating a framework for practice protocol development, defining the foundations of the evidence-based frame for advanced practice standards of performance.
- Constructs an organized and systematic identity in the structure of the organization for advanced practice nurses from which role identity, colleague relations, professional support, and contributions to the discipline and to the organization can be clearly demonstrated.
- Locates a specific place for advanced practice nurses in the organization where case review, quality activities, continuing professional education, role refinement and clarification, and role-specific problem solving can occur that are unique to the issues and circumstances of advanced practice nursing.
- Links advanced practice nurses in a formal and structural way to the organized nursing service with clarity around role, contribution, intersection, and advancing the interests and impact of nursing at every level of practice.

One of the more significant problems with NPs and other advanced practice nurses is their identity and locus in the organized health care system. Clearly, they must be validated as the nurses they are, but in a capacity that recognizes their unique role and contribution in the profession. By so doing, these nurses are both validated and valued with particular recognition of the unique contribution they make, within a context that can validate their membership in the broader nursing community and recognize the significant contribution they make in advancing its interests and impact on patient care (Figure 9.4). Furthermore, because of their inclusion and incorporation in the broader nursing community, they are able to advance their identity and to build on a support system whose numbers and capacity extend the opportunity to advocate for the value of the role and its importance in strengthening the health of the broader community (Porter-O'Grady, 2009).

Just a short word on bylaws. Formal professional organizations operate in partnership with the systems of which they are part. Formalization is required in order to establish a frame for self-governance and for defining the nature of the relationship of each member of the profession with each other, with the profession, and with the organization with

FIGURE 9.4 Structural elements of professional governance.

which they partner. Bylaws set out the rules of the profession's corporate or collective behavior. Establishing a formal and structured framework for how members operate within the profession and how the profession operates as a whole disciplines the action of the discipline. Every professional community that identifies itself as a distinct and independent profession operates through use of a formal set of bylaws. These bylaws set out the rules of membership, operating conditions of the profession and its relationship to its service and organizational partners, expectations of performance and behavior personally and within the operating formal profession. In addition, the bylaws define rules governing ethics, normative processes for sanctioning or removing members from the professional body who do not meet its standards, ethics, or obligations, and the functional and operational mechanisms that articulate the methods of doing business in the professional community. Any other rules and regulations that are unique to the role and performance of the profession are generally included in the bylaws. All organizational practices of nursing should have operating bylaws, be they in medical practice models, hospitals, or other community and agency structures. Without them, professionals soon become functional employee groups with no identity or sustainable power locus within the communities of practice.

Bylaws are formal governance instruments. They require approval of the professional body they address, support and approval of the organization with whom the professional body partners, and at least an annual opportunity to refine, advance, or revise them, consistent with the methods for doing so incorporated into the bylaws and subject to the approval of the nursing body covered by the bylaws and of the organizational governance leadership that authorizes them. Nursing has not historically operated at the level of maturity where bylaws become the foundational structural instrument for governing the profession. Bylaws provide a framework for acting collaboratively and consistently with the professional bodies with whom the organized discipline of nursing relates and provide equitable credibility in that relationship. Bylaws serve as an elemental and, some would suggest, essential tool for structuring the profession. Since bylaws have not historically been a part of the organizational construct of the profession of nursing, designers and advocates for developing professional governance tools will confront varying levels of resistance as a part of the normative initial steps of changing organizational consciousness with regard to constructing this formal legitimacy for the profession of nursing. Nursing leaders incorporating bylaws into the organizational relationship will be well advised to expect challenge, questions, concerns, and some opposition. Building good change strategies into the transition to professional bylaws will be as critical as the clarity and effectiveness of the bylaws themselves. Advanced practice nurses must assure that the section of the bylaws that relates specifically to their role clearly enumerates their relationship to the organization, to the profession and to each other, and substantiates the functional value and significance of their role in contributing to both the profession and the organization.

Full Membership in the Nursing Professional Community

Structuring for the construction and maintenance of the nursing professional community is certainly the cornerstone within which patterns of behavior and relationships between nursing professionals unfold. The needs of the nursing professional community become especially apparent for advanced practice nurses as they seek to clarify, differentiate, and enumerate their specific role and contribution to the interdisciplinary health community. Yet, in addition to structure, there is a need for the individual professional to recognize personal obligations of membership in the professional community. As mentioned above, all professionals represent in their person the whole of the profession and the expectation that as individuals they manifest the obligation of the profession to fulfill its social mandate to act in the best interests of the community, which empowers them to express the full scope of their practice.

All advanced practice nurses must recognize that at any given moment of interaction, they hold on their shoulders the full weight of the profession since, in that moment, they are all that any other person sees or knows of the profession, an image that will remain with them wherever they may take it and with whomever they may dialogue regarding it. This clearly calls for a rather well articulated delineation of who the practitioner is as an individual and how consistently he or she manifests the character and content of the profession within the context of his or her own behavior. Nurses must first know they are professional, see that as cohabitating with their pattern of behavior, and consistently demonstrate that in their relationships and performance as an expression of their person as professional. Informed by the structural requisites, code of conduct, and consistent professional behaviors within the discipline, the nurse is better able to consistently represent that pattern of behavior in dealings with disciplinary partners, leaders, patients, and the community at large. As more advanced practice nurses obtain their practice doctorates (DNP), and are introduced as such, they will need to emphasize the nurse attribution in language and action in order to both validate their connection to nursing and to affirm to the patient and other practitioners the legitimate scholarly knowledge foundations of nursing learning and practice.

There is a temptation on the part of NPs and other advanced practice nurses to create a niche for themselves that places them between "the devil and the deep blue sea." Within their unique and special category of nursing practice, NPs and other advanced practice nurses can get "lost" from their roots and create an ambiguous and uncertain context for their role that neither validates them nor advances their interests. While the medical staff certainly values their contribution, that value can never be enumerated within the medical model in any way other than a subordinating and subsequent role. At the same time, unless clearly enumerated, structured, and incorporated as a contributing component of the broader nursing community, the NP and other advanced practice nurses can lose connection to their legitimate membership community and can fail to sense the value and significance of their role and contribution in the profession. This demonstrates the importance of formal structuring of the advanced practice role within the nursing clinical service structure and of delineating and clarifying the particular value, specific role, and unique contribution these nurses represent through advanced and advancing nursing practice.

Professional role performance expectations require a level of self-perception, maturity, and expectation in a way that reflects a healthy self-image and a fully embraced sense of self. It is this behavioral arena that may perhaps be the most significant challenge for most nurses, especially advanced practice nurses. It is not a stretch to assume that working and practicing in a work setting reflecting a history of hierarchy, subsidiarity, and gender inequity will ultimately fail to generate the conditions necessary for assertive, engaged, and mature self-expression (Stone, 2004). Much of the work to obtain this pattern of behavior must also be intentional and be inculcated into the structural expectations for both membership in and participation in the professional nursing community (Exhibit 9.2). Through the development of the appropriate professional infrastructure and the membership, relational, and functional frames of behavior, it is simply a matter of time before the behavioral patterns consistent with the

> ### EXHIBIT 9.2   Expectations of APN Team Leadership
>
> - Advise standards and practices
> - Lead policy development
> - Facilitate decision making
> - Share specialized knowledge
> - Lead practice changes
> - Problem-solve as a team

structural imperatives begin to change self-perceptions and expressions of the individual and, ultimately, of the nursing professional community. In the change in self-perceptions, mature patterns of adult-to-adult behaviors and self-expectation begin to shift. This transition occurs when one changes self-expectations, one alters others' behaviors (Bonvillain, 2007). After all, one is always treated precisely as one expects to be treated, and no differently.

Representing the Nursing Community to Others

Whatever image the nursing community has in the eyes of others is a reflection of the self-perceptions nurses project about who they are and how they represent that to the world. So often one is heard repeating how poorly nurses are perceived or treated by others. They do so without fully realizing that however they are treated is a reflection of how they behave in the world and how nurses generally relate to others. Group oppression often has as much to do with the group as it does with the identified oppressor (O'Connor, 2002).

Nursing has done much work along the path to full maturity to create the conditions of equity, establish a body of scholarship and practice, and to establish real value in the practice arena. What may not have kept up with the work to establish content value is the effort to establish relational value. Membership at the interdisciplinary table means that nursing and, notably, the NP must sense the right to be there and have a real impact to make their contribution comparable to the efforts made by any other participant at the table. The challenge here is the confidence in the role and the competence at expressing its comparable value to others. At a time when the health system is reconfiguring around primary care realities, the centrality of the practitioner's role in that reformed system has been well established.

Interdisciplinary teams are becoming increasingly an essential component of health care design and organizational work within the contemporary post-reform environment. The growing complex nature of multifocal clinical services now drives the system more intensely toward well-calibrated and clearly accountable interdisciplinary teams (Phillips & Bazemore, 2010). The complexity and depth of knowledge of specific disciplines across a range of services in the continuum of care now require a stronger, more clearer articulation and intersection of those sources of expertise in a way that best benefits the patient and the circumstances that affect patient's health. Research has increasingly demonstrated a strong and effective interdisciplinary communication as a positive impact on clinical and relational outcomes, which ultimately affects the cost and quality of service delivery (Winowiecki et al., 2011). There is perhaps no more significant opportunity and partnering role for which the NP is better prepared. Here the normative skills embedded in the NP's role become critical to the effectiveness of the work of the clinical team.

From the perspective of the nursing community, basic requisites for establishing leadership and partnership in team relationships reflects much of what has been said in this chapter. Before effectiveness can be experienced by the interdisciplinary team, the NP must have a firm understanding of her value and role individually and have a strong collective network, professional community, and strong discipline-grounded value system and set of relationships in order to successfully exercise the clinical leadership role that is normative in team-based clinical practice. All of these serve as a strong backdrop, which advances the confidence and the competence of the NP. Competence in the leadership role is essential to the exercise of team-based leadership (Figure 9.5).

Effective communication structures will be essential to formalizing the relationship and role of the NP on the interdisciplinary team (Carroll & Ameson, 2003). It is important to align the communication infrastructure with the nature and character of the team and to clearly delineate the role of each of the participants in a way that best values their contribution and demonstrates the strongest use of their skills and applications on the clinical team. Increasingly, the notion of equity is becoming a driving value in understanding how effective teams operate, and an understanding

FIGURE 9.5   Model of APN leadership.

of situation-based emergent leadership capacity and its implications in team function is becoming more critical to assuring effective interdisciplinary teamwork (Foti & Hauenstein, 2007). The "captain of the ship" notion of team function actually acts as a deterrent to building effective teams and in many ways diminishes the potential for effectiveness by eliminating essential elements of emergent leadership driven by particular clinical scenarios, the need for specific competencies, and the need for an appropriate interdisciplinary interface around an existing critical clinical issue (Wright et al., 2008).

For the NP, it is critical to both expect and recognize the opportunities for providing particular clinical leadership in interdisciplinary teams. Traditional assumptions that the physician must always either direct, coordinate, or lead the clinical team in all circumstances are simply not supported by the evidence. At the same time, the NP must recognize the opportunities, availability, and conditions that either constrain or support the situational or emergent leadership role opportunity for the NP. Of course, the assumptions regarding all that has been identified in this chapter about the person and the role of the NP operates as a driver for taking advantage of the opportunities and obligations to provide leadership on interdisciplinary clinical teams. (A hot topic for NPs is admission to the hospital as the "attending provider." This section is very relevant to that debate.) The NP must confidently depend on the support of the nursing community, and on structures and relationships that advance the collective support system validating the NP leadership capacity. As primary care becomes a growing frame for the delivery of health service across the continuum of care in the United States, advanced practice nurses will be central to both the leadership and team-based delivery of health services to a broader population of users within a stronger health script. Collectively and assertively translating and applying the role of advanced practice requires personal commitment and action, but in so doing the NP should reflect the collective and community valuing and support of individual nursing leadership action.

Mentors in the Nursing Community

Capacity to grow in membership, relationship, and leadership in the professional nursing community as an advanced practice nurse requires a deep understanding and embracing of the interdependence professionals must have to advance the interests of the discipline. One cannot grow and mature in isolation. Without the opportunity to both share and invest in broader and deeper insights about role, relationship, interaction, and self-development, such development simply does not occur. For professionals, and especially for leaders, it is important to be able to establish particular relationships with individuals who best represent the talents, skills, and capacities we most idealize as exemplars of excellence, leadership, and personal commitment (Whitworth et al., 2007). Identifying and establishing relationships with those who represent the best in our practice provides an opportunity to deepen our understanding of the character of these individuals and of the principles, processes, and practices that demonstrate the best of who we are and what we can become. These individuals provide an opportunity to act as exemplars for excellence and best practice and when used as a vehicle for dialogue and discernment, they can provide insights that inform our own personal professional and leadership journey.

It goes without saying that almost all leaders in practice have identified particular individuals whom they accessed and with whom they related, to act as a personal mirror, medium, and mentor for their own personal professional and leadership journey (Crane & Patrick, 2007). Mentors provide an opportunity to refocus and recalibrate the professional experience and leadership capacity. Mentorship is a personal relationship with another that allows for a deeper engagement and insight into patterns of thinking and behavior which drive particular practices and help challenge and influence the refinement and advancement of deeper principles and stronger best practices.

The search for mentorship need not be generated out of deficit but is actually a better representation of a clear commitment to a deeper and broader "becoming." Mentors simply provide additional insights and tools, which facilitate self-choice-making and even insights with regard to one's personal and professional journey. Mentors play a wide-ranging number of roles, depending on the situation and needs to facilitate the individual's personal capacity in communicating, goal setting, reflection, and choice-making. Careful consideration of the selection of a mentor means careful consideration of need, purpose, and value obtained from such a relationship. Rather than dependency interaction, the mentor relationship operates at a peer level and reflects the maturity of adult-to-adult communication and interaction. The mentor interaction is best exemplified in a broader clarity of understanding, a deeper articulation of meaning, more specific and achievable goals, and a better understanding of means and methods to advancing one's choices, career, or life processes.

An effective and generative professional community seeks to include both the value and role of mentorship as a fundamental part of its structure and mosaic of relationships. Mentorship in the professional community represents a fundamental engagement between and among the members of the community in ways that serve to build equity, relationship, trust, mutuality, and real collective competence around advancing both the professional and the profession. Mentorship represents what's best in a group and depends on the unique skills and capacities of each member of the group in relationship to the other, allowing for full utilization of the talents and abilities of members in ways that aggregate to the collective benefit of the discipline. Seeking these opportunities for mentorship demonstrates a level of personal maturity and professional value that accrues positively to the benefit of each person and to one's impact on the profession.

CONCLUSION

Professions are fundamentally and essentially membership communities. Members of professions hold this membership and in so doing represent access to both opportunity and obligation. The professional community is designed to advance the interests of those it serves and to provide a collective form and format for members of the discipline through collective action and individual commitment to continuously and effectively work to advance those interests. This greater social mandate creates an internal milieu that requires both formal and informal infrastructure, relationships, and interactions, which continually make it possible for the action of the discipline to be both relevant and meaningful.

While having an impact on those the nursing profession serves, the nursing professional community works to preserve the integrity of the discipline, create opportunities for it to advance its value and work, build a framework for advancing the relationship and effectiveness of the members of the profession, and establish opportunities for creating an ever-growing and effective community of practitioners. Building internal structures and supports as well as exercising the dynamics of real community provides the frame and the operating context for the intradisciplinary dynamics necessary to lead to competence, confidence, relationship, and effective practice. The structures of professional shared governance; the expectations of member engagement in the life of the profession; and the construction of interactive equity, value, and clinical leadership all converge to create the conditions for sustainability and for strong interdisciplinary interaction. With both mentorship and mutual support of each other within the professional community, the benefits cascade throughout and create in the community a force for positive clinical and relational impact, commitment to high levels of competent service, assurance of a dynamic commitment to high quality, and a growing sense of value. This is especially true with regard to the contribution and considerable impact of NPs and other advanced practice nurses. Through their unique capacity in the profession to provide leadership, to act as a bridge between the disciplines, to exemplify the highest levels of excellence in practices, and to push the walls of practice competence for all nurses, NPs and other advanced practice nurses make a particularly unique contribution. This value is best represented in the equitable relationship within the community and with other communities of practice whose convergence with the nursing community is essential to advance the interests of those that are mutually served by them. In this way the community of nursing practice provides to the world a clear representation of what is best in health care and how that gets translated into individual and collective practice. In the mature and effective practice community, its members demonstrate the fulfillment of the desire to serve in a way that advances and positively impacts the sustaining health of the community. At the center of this opportunity and obligation is the emerging practice leadership role of NPs and other advanced practice nurses, demonstrating the potential embedded in the fullness of practice competence and their engagement in advancing the health of the community.

REFERENCES

American Association of Grant Professionals. Research and Authority Committee. (2006). *Monograph: A series of papers on the topic of professionalization in the grant field*. Kansas City, KS: American Association of Grant Professionals.

Arnold, L. (2002). Assessing professional behavior: Yesterday, today, and tomorrow. *Academic Medicine, 77*(6), 502–517.

Ashley, J. A. (1976). *Hospitals, paternalism, and the role of the nurse*. New York: Teachers College Press.

Balogh, R., & Cook, M. (2006). Achieving magnet accreditation in the UK: A case study at Rochdale NHS Trust. *Journal of Nursing Management, 14*(5), 366–376.

Bednarski, D. (2009). Shared governance: Enhancing nursing practice. *Nephrology Nursing Journal, 36*(6), 585.

Bergquist, W., Robertson, D., & Gillespie, K. (2010). *A guide to faculty development*. San Francisco, CA: Jossey-Bass.

Bonvillain, N. (2007). *Women and men: Cultural constructs of gender*. Upper Saddle River, NJ: Pearson Prentice Hall.

Carroll, L., & Ameson, P. (2003). Communication in a shared governance hospital: Managing emergent paradoxes. *Communication Studies, 54*(1), 35.

Chaska, N. L. (2001). *The nursing profession: Tomorrow and beyond*. Thousand Oaks, CA: Sage Publications.

Cody, W. K. (2003). Paternalism in nursing and healthcare: Central issues and their relation to theory. *Nursing Science Quarterly, 16*(4), 288–296.

Collard, J., & Reynolds, C. (2005). *Leadership, gender and culture in education: Male & female perspectives*. Maidenhead, New York: Open University Press.

Crane, T., & Patrick, L. (2007). *The heart of coaching: Using the transformational coaching to create a high-performance coaching culture*. San Diego, CA: FTA Press.

Erickson, J., Hamilton, G. et al. (2003). The value of collaborative governance/staff empowerment. *Journal of Nursing Administration, 33*(2), 96–104.

Foti, R., & Hauenstein, N. (2007). Pattern and variable approaches in leadership emergence and effectiveness. *Journal of Applied Psychology, 92*(2), 347–355.

Institute of Medicine. (2010). *The future of nursing* (pp. 1–11). Washington, DC: Institute of Medicine.

Kritek, P. B. (2002). *Negotiating at an uneven table: Developing moral courage in resolving our conflicts*. San Francisco: Jossey-Bass

Long, K. P. (2010). *Gender and scientific discourse in early modern culture.* Farnham, Surrey, England; Burlington, VT: Ashgate.

Malloch, K. (2010). Creating the organizational context for innovation. In: T. Porter-O'Grady, & K. Malloch (Eds.), *Innovation leadership: Creating the landscape of healthcare.* Boston: Jones and Bartlett.

Naylor, M., & Kurtzman, E. (2010). The role of nurse practitioners and reinventing primary care. *Health Affairs, 29*(5), 893–899.

O'Connor, P. (2002). *Oppression and responsibility : A Wittgensteinian approach to social practices and moral theory.* University Park, PA: Pennsylvania State University Press.

Oermann, M. H. (1991). *Professional nursing practice: A conceptual approach.* Philadelphia, PA: Lippincott.

Phillips, R., & Bazemore, A. (2010). Primary care and why it matters for US health system reform. *Health Affairs, 29*(5), 806–810.

Pinkerton, S. (2008). The unit practice council: The center of professional practice. *Nursing Economics, 26*(6), 401–407.

Pohl, J., Hanson, C., Newland, J., & Cronenwett, L. (2010). Unleashing nurse practitioners potential to deliver primary care and lead teams. *Health Affairs, 29*(5), 900–905.

Porter-O'Grady, T. (2001a). Is shared governance still relevant. *Journal of Nursing Administration, 31*(10), 468–473.

Porter-O'Grady, T. (2001b). Profound change: 21st century nursing. *Nursing Outlook, 49*(1), 182–186.

Porter-O'Grady, T. (2009). *Interdisciplinary shared governance: Integrating practice, transforming healthcare.* Boston: Jones & Bartlett.

Rivington, W. (1879). *The medical profession.* Dublin: Fannin: xii, p. 477.

Schuman, S. and International Association of Facilitators. (2006). *Creating a culture of collaboration: The International Association of Facilitators handbook.* San Francisco, CA: Jossey-Bass.

Scully, J. L., Baldwin-Ragaven, L. et al. (2010). *Feminist bioethics: At the center, on the margins.* Baltimore, MD: Johns Hopkins University Press.

Spalding, E. K. (1954). *Professional nursing: Trends and relationships.* Philadelphia: Lippincott.

Stone, F. M. (2004). *The essential new manager's kit.* Chicago: Dearborn Trade Pub.

Styer, K. (2007). Development of a unit-based practice committee: A form of shared governance. *Association of Operating Room Nurses. AORN Journal, 86*(1), 85.

Tanner, C. (2006). Thinking like a nurse: Research-based model of clinical judgment and nursing. *Journal of Nursing Education, 45*(6), 204–212.

Waltenburg, E. N. (2002). *Choosing where to fight: Organized labor and the modern regulatory state, 1947–1987.* Albany: State University of New York Press.

Whitworth, L., Kimsey-House, K. et al. (2007). *Co-active coaching: New skills for coaching people toward success in work and life.* Mountain View, CA: Davis–Black Publishing.

Winowiecki, L., Smulder, S. et al. (2011). Tools for enhancing interdisciplinary communication. *Sustainability: Science, Practice & Policy, 7*(1), 74–83.

Wright, M., Phillips-Bute, B., Petrusa, E., Griffin, K., Hobbs, G., & Taekman, J. (2008). Assessing teamwork in medical education and practice: Relating behavioural teamwork ratings and clinical performance. *Med Teach,* 1–9.

10

Quantifying the Value of the Hospital-Based NP: Billing for Clinical Services

Robert P. Blessing

This chapter describes the value of nurse practitioners (NPs) in the inpatient setting. Several key components are identified, including the clinical impact of NPs as well as considerations important for financial success. In determining NP value within a health care system, it is important to discuss roles, regulations, and outcome metrics that impact delivery of patient care. Understanding basic concepts of billing is required to maximize legitimate reimbursement and increase billing opportunities. All of these factors are required for a successful NP practice.

THE NEED FOR NPs FOR INPATIENT CARE

Inpatient hospital care is an integral part of our health care system utilizing much of our health care resources. The demand for inpatient services is growing rapidly. The average acuity of hospitalized patients is rising with the growth of the elderly population. The ability of hospitalized patients to receive adequate care depends upon a number of factors, including the availability of highly trained health care professionals. Physician manpower is not sufficient to keep up with the overwhelming increase in patient population. To compound this problem, many teaching hospitals are experiencing restricted growth of medical training programs due to financial limitations.

One reason for the shortage of hospital care providers is the limitation of work hours imposed by the Accreditation Council for Graduate Medical Education (ACGME). In 2003, ACGME required all accredited residency-training programs to comply with an 80-hour workweek limiting available daytime and on-call duty hours to education-based activities for all physicians-in-training (Nasca, Day, & Amis, 2010). This resulted in a shortfall of resident and subspecialty fellow duty hours to provide patient care services and has driven hospitals to find alternatives to care delivery. Further reduction in resident duty hours were implemented by ACGME in July 2011, increasing this deficit by an estimated 6,000 providers (Iglehart, 2008). The impact of these changes is unclear, but the cost associated with shifting the services performed by residents to alternative providers is estimated at $1.6 billion annually (Pastores et al., 2011).

With the shortage of highly trained physicians, an alternative method for delivering care must be implemented. NPs have become a valuable resource as health care providers. The growth of NP and PA (physician's assistant) workforce has exceeded physician growth in the United States (Moote, Krsek, Kleinpell, & Todd, 2011). The integration of specialty-trained NP patient care teams is one solution for the gap in coverage (Angus et al., 2006). These teams are compatible with many professional values as there is literature supporting their use from medical, nursing, and administrative communities (Kleinpell, Ely, & Grabenkort, 2008). Horrocks, Anderson, and Salisbury (2002) reviewed 34 papers that looked at patient outcomes and found no differences between the primary care delivered by NPs and care delivered by physicians. Similar findings extend to critical care settings when teams composed of residents were compared to teams composed of NPs (Hoffman, Tasota, & Zullo, 2005).

There are other alternative staffing models utilizing intensivists and hospitalists exclusively, but they are more costly with outcome metrics that are equivocal compared to models incorporating advanced practice nurses. Table 10.1 represents an example of a cost comparison made between a group practice team composed of ACNPs (acute care nurse practitioners) + physicians and an all-physician staffing model for a typical eight-bed ICU (intensive care unit). Many models will incorporate residents, fellows, or interns into staffing models if these resources are available, but their services are not reimbursable by Medicare. The schedules required for an all-physician model have significant negative effects on physician job satisfaction, and morale (Dorman & Pauldine, 2007). With a limited number of available hospitalists and intensivists, this staffing model is not widely applicable (Gajic et al., 2008).

TABLE 10.1 Costs Comparison of ICU Staffing Models

STAFFING MODEL	AVERAGE SALARY	# FULL TIME EQUIVALENTS NEEDED	TOTAL COSTS ($)
Critical Care/Hospitalists (Physicians Exclusively)	$ 225,344*	5 Physicians	$ 1,126,720
Physicians + ACNPs***	$ 90,770**	5 ACNPs + 1 Physician	$ 453,850 $ 225,344 =$ 679,194

* Average salary based on 2010 Medical Group Management Association and Society of Hospital Medicine survey (Nelson, 2010).
** Average salary from National Salary Report 2010 (Pronsati & Gerchufsky, 2011).
*** ACNPs = acute care nurse practitioner.

ROLES OF THE INPATIENT NURSE PRACTITONER

The role of the NP functioning in the inpatient setting has evolved over the years. Integrating NPs into a successful multidisciplinary practice model requires careful consideration of their roles and services. Understanding and optimizing the NP role to the full scope of practice is key for the success of the care team. Failure to utilize NPs to their full scope of practice can decrease job satisfaction as well as potential billing opportunities.

NPs are primarily engaged in activities related to direct patient care. The most frequently reported activities include conferencing with patients and families, conducting physical examinations, obtaining medical histories, writing orders, conducting rounds, initiating consultations, and performing transfers and discharges (Kleinpell, 2005). Another change in the evolving NP role is the expansion of duties beyond direct patient care. These roles include rapid response team provider, educator, researcher, coordination of care, and quality assurance (Kleinpell, 2008). Clearly defined roles are essential to the success of the NP, and without them, the result is confusion and dissatisfaction for the entire practice group. According to Kleinpell (2005), NPs are generally satisfied with their roles and cite autonomy, involvement with patient care, and physician collaboration as important contributors. The role has become more autonomous with a reported increase in respect and trust from physicians and staff.

Defining the role and exact job description will be imperative for building a billing model for the NP practice. Once there is consensus from all vested parties, then a billing structure and effort report can be generated. NP efforts that are not considered physician services are not eligible for direct reimbursement. For the portion of the non-physician services provided, salary support may be provided by the hospital or other funding sources. An example is a critical care NP practice where the majority of efforts performed are direct physician services, accounting for 70%, but a portion of the job includes education, research, and other nonphysician services, accounting for the remaining 30%. In this case, 70%, of the NP time may be reimbursed if the NP is providing physician services, if the services are documented appropriately, and if all other criteria have been met.

While only some of the NP functions qualify for direct reimbursement, many have positive financial impacts. Incorporating the use of NPs can increase physician productivity, improve patient throughput and access to care, improve continuity of care, and promote positive outcomes. Examples of outcomes that measure the direct impact of NP involvement may include length of stay, ventilator-free days, and adherence to clinical practice guidelines (Kleinpell et al., 2008). Other outcomes that are not directly reimbursed include improving mortality, reducing adverse events, collaboration, education, and improved safety and communication. Documenting outcomes related to patient care is essential for quality improvement, but also for determining financial impact of the practice.

Many of the outcomes may have a financial benefit in reimbursement rates from third-party payers. Only 31% of academic medical centers report documenting the financial impact of NPs and PA practice (Moote et al., 2011). Measuring outcomes attributed solely to NP practice is challenging as there is no standardization of the roles and there is often blurring of roles between NPs and physicians (Rosenthal & Guerrasio, 2009). Many of the health care centers are not tracking outcomes associated with individual NP care but rather across service lines.

FINANCIAL CONSIDERATIONS FOR HOSPITAL BASED NP PRACTICES

There are several issues that will need to be considered prior to the introduction of NPs into a practice. One consideration is the number of NPs required. The factors impacting staffing include patient census, patient acuity, staff support, organizational structure, and staffing ratios. There is a paucity of data describing staffing ratios for providers, especially for NP practice. Shorter ICU length of stay has been reported with lower intensivists-to-bed ratios (Dara & Afessa, 2005). For critical care NPs, common provider-to-patient ratios observed are between 1:6 and 1:10. Determining the optimal staffing is difficult due to the variability in staffing models. Research often includes ICU teams comprised of inconsistent numbers of providers such as interns, residents, fellows, and NPs.

Inclusion of essential hospital personnel is necessary for introducing NPs. The practice group will need support from not only the physician group but also from nursing departments, credentialing, billing and compliance departments, quality improvement, and hospital administration. This model of interdisciplinary collaboration can be a complex project, but the relative advantage is potentially high. These advantages include improved clinical outcomes, patient safety, job satisfaction, and financial benefits.

\Another consideration is NP salary. The department from which the NP salary originates may also impact billing potential. For NPs receiving their salary support from the hospital, if the salary is included on the cost report, then the NPs cannot bill for their services. Medicare reimburses hospital salaries under Part A and considers compensation already provided. Billing criteria and Medicare Part A and B will be described later in this chapter. A leasing plan may be arranged to allow physicians that are not employed by a hospital to bill for the services of the hospital-employed NP as long as other criteria are met. "It is the entity employing the nurse practitioner, whether by W-2 employment or lease, that has the opportunity to bill for the nurse practitioner's service" according to Buppert (2006).

All of these factors can affect success and must be considered when determining the feasibility of a billing program for an inpatient NP practice, which depends on many variables (Buppert, 2005; see Figure 10.1).

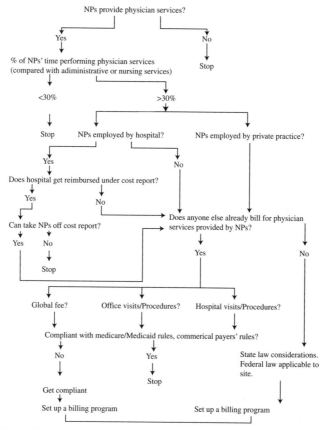

FIGURE 10.1   Should a hospital set up a billing program for nurse practitioner (NP) services?
Source: Buppert (2005).

Getting Started

Once the hospital administration has determined that NP services are required, billing for services is appropriate, and collaboration with NP/ state and federal laws is ensured, the NP must then be educated regarding reimbursement practices. The health care systems' billing, compliance, finance and advanced practice nursing departments can provide education for the NP practice. Collaboration between all of these departments is crucial for the success of the program. Consultation with billing experts familiar with NP practices is another option available to help capture potential billing opportunities and ensure compliance. Education must include federal and state regulations for billing as well as requirements demanded by third-party payers. NPs must be actively engaged in the billing practices and must maintain relationships with their billing departments. Monitoring billing and collections can improve the financial success of the NP practice and can be used for leverage for benefits and salary. Exhibit 10.1 is a list of useful resources for information regarding coding and billing.

MEASURING PRODUCTIVITY FOR NPs

NPs' salary, benefits, and bonuses are often based on the value added and revenue generated for a practice. There are various methods and formulas for calculating value earned for practices. The formulas offered by employers are often vague and difficult. There are legal considerations regarding salary and bonuses. Additional pay or bonuses should not be determined by offering additional care that is not deemed necessary nor omitting necessary care for cost savings. It is important for NPs to understand the verbiage and formula outlined in their contract. Measurements for productivity might also be considered in salary adjustments.

Productivity and reimbursement are not the same. Productivity measures may include any of the following:

• Gross patient charges
• Total revenue minus expenses

EXHIBIT 10.1:   Useful Resources on Coding and Billing Can Be Found at the Following Websites

• For Medicare patients, this FAQ will reflect the language in Transmittal 1548.
  www.cms.hhs.gov/Transmittals/Downloads/R1548CP.pdf,   www.cms.hhs.gov/MLNMattersArticles/downloads/MM5993.pdf
• The Medicare Learning Network at www.hcfa.gov/medlearn will provide you with educational materials and resources on the basics of medical coding and billing.
• For assistance with proper coding and billing instructions, visit the Medicare Carrier's Website at www.hcfa.gov/medicare/incardir.htm
• Contact your Medicare Carrier. The toll free number can be found at www.hcfa.gov/medlearn/tollnums.htm
• Contact Centers for Medicare and Medicaid Services directly regarding coding and billing at doctor11cms.hhs.gov
• Get information on the Medicare Integrity Program at the following websites: www.hcfa.gov/pubforms/83pim/pim83cO1 www.hcfa.gov/medicare/mip/mip.rtf
• For more information on Evaluation and Management (E&M) documentation, visit the website at www.hcfa.gov/medlearn/emdoc.htm or at www.hcfa.gov/medicare/incardir.htm
• View the Office of Inspector General's Compliance Program for Individual and Small Group Physician Practices, at oig.hhs.gov/oigreg/physician.pdf

Source: The Centers for Medicare and Medicaid Services.

- Hospital admissions, transfers, or discharges
- Number of patient encounters
- Number of consults
- Number of hours worked
- Number of procedures

Depending on how a health care system utilizes NPs, hospital bylaws, and regulations, NP collections may not be a true reflection of the services they provide. NP services might be captured under the physician's provider number. Tracking software is available to help capture the contributions of the NP. Another way to capture productivity is measuring relative value units (RVUs). Historically, RVUs have been used to measure physician productivity but more recently some practices are tracking RVUs as a measurement of NP productivity. An RVU assigns a value to each CPT code relative to time and resources expended to perform the RVU. This system is known as the resource-based relative value scale (RBRVS); it was developed by the Health Care Financing Administration (HCFA). There are three components to a relative value: practice expense, work, and malpractice component. These components help quantify the technical skill and physical effort required as well as the mental effort and judgment required and the potential risk of each service.

PAYING FOR THE HEALTH CARE MODEL

The American health care system has incorporated advanced practice providers performing services traditionally performed by physicians since the 1960s (Moote et al., 2011). NPs were initially paid as employees of individual physicians, physician group practices, or hospitals. Reimbursement of NP services was captured from activities performed under the physicians' provider number. This lack of direct NP reimbursement remained a significant barrier for NP practice and impacted the progression and utilization of their roles as providers (O'Brien, 2003). Without direct reimbursement for services rendered, NPs lacked the recognition as independent health care providers. In 1977, one of the first federal actions recognized the services provided by NPs and mandated 50% of services in funded rural health clinics be provided by NPs, certified nurse midwives, and PAs (O'Brien, 2003). Since then, the number of NPs has continued to grow along with years of research aimed at establishing value (Mundinger et al., 2000). As the number of NPs increased, so did national NP organizations with a primary objective of direct reimbursement by Medicare, Medicaid, and commercial insurers. This change developed through years of effort by individual NPs, professional organizations, as well as professional lobbyists. In 1997, The Balanced Budget Act granted provider status to NPs and allowed direct Medicare billing for their services in any setting (Balanced Budget Act, 1997).

As the environment of providers changed, so did the reimbursement of hospitals. In the past, hospitals would receive reimbursement from the federal government to help offset costs of providing care, regardless of the amount. This Medicare system was adopted from the private health insurance sector's cost-based reimbursement. As medical costs increased and charges were passed along to the government, this system was forced to change. Medicare's hospital costs increased between the years 1967 and 1983 from $3 billion to $37 billion annually (Centers for Medicare and Medicaid Services White Paper, 2001). In 1982, Congress imposed mandates changing the mechanism for hospitals' reimbursement. No longer was payment based on hospital charges, but instead on patient diagnosis. Under the prospective payment system (PPS), a set amount is paid depending on a patient's diagnostic related group (DRG). DRGs are based on many factors, including patient diagnosis(es), procedures, and complications. Hospitals may receive additional payments depending on variables such as location, teaching capacity, and patient-payer mix. For example, if a hospital cares for a high percentage of low-income patients, then it receives a percentage add-on to help offset these costs. Payments under the acute inpatient PPS system totaled about $110 billion and accounted for about 25% of Medicare spending in 2009 (MedPAC). Hospitals are now required to submit quality data related to patient care that can impact reimbursement. Quality data with negative financial consequences may include vascular associated infections, thromboembolic events or surgical site infections. Capturing these outcome metrics may be another way to evaluate NP practice. Medicare payments to the hospital are paid under Medicare Part A. These payments cover a variety of hospital expenses and personnel (Buppert, 2005). Efficient hospitals are now rewarded and inefficient hospitals have an incentive to become more efficient.

BILLING AND REIMBURSEMENT

Compliance

As health care costs continue to increase, hospitals are faced with optimizing potential income sources and improving quality care. Generating revenue through reimbursement requires compliance and training. Compliance is essential for hospitals to avoid penalties and potentially even repayments due to inconsistencies between documentation of care provided and charges submitted. The potential risk for improper billing practices may include not only loss of revenue but also financial sanctions, disciplinary actions, and exclusion from participating in governmental programs. Monitoring of billing practices is a major focus of the Office of Inspector General (OIG) within the US Department of Health and Human Services (DHHS).

Improper billing accounts for billions of dollars annually representing greater than 6% of Centers for Medicare and Medicaid costs (Adams,

Norman, Burroughs, 2002). Due to the rising costs of billing errors, other federal and state agencies have joined DHHS in investigating billing practices, including Department of Justice, Medicaid Fraud Units, and U.S. Attorneys General office. The OIG lists common high-risk billing patterns of physicians, including billing for services not provided or not necessary, misuse of provider identification numbers, and misuse of coding modifiers (Federal Register Compliance Program Guidance for Small Group Physician Practices; see Exhibit 10.2).

All third-party payers use similar mechanisms for reviewing medical claims, although Medicare has the most rigorous standards. Federal and state laws establish regulations for reimbursement of claims but it is often the claims processors, adjudicators, and auditors who review these claims and determine reimbursement.

There are several strategies designed to improve billing compliance, including formal training programs, audits, and quality-improvement audits linked to compliance data. OIG also lists compliance strategies such as designating a compliance officer, implementing written policies for billing practices, conducting internal monitoring/auditing, responding promptly to the audits with publicized corrective action, and disciplinary guidelines. Compliance training should include instruction on proper documentation. The OIG lists important elements for documentation, including timeliness of documentation, appropriate use of diagnostic codes, complete and legible notation of a patient encounter, including reason for encounter, pertinent physical examination findings, diagnostic studies, clinical diagnoses, and plan of care (Federal Register Compliance Program Guidance for Small Group Physician Practices). Standardized templates permitting reproducible and consistent documentation could be one method to improve compliance (Butler, Calabrese, Tandon, & Kirton, 2011).

Reimbursement

With the drive to become more efficient and thus more profitable, it is imperative for all providers to understand some basic concepts of generating income. Billing for inpatient care is complex and can be confusing with

---

EXHIBIT 10.2:   Common Risk Areas for Providers

- Billing for services not provided
- Billing for nonphysician services
- Submitting for unnecessary services, medical supplies, or equipment
- Billing for duplicate services
- Misuse of provider identification numbers
- Billing for bundled services under separate service
- Upcoding the level of service provided
- Improper use of coding modifiers

legislation constantly changing. The question becomes: who pays for the physician services provided by NPs? Third-party payers include Medicare, Medicaid, commercial managed care organizations (MCOs) or health maintenance organizations (HMOs), and commercial indemnity insurers. The rules that govern reimbursement for each of these third-party payers vary. The following discussion will focus on Medicare rules that pertain to inpatient care provided by the NP and provider team. Many of the regulations presented in this chapter are available on the Center for Medicare and Medicaid Services (CMS) website and can be obtained in CMS manuals and transmittals.

GENERAL MEDICARE RULES TO CONSIDER FOR NP BILLING

There are some general rules regarding Medicare conditions and qualifications for NPs. Listed in Exhibit 10.3 are some of these requirements, which and will be discussed in subsequent sections.

Medicare requires NPs to be registered as professional nurses by the state in which they provide services as NPs in accordance to state law, and meet one of the following:

If the NP obtained Medicare billing privileges as an NP for the first time on or after January 1, 2001–2003, then the following applies:

- Must be certified as an NP by a recognized certifying body (American Academy of Nurse Practitioners, American Nurses Credentialing Center, National Certification Corporation, National Certification Board of Pediatric Nurse Practitioners and Nurses, Oncology Nursing Certification Corporation, Criteria Care Certification Corporation).
- NP must have a Master's Degree in nursing or a Doctor of Nursing Practice (DNP) degree.

EXHIBIT 10.3:   General Rules for NP Reimbursement

- The NP meets Medicare qualifications
- The NP obtains a national provider identifier (provider number)
- Services performed are medically necessary
- The services performed are physician services
- The services performed cannot be just one part of a bundled service
- The services performed are in collaboration with a physician
- The NP is legally authorized to provide the services defined by scope of practice and state law
- No other provider had billed or been reimbursed for the same services
- The institution accepts Medicare's payment
- The services of residents, interns, or students cannot be billed under the NPs provider number

REIMBURSEMENT FOR CENTERS OF MEDICARE AND MEDICAID SERVICES

Medicare was created in 1965 as a federal health insurance program designed for the elderly and disabled. It has become the largest single health payer entity in the United States. Medicare consists of two programs. Medicare Part A covers inpatient care in hospitals, skilled nursing facilities, hospice, and home health care. NPs services were once covered under this program. Medicare Part B covers medically necessary services such as outpatient care, durable medical equipment, and physician services. The Balanced Budget Act of 1997 removed Medicare Part B restrictions regarding NP practice and now direct reimbursement is permissible for NPs to bill under Part B (Balanced Budget Act 1997). There are strict guidelines governing the reimbursement of NPs that must be followed to be in compliance with federal and state regulations. Unfortunately there is not a single document stating NP regulations required for billing. Regulations are scattered among various federal documents, as well as in state regulations that are constantly changing or reinterpreted. Many of these rules are vague in particularly important areas pertaining to NP practice such as physician participation, collaboration, and initial services rendered.

Public agencies or private organizations have participated in the administration of the Medicare program since 1965 (Federal Register Compliance Program Guidance for Small Group Physician Practices). These medical contractors, known as fiscal intermediaries (FIs), serve as the federal government's agents in the administration and payment the CMS program. There are two primary functions of the FIs: reimbursement review and medical coverage review. Interpretation of CMS regulations may differ from region to region depending on individual FIs. They are often involved in performing medical reviews to determine whether services billed are necessary, billed at appropriate levels, and are adequately documented. Congress appropriates funds to help support FI activities. A portion of the federal funds received is to detect and deter Medicare fraud (Federal Register Medicare Program; Medical Integrity Program). Provider practices should maintain a relationship with their regional FIs.

As providers, it is important to understand the Medicare payment structure. Under Medicare Part B, physicians are reimbursed at 80% of the total physician charge, leaving the patient responsible for the remainder 20% of the bill. NPs are reimbursed at 85% of the physicians' schedule. An example would be a service provided to a patient and the physician fee schedule was $100.00 for the service. The physician would have collected $80.00 from Medicare and $20.00 from the patient. If the NP provided the service, collections from Medicare would be 85% of the $80.00 or $68.00 and $17.00 dollars from the patient (Buppert, 2002). Although the NP collected 15% less revenue than the physician for the Medicare patient, from a pure financial perspective the 15% loss of revenue does not exceed the difference in salary. In many circumstances, Medicare requires the services billed under the actual provider responsible for the services. There are some situations where NP services can collect 100% of the physician fee schedule including "incident to" billing and shared visits. Incident-to billing applies only to outpatient settings therefore will not be further discussed in this chapter.

Shared Visits

An inpatient encounter may be shared between a physician and an NP from the same practice group. Each provider must perform a substantive portion of the evaluation and management service with face-to-face interaction between the patient and both the NP and physician (Centers for Medicare & Medicaid Services, *Medicare Claims Processing Manual*). A substantive portion of the visit involves all or some portion of the history, exam, or medical decision making. The physician and NP must be in the same group practice or be employed by the same employer. The encounter may occur at different times but must be on the same calendar day. This service may be billed under the physicians' provider number at 100% of the scheduled fee or under the NP's provider number at 85% of the scheduled fee. Shared visits do not apply to procedures, consultations, or critical care billing (Centers for Medicare & Medicaid Services, *Medicare Claims Processing Manual*). The requirements for billing shared visits are listed in Exhibit 10.4.

Evaluation and Management Services

Medicare will pay for evaluation and management (E/M) services for physicians and specific nonphysician providers (NPPs), (i.e., NP, clinical nurse specialist (CNS), and certified nurse midwife (CNM)), who meet Medicare's conditions. There is a common set of codes used to bill for E/M and it is up to the provider to ensure that the submitted claim accurately reflects the services provided. Documentation must support the level of service. In selecting the service or code that best reflects care, three components

---

EXHIBIT 10.4:   Medicare's Requirements for Shared Visits

- Services are considered physician services and are medically necessary
- No other provider has billed for same service
- Service must be within NP's scope of practice
- Encounter must be in collaboration with physician and must occur on same calendar day and by same practice
- Face-to-face encounter with patient and both NP and physician
- Code appropriate for service provided and reflective of documentation

should be considered; patient type, setting of the service, and level of E/M performed. Patient type for the purposes of E/M billing represents either a new patient or an established patient. If the patient has not received care from the same specialty or practice within 3 years, he or she is be considered a new patient. The settings include office or outpatient, hospital inpatient, emergency department, and nursing facility. Level of evaluation is organized by complexity of the visit. There are three key components to consider when selecting level of service: history, examination, and medical decision making. See Tables 10.2 and 10.3. Patients requiring a more comprehensive history, examination for diagnosis, and/or treatment regimens should be billed at a higher E/M code. These services must be medically necessary and compliant with standards of good medical practice. It would not be medically necessary to bill at a higher level when a lower-level encounter is warranted. The duration of the encounter is an ancillary factor and does not control the level of service to be billed unless requiring that more than 50% of the floor time is spent on providing counseling or coordination of care. Time in this case is the controlling factor in selecting level of service. An example would be for a cancer patient deciding therapeutic options—the provider discussing the effects of therapies on quality of life and lifestyle changes. In this case, documentation regarding physical examination is not required but proper documentation reflecting the discussion is warranted. For inpatient care, the encounter must take place at the patient's bedside or on the patient's hospital floor or unit (Centers for Medicare & Medicaid Services, *Medicare Claims Processing Manual*).

Both Initial Hospital Care and Subsequent Hospital Care codes are "per diem" services according to CMS and may be reported only once per day by the same physician or physicians of the same specialty from the same group practice. If two visits are required in the same calendar day, the provider should select a code that best reflects all services provided during the date of service. If two providers are each responsible for a different aspect of the patient's care, both visits may be reimbursed if their practices are different specialties AND they are billing different diagnoses.

TABLE 10.2   Initial Evaluation and Management Codes for Inpatient Services

CPT CODE	HISTORY/EXAM	DECISION MAKING	PRESENTING PROBLEM(S)	TIME*
99221	Detailed	Low	Low severity	30 min
99222	Comprehensive	Moderate	Moderate severity	50 min
99223	Comprehensive	High	High severity	70 min

*Time is an ancillary factor representing only usual time spent.

TABLE 10.3 Subsequent Hospital Visits for Inpatient Services

CPT CODE*	HISTORY/EXAM	DECISION MAKING	PRESENTING PROBLEM(S)
99231	Problem focus	Low	Stable, recovering
99232	Expanded focus	Moderate	Responding inadequately or minor complications
99233	Detailed	High	Not responding to therapy or new serious problem/complication

*Two out of three components of history, exam, and medical decision making must meet to assign a code (1 of the 2 has to be medical decision making).

Hospital Evaluation/Management and Critical Care on Same Day

When an inpatient hospital E/M service is provided a time that patient does not meet criteria for critical care and the patient subsequently deteriorates, requiring critical care, both the critical care services (CPT codes 99291 and 99292) and the previous E/M service may be reimbursed on the same day of service. The exception to this rule is if it occurs in the hospital emergency department. Some payers require adding a modifier "25" to the noncritical care E/M service. This however is not allowable in the emergency department. CMS Transmittal 1548 specifically addresses this situation and states that when critical care services are required upon arrival into the emergency department, only critical care codes (99291-99292) may be reported. Emergency department E/M codes (99281-99285) may not be reported (Centers for Medicare & Medicaid Services, *Medicare Claims Processing Manual*).

Hospital Discharge Day Management Services

Hospital Discharge Day Management Services (CPT codes 9238 or 99239) is an E/M service between the attending physician of record and the patient. This service must be reported for the date of the actual visit by the physician or nonphysician provider (NPP) even if it is not the actual discharge date. Reimbursement is not allowed for both the hospital discharge day management service and a separate E/M subsequent hospital visit on the same day.

Consultation Services

Medicare Part B no longer recognizes consultation codes, effective January 1, 2010. Instead of billing consultation codes, practitioners may bill the most appropriate initial care codes (99221-9923), or subsequent hospital codes (99231-99233) that best reflect the services provided. Contact other third-party payers since some may still recognize consultative services.

Reimbursement for E/M Services Provided During Global Period of Surgery

All care provided during a global period of surgery for inpatient setting is compensated through the surgical payment UNLESS the physician is treating another medical condition unrelated to the surgery. In this case, a CPT Modifier "24" and appropriate documentation is required. If the services are provided by the same physician on the same day of surgery and are a separately identifiable E/M service, then a modifier "25" is added to the E/M code on the claim. Hospital discharge day management codes (CPT 99231-99239) that are part of the global service payment are not reimbursed when the bill is fragmented for staged procedures.

Critical Care Services

Critical care services are defined by CMS as "the direct delivery by a physician(s) of medical care for a critically ill or critically injured patient. A critical illness or injury acutely impairs one or more vital organ systems such that there is a high probability of imminent or life threatening deterioration in the patient's condition" (Centers for Medicare & Medicaid Services, *Medicare Claims Processing Manual*). There are several criteria that must be met in order to bill critical care services.

1. Critical care must involve high-complexity decision making to assess, manipulate, and support vital system functions, to treat vital organ system failure, and/or to prevent further life-threatening deterioration. Examples of vital organ system failure include central nervous system failure; circulatory failure; shock; and renal, hepatic, metabolic, and respiratory failure. Both the illness or injury and the treatment being provided must meet the above criteria to bill critical care. Critical care services do not always occur in ICUs. Payment may be made for these services despite location as long as the care and documentation meet the above definition of critical care.
2. Critical care services must be medically necessary and reasonable. If the patient does not meet these criteria, then other appropriate codes such as subsequent hospital care may be more appropriate. CMS lists examples of patients that are commonly cared for in ICUs that do not meet critical care criteria. Examples include daily management of a patient receiving chronic ventilatory management and patients admitted to the ICU only for close monitoring of vital signs.
3. Critical care services require immediate availability either at the bedside or on the unit where the care is provided. The physician or

qualified nonphysician practitioner must devote full attention to the patient.

4. To qualify for critical care services, BOTH the illness and the treatment being provided must meet the above criteria and reflect that in the documentation. For each date and encounter entry, the note shall document the total time that the critical services were provided. For noncontinuous time, the services are aggregated and documented. Documentation must reflect the severity of the illness as defined by critical care codes.

Duration of critical care services must be reported in time spent evaluating, providing care, and managing the critical illness. Critical care codes are time based. Time is aggregated throughout the calendar day, and documentation should reflect the time providing this service. Payment is not restricted to one provider per service per calendar day as is the case with E/M services. Multiple providers can provide critical care as long as the services are necessary and not duplicative care. Multiple providers cannot however bill for critical care services for the same patient at the same time. If the physician and hospital staff or multiple hospital staff members are simultaneously engaged in this active face-to-face care, the time involved can only be counted once. Payment is not restricted to a fixed number of hours or a fixed number of days, as long as the patient meets the requirements for critical care services. Physicians of the same specialty within the same group practice bill and are paid as though it was a single provider. The NPP however will be reimbursed at 85% of the physician fee. Interpretation of this regulation may vary depending on the fiscal intermediaries of a region.

Critical care services include both CPT code 99291, used to report the first 30–74 min of critical care on a given calendar date of service, and CPT code 99292, used to report additional block(s) of time, of up to 30 min each beyond the first 74 min of critical care (See Table 10.4). Critical care of less than 30 min total duration on a given calendar date is not reported using the critical care codes. This service should be reported using appropriate E/M code such as subsequent hospital care. It is important to note that

TABLE 10.4 Critical Care Codes, Based on Duration

LESS THAN 30 MIN	NO CRITICAL CARE MAY BE BILLED
30–74 min	99291 × 1
75–104 min	99291 × 1 and 99292 × 1
105–134 min	99291 × 1 and 99292 × 2
135–164 min	99291 × 1 and 99292 × 3
165–194 min	99291 × 1 and 99292 × 4
194 min or longer	99291 × 1 and 99292 as appropriate

only one unit of CPT code 99291 may be billed by a provider on a given date and must be met by a single physician. This can be in a single period of time or cumulative over the calendar day. CPT code 99292 indicates subsequent critical care time and may represent aggregate time met by a single provider or providers in the same group practice in the same specialty. Multiple specialties billing critical care are allowable as long as the services are not duplicative. For example, if a pulmonary intensive care group is managing acute respiratory failure in a patient who also has a stroke requiring a neuro-intensivist and the patient requires critical care for both problems, then both services may bill critical care services. The care must be unique to the respective specialties.

A split/shared E/M service performed by a physician and a qualified NPP of the same group practice cannot be reported as a critical care service. Critical care codes shall reflect the evaluation, treatment, and management of a patient by an individual physician or qualified nonphysician practitioner (NPP) and shall not be representative of a combined service between a physician and a qualified NPP.

Critical Care Services and Other Common Procedures

Critically ill patients often require procedures during their ICU stay. For providers who bill critical services, many of these procedures are considered bundled and cannot be billed separately with either 99291 or 99292 critical care codes. Below is a list of bundle procedures and nonbundled services. Nonbundled services may be billed separately but the time required to perform these procedures may not be added to critical care time and should be reflected in documentation. Some providers may require the addition of a "25" modifier if billing both critical care and nonbundled services.

Bundled services (not billable separately)

- The interpretation of cardiac output measurements (CPT 93561, 93562)
- Pulse oximetry (CPT 94760, 94761, 94762)
- Chest x-rays, professional component (CPT 71010, 71015, 71020)
- Blood gases and patient information data stored in computers (e.g., ECGs, blood pressures, hematologic data-CPT 99090)
- Blood draw for specimen (CPT 36415)
- Gastric intubation (CPT 43752, 91105)
- Temporary transcutaneous pacing (CPT 92953)
- Ventilator management (CPT 94002-94004, 94660, 94662)
- Vascular access procedures (CPT 36000, 36410, 36415, 36591, 36600)

Nonbundled services (billable separately)

- CPR (92950) (while being performed)
- Endotracheal intubation (31500)

- Central line placement (36555, 36556)
- Arterial line placement (36620)
- Spinal puncture lumbar (66270, 66272)
- Intraosseous placement (36680)
- Tube thoracostomy (32551)
- Temporary transvenous pacemaker (33210)
- Electrocardiogram—routine 12-lead ECG interpretation and report only (93010)

REIMBURSE FOR COMMERCIAL MANAGED CARE ORGANIZATIONS (MCO)/HEALTH MAINTENANCE ORGANIZATIONS (HMO)

Commercial managed care plans provide health coverage using only a specific group of providers in a particular service area. Providers may be under contract with a commercial health insurer and may receive payment based on a capitation payment (number of patients seen). In general, only those providers within the designated network will be reimbursed unless prior authorization is obtained in cases of referral. Some HMOs will reimburse the care of NPs if the care provided is under the supervision of a participating preferred physician. In many cases, NPs remain silent in terms or reimbursement or even policies regarding reimbursement (Buppert, 2002). In these cases, the practice group may elect to ask for written authorization for reimbursement for physician care provided by the NP.

For many health plans, there is a shift in strategy from competing for the bottom line in terms of cost to quality and service. Improvement on mutually agreed-upon performance objectives is becoming the focus. This may require partnering with providers for a period of years, in order to actually improve health care value. NPs may have a role in helping establish these criteria assessing quality outcomes of patient care.

REIMBURSEMENT FOR COMMERICAL INDEMNITY INSURERS

There is no one standardized policy for reimbursement from commercial indemnity insurers. Each commercial indemnity insurer may have different rules on NP reimbursement and understanding these regulations will be important for optimizing reimbursement potential. It is important for each practice to review the policies. Regulations to consider include the following: whose provider number will the service be billed under, payment fee schedule for NPs, and denial of payments from NPs. The ability to bill for NP practice will also be influenced by scope of practice and state regulations. Some states require commercial insurers to reimburse NPs for physician services. Commercial insurers may even elect to adopt Medicare's regulations for billing.

Commercial insurers historically have reimbursed providers on a fee-for-service basis. This payment model gives an incentive to providers to perform more treatments, as payments are dependent on quantity of care, not necessarily on quality. Since this method discourages efficiencies in health care, there are efforts for reform moving toward pay for performance. Pay for performance introduces both quality and efficiency incentives instead of relying solely on quantity.

PAY FOR PERFORMANCE

Creating a practice model with an emphasis on safe, patient-centric quality care that is data-driven while ensuring cost-effective coverage for the inpatient setting is challenging. There has been a recent focus on measuring quality and paying for quality care by governmental health care programs, third-party payers, and by individual consumers. Most of the focus has been on physician-driven care initiatives in both inpatient and outpatient settings.

As the face of health care providers changes to include more advanced practice providers, accountability of care will be more equally distributed regardless of provider type (O'Grady, 2009). These changes will require advanced practice providers to become more involved with the development of evidence-based protocols, health information systems, and research endeavors. But how do you promote these changes in an environment of extended work hours, heavy workloads, and limited resources?

For years, business organizations have rewarded and set salaries based on job performance. Incentivized pay can lead to increased productivity and help companies achieve desired outcomes. In health care, however, there has been resistance until recent years, primarily due to ethical concerns. To be successful, pay-for-performance (PFP) models must include benchmarks and clearly defined goals consisting of both financial and nonfinancial incentives (Mackey, Roone, & Skinner, 2009). Pay-for-performance programs are attractive to many NPs as a way to enhance personal income as well as improving patient care. A successful PFP plan can also be useful as a strategy for retention.

Although new to health care, PFP programs are found in both academic and clinical practice areas. Components of pay-for-performance programs should include both patient outcome metrics as well as nonclinical outcomes. Measures of quality outcomes are aimed at safety, equitability, and other clinical benchmarks established by private and governmental agencies as well as academic institutions (Mackey et al., 2009). Examples of clinical outcome incentives include management of hemoglobin A1C bloodstream infections and prophylactic management of thromboembolic events. Tracking quality outcome metrics used for inpatient care area is difficult since they are usually reflective of a care team or service line. Incorporating clinical outcome measures in a PFP program in this setting may foster collaboration and a dedicated team approach to achieve these benchmarks. Nonclinical outcomes included in PFP may include use of established best practices such as administration of bundled services, patient satisfaction, and patient safety reporting. Although there is an increasing number of quality-based pay-for-performance plans, not all research has shown improved clinical outcomes with financial incentives. More research in this area is warranted to evaluate the success of these programs.

A pay-for-performance plan should be predicated on an individual practice setting, and should include basic principles. Programs should offer voluntary participation and include the following: transparency with equitable incentives, accessibility for review, foster provider/patient relationships, and they should utilize evidenced-based practices with recognized benchmarks such as quality of care indices or patient satisfaction (American Medical Association, Principles for pay-for-performance). The benchmarks should emphasize the organizational strengths and work to improve weaknesses as well as focus on compliance metrics.

In developing a pay-for-performance plan, one of the first components to address is the provider's financial contribution to the practice. There are multiple calculations used to determine benchmarks related to revenue. Practice expenses or overhead must be calculated and compared with provider collections or total billable revenue, and a percentage of profit for the practice must be determined to set the benchmark and overage given to NP as the performance incentive. In some PFP plans, the financial incentive is not granted unless the quality performance is met. The quality performance is often preset quality-based initiatives based on the practice values or goals and may include CMS or Physician Quality Reporting Initiative (PQRI) quality measures. Other components of PFP may include professional development strategies such as patient satisfaction benchmarks, scholarly activity, and research.

Evaluation of PFP plans is equally important for successful implementation. Data collected must be accurate, reflecting provider practice, and must be readily available for review. Quality data are often embedded within the institutions, health information system, and easy accessibility allows the provider an opportunity to periodically review their current data. Without prompt feedback, providers will not be able to adjust actions to achieve performance benchmarks.

Efficient implementation and utilization of NPs will be key to the success an inpatient health care team. Maintaining appropriate billing practices and ensuring ongoing competency can lead to increased billing opportunities and revenue. Future studies are needed to assess the value added with inpatient NP practices. Outcomes associated with NP services must be a priority in order to advance our roles as providers in the hospital setting.

REFERENCES

American Medical Association. *Principles for pay-for-performance*. Retrieved November 2, 2011, from http://www.amaassn.org/amal/pub/upload/mm/368/principles4pay 62705.pdf

Angus, D. C., Shorr, A., Whits, A., Dremisizov, T., Schmitz, R., & Kelley, M. (2006) Distribution of services and compliance with leapfrog recommendations. *Critical Care Delivery in the United States, 34*, 1016–1024.

Adams, D. L., Norman, H., & Burroughs, V. J. (2002). Addressing medical coding and billing. Part II: A strategy for achieving compliance. A risk management approach for reducing coding and billing errors. *Journal of the National Medical Association, 94*(6), 430–447.

Balanced Budget Act of 1997, Pub L. No. 105–33.

Buppert, C. (2002). Billing for nurse practitioner services: Guidelines for NPs, physicians, employers, and insurers. *Medscape Nurses*, Retrieved November 30, 2011, from http://www.medscape.com/viewarticle/422935_print

Buppert, C. (2005). Capturing reimbursement for advanced practice nurse services in acute and critical care: Legal and business considerations. *AACN Clinical Issues, 16*(1), 23–35.

Buppert, C. (2006). Who can bill for services when a nurse practitioner is a leased employee? *Medscape Nurses*, Retrieved October 25, 2011, from http://www.medscape.com/viewarticle/541659_print

Butler, K. L., Calabrese, R., Tandon, M., & Kirton, O. C. (2011). Optimizing advanced practitioner charge capture in high-acuity surgical intensive care units. *Archives in Surgery, 146*(5), 552–555.

Centers for Medicare and Medicaid Services. (2001). *CMS white paper on Medicare hospital prospective payment system*. How DRG rates are calculated and updated [white paper]. Retrieved November 2, 2011, from http://oig.hhs.gov/oei/reports/oei-0900-00-00200.pdf

Centers for Medicare and Medicaid Services. (2011). *Medicare claims processing manual: Chapter 12*, Retrieved on November 2, 2011, from www.cms.hhs.gov/manuals/downloads/clm104c12.pdf

Dara, S. I., & Afessa, B. (2005). Intensivist-to-bed ratio: Association with outcomes in the medical ICU. *Chest, 128*, 567–752. doi:10.1378/chest.128.2.567.

Dorman, T., & Pauldine, R. (2007). Economic stress and misaligned incentives in critical care medicine in the United States. *Critical Care Medicine, 35*(2), S36–S43.

Federal Register. (2005). The Daily Journal of the United States Government. *Medicare program; medicare integrity program, fiscal intermediary and carrier functions, and conflict of interest requirements*, Retrieved October 25, 2011, from http://www.federalregister.gov/articles/2005/06/17/05-11775/medicare-program-medicare-integrity-program-fiscal-intermediary-and-carrier-functions-and-conflict

Federal Register. The Daily Journal of the United States Government. *Compliance program guidance for individual and small group physician practices*. Retrieved November 2, 2011, from http://www.oig.hhs.gov/authorities/docs/cpgphysiciandraft.pdf.

Gajic, O., Afessa, B., Hanson, A., Krpata, T., Yilmaz, M., & Mohamed, S. F. (2008). Effect of 24 hour mandatory versus on demand critical care specialist presence on quality of care and family and provider satisfaction in the intensive care unit of a teaching hospital, *Critical Care Medicine, 35*, 36–44.

Hoffman, L. A., Tasota, F.J., & Zullo, T. G. (2005). Outcomes of care managed by an acute care nurse practitioner/attending physician team in a subacute medical intensive care unit. *American Journal of Critical Care, 12*, 436–443.

Horrocks, S., Anderson, E., & Salisbury, C. (2002). Systematic review of whether nurse practitioners working in primary care can provide equivalent care to doctors. *BMJ, 324*(7341), 819–823.

Iglehart, I. K. (2008). Revisiting duty-hours limits-IOM recommendations for patient safety and resident education. *New England Journal of Medicine, 359*, 2633–2635.

Kleinpell, R. M. (2005). Acute Care Nurse Practitioner practice: Results of a 5-year longitudinal study. *American Journal of Critical Care, 14*(3), 211–219.

Kleinpell, R. M. (2008). Hospital services: An evolving opportunity. *The Nurse Practitioner, 33*(5), 9–10.

Kleinpell, R. M., Ely, E. W., & Grabenkort, R. (2008). Nurse practitioners and physician assistants in the intensive care unit: An evidence based review. *Critical Care Medicine, 36*, 2888–2897

Mackey, T. A., Rooney, L., & Skinner, L. (2009). Pay for NP performance? *The Nurse Practitioner, 34*(4), 48–51.

MedPAC. *Payment basics.* Retrieved October 12, 2011, from www.medpac.gov/payment_basics.cfm

Moote, M., Krsek, C, Kleinpell, R., & Todd, B. (2011). Physician assistant and Nurse Practitioner Utilization in Academic Medical Centers. *American Journal of Medical Quality, 26*(6), 452–460.

Mundinger, M. O., Kane, R. L., Lenz, E. R., Totten, A. M., Tsai, Y. W., Cleary, P. D., ... Shelanski, M. L. (2000). Primary care outcomes in patients treated by nurse practitioners or physicians. *JAMA, 283*, 59–68.

Nasca, T. J., Day, S. H., & Amis, E. S. (2010). The new recommendations on duty hours from the ACGME Task Force. *New England Journal of Medicine, 363*(2), e3(1–6).

Nelson, J. (2010). Hospitalist salary spike. *The Hospitalist.* Retrieved November 2, 2011, from http://www.the-hospitalist.org/details/article/747187/Hospitalist_Salary_Spike.html

O'Brien, J. M. (2003). How nurse practitioners obtained provider status: Lessons for pharmacists. *American Journal of Health-System Pharmacy, 60*(22), 2301–2307.

O'Grady, E. (2009). Advanced practice registered nurses: The impact on patient safety and quality. Ronda Hughes, Patient Safety and Quality: An Evidenced-Based Handbook for Nurses. Retrieved from http://www.scribd.com/doc/7609817/AHRQ-Nurses-Handbook.

Pastores, S. M., O'Connor, M. F., Kleinpell, R. M., Napolitano, L., Ward, N., Bailey, H., & Coopersmith, C. M. (2011). The accreditation Council for Graduate Medical Education resident duty hour new standards: History, changes, and impact on staffing of intensive care units. *Critical Care Medicine, 39*(11), 2540–2549.

Pronsati, M. P., & Gerchufsky, M. National salary report 2011: Inching forward with mixed results. *ADVANCE for NPs & PAs*, Retrieved November 2, 2011, from http://nurse-practitioners-and-physician-assistants.advanceweb.com/Features/Articles/National-Salary-Report-2010.aspx

Rosenthal, L. D., & Guerrasio, J. (2009). Acute care nurse practitioner as hospitalist: Role description. *AACN Advanced Critical Care, 20*(2), 133–136.

11

Measurement of Success

Clare Thomson-Smith, April N. Kapu, and Elizabeth Zink

Health care delivery systems, organizations, and individual providers must continually employ strategies to meet the triple aim of better health, better health care delivery, and lower costs. Each organization utilizing the expertise of the nurse practitioner (NP) provider seeks to define measures of success in the context of the NP's ability to deliver measurably better care, with greater efficiency, producing better patient care outcomes. Individually, each NP must also define personal and professional measures of success that align with the strategy of the organization to meet the goals of the triple aim. At the organizational level, a number of objective measures of success exist, driven both by external and internal regulatory mandates. External regulatory mandates are usually driven by the imperative to protect the public, so demonstrating a culture of safe, quality-driven care is the cornerstone of measuring an organization's success.

A variety of organizational and individual performance measures exist. Not all will be appropriate for all situations. Transparency of purpose and clarity of goals will facilitate the process for both NPs and the organizations that employ them. In evaluating the decision to implement NP practice, the organization must be very clear about why the decision was made. Clear, measurable goals must be established at the outset so that aggregate NP practice can be evaluated, congruent with those goals. This chapter will present strategies for measuring NP success as they relate to professional and organizational goals. We will conclude with the presentation of a model of a comprehensive outcomes performance assessment program that combines external regulatory forces with other safety and quality indicators critical to the NP.

NP MEASURES OF SUCCESS

Critical to the definition of success in an NP role is establishing clinical competence of core behaviors, as well as the development of a comprehensive skill set. Universal measurements of competence include validation of procedural competence (delineation of practice), initial and ongoing credentialing, and interval performance reviews. Although these processes are essential, they do not adequately capture the knowledge, skills, and abilities expected of NP practice. A comprehensive evaluation process to develop and measure NP outcomes of success should be a goal for organizations. It is essential that NPs, physicians, managers, and administrators remain current and knowledgeable of the regulatory and organizational competency review processes as they relate to the hospital-based NP.

The NP Credentialing Process

Credentialing an NP to function in a specialty role within a hospital is a fairly simple, but detailed process. Hospitals are obligated to ensure their providers meet a threshold of criteria to minimize their own liability and, more importantly, to protect their patients. The imperatives on the hospital to ensure their providers are educated and trained to provide safe care is driven by accrediting agencies, by the insurance companies who pay for services rendered, by the various state boards governing practice, by the legislatures tasked with ensuring the safety and welfare of its citizens, and by national specialty boards who set the thresholds for competency.

Hospital Credentialing and Privileging Processes

The approved credentialing and privileging processes for all providers is typically found within the hospital bylaws, rules and regulations, policies and procedures. Most hospitals by virtue of necessity have had to amend their bylaws, rules, and regulations to accommodate the growth in the utilization of the NP as provider. As a general rule, hospitals have a dedicated office or department responsible for ensuring the credentialing and privileging process for providers is consistent not only with the institutions, own approved rules, but is compliant with state and federal law, accrediting agency standards, and meets the contractual needs to the third-party payers. Staff in these offices may be potential resources for measuring NP performance outcomes.

Ongoing Evaluation of Competency

Basic competence is necessary but not sufficient to define success for the NP's practice. The NP must have the opportunity to define additional goals and practice learning opportunities that will lead to professional fulfillment within the scope of practice and the mission of the organization. The extent to which these professional goals are encouraged and facilitated within the organization and considered in the value of the NP will contribute to the satisfaction and success of the NP, and therefore the success and the stability of the organization.

Professional growth can be accelerated with an effective performance evaluation program. Competency assessment via performance evaluation programs should be standardized and objective. Performance feedback, separate from the evaluation and provided on a frequent and regular schedule, will benefit both the NP and the organization by encouraging the NP's path to successful growth. Ongoing individual NP performance measurement documents may improve procedural competence, clinical judgment, documentation, professional practice behaviors, and interpersonal skill. Delaying feedback until an annual performance evaluation may actually be harmful in promoting the development of the NP.

The individual NP is responsible for ongoing self-evaluation and the organization will require evidence of ongoing clinical, financial, and improved outcomes data to account for the NP's practice to the organization. It is therefore important that the system in place to measure these outcomes be easy to use and understand. Limitations in the data-collection vehicle will limit later interpretation and, worse, cause the reviewer to draw incorrect conclusions. This is especially essential for the NP attempting to collect outcomes data in a multifactorial environment. The NP's impact on organizational outcomes and performance improvement is discussed in more detail in Chapter 12.

An evaluation instrument is a necessary tool for assessing NP performance of core competencies and for identifying areas of growth. NP specialty core competencies and standards are well documented by organizations such as the National Organization of Nurse Practitioner Faculties (NONPF) in 2011 and the American Association of Colleges of Nursing (AACN), as well as by national credentialing bodies. These documents describe foundational competencies for all NPs that can be used to guide development of the NP evaluation process and to identify specific performance measures of success (see Figure 11.1).

Ongoing Professional Practice Evaluation

The Ongoing Professional Practice Evaluation (OPPE) process was designed to move away from a cyclical to a continuous evaluation of a practitioner's performance. In many institutions, practitioners are evaluated every year with annual performance reviews and/or every 2 years at the time of reappointment through the institution's credentialing and privileging process. These cyclical reviews are not the ideal measure of a practitioner's day-to-day performance. An evaluation every 2 years is a snapshot in time rather than an ongoing monitoring process. It is recommended that a practitioner be evaluated based on several standardized data points for reference, every 6 to 8 months and at the time of renewal of privileges. The key is developing on ongoing evaluation system that accurately reflects the practitioner's practice. The general competency measures suggested by The Joint Commission (TJC) as a framework for guiding

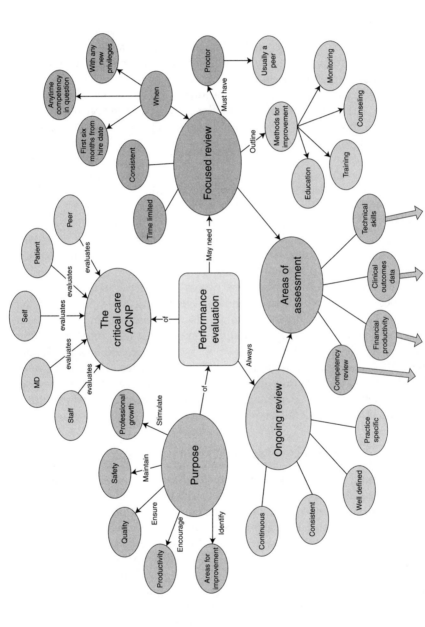

FIGURE 11.1 Critical Care Advanced Practice - Focused Professional Practice Evaluation. *Source:* Used with permission by A. Kapu.

TABLE 11.1   American Council on Graduate Medical Education Core Competencies

ACGME COMPETENCY	DESCRIPTION
Patient Care	Provides patient care that is compassionate, appropriate, and effective for the promotion of health, prevention of illness, treatment of disease, and care at the end of life.
Medical/Clinical Knowledge	Demonstrates knowledge of established and evolving biomedical, clinical, and social sciences and the application of knowledge to patient care and the education of others.
Practice Based Learning and Improvement	Able to use scientific evidence and methods to investigate, evaluate, and improve patient care practices.
Interpersonal and Communication Skills	Demonstrates interpersonal and communication skills that establish and maintain professional relationships with patients, families, coworkers, and other members of the health care team.
Professionalism	Demonstrates behaviors that reflect a commitment to continuous professional development, ethical practice, an understanding of and sensitivity to diversity, and a responsible attitude toward patients, profession, and society.
Systems-Based Practice	Demonstrates both an understanding of the contexts and systems in which health care is provided and the ability to apply this knowledge to improve and optimize health care.

Source: Accreditation Council on Graduate Medical Education (ACGME)

evaluation correlate with the six major competencies used by the Accreditation Council on Graduate Medical Education (ACGME); see Table 11.1. These general competency areas were designed for assessment of residents but apply equally to all licensed, privileged health care providers.

Focused Professional Practice Evaluation

The other component of professional practice evaluation is the Focused Professional Practice Evaluation (FPPE). A focused review is a time-limited review of a particular aspect of the NP's practice, typically related to specific privileges. There are four indications for FPPE.

(a) *For newly hired practitioners*—An institution's credentialing and privileging process is to verify the NP's credentialing file through licensure, certification, background checks, peer recommendations, and so forth. However, fundamental to privileging an NP to work independently in the institution is that the NP's core competencies are verified. The NP remains in a period of focused review during the first few months of employment to verify that the NP is competent in core competencies. At the end of this FPPE, the proctor either releases the NP from the FPPE or continues the NP in the FPPE, setting a new time limit and a measureable process for improvement.

(b) *Each time the NP applies for a new privilege*—When an NP is granted an additional privilege, FPPE is again triggered. For example, placement of arterial lines. Once the NP has demonstrated competency, a proctor documents the NP is competent to insert arterial lines, and the FPPE ends with inclusion of the document in the credentials file.

(c) *Whenever performance is in question*—An FPPE could be triggered by an event that puts into question the NP's medical/clinical knowledge, technical skill, or professional behavior.

(d) *Triggered by an OPPE*—An FPPE can be triggered via the process of OPPE. If there are consistently poor outcomes, poor patient satisfaction ratings, or other patterns that question competency, an FPPE can be implemented.

The key to an effective FPPE is to clearly outline a plan for improvement. After selecting the target or target range, calculate what would be a statistically significant negative variance that would warrant a focused review or FPPE. The NPs in the practice should be able to understand and identify their target for each quality indicator and what variable would be seen as suboptimal and poor practice. They would need to know what to expect in this situation, which would be a time-limited focused review with a detailed plan for improvement. The review usually would be conducted by one proctor (usually a peer), but can be more than one proctor if warranted. The proctor must understand his or her responsibility in the focused review. There should be a clear time limit with interval times to review progress if needed. The plan for improvement should be specific, with methods established for measurement. For example, workshops, training classes, simulation, and counseling would all be examples of assignments to include in improvement plans. Examples of methods for monitoring during an FPPE are listed in Exhibit 11.1. Focused reviews can be meaningful and beneficial to the NP's professional growth and can optimize quality of practice.

EXHIBIT 11.1   Sample Measures Used in a Focused Professional Practice Evaluation

Chart audit
Monitoring clinical practice patterns
Simulation
Peer pre- and post-evaluation
Discussions with other individuals involved in the care of the patient
Attendance at counseling sessions
Completion of training classes
Continuing education credits

PATIENT SAFETY AND HEALTH CARE QUALITY

Just as success for an individual NP is measured in terms of safe, high-quality, cost-effective, and patient-centered care, organizational success is measured in high-quality care delivered in a safe environment. Measuring the impact of NP practice on patient outcomes, safety in health care, and health care quality is integral to advancing this role and solidifying a lasting and important role in health care. Aligning outcomes measurements with the organizational mission is key to demonstrating the value of NP practice in achieving performance metrics (Newhouse et al., 2011). It is important to determine which productivity measures will be tracked based on the organizational mission and current priority. For instance, if attaining accreditation in a specialty such as heart failure, stroke, or orthopedics is identified as key to achieving the organizational mission, it is important that the NPs measure and document their contribution to accomplishing these specific measures. In many circumstances, NPs have an enhanced ability to influence positive outcomes, particularly in these specialty areas, because of their knowledge of how the system of care delivery interoperates and how it can be changed or organized to accomplish particular goals or outcomes. It is imperative that this unique asset of the NP be continually illustrated and recognized.

Donabedian's 1985 model of structure, process, and outcome provides a meaningful foundation for approaching issues of health care quality and patient safety. In this model, structure refers to the tools, equipment and physical infrastructure needed to accomplish a process or set of actions, which then produce outcomes for patients. These variables can be assessed independently or as an overall model to evaluate NP practice. Initiating a quality improvement project can seem daunting, but is intended to simplify processes to rapidly improve quality of care. Langley, Nolan, Nolan, Norman, and Provost (2009) recommend asking three basic questions when designing the process:

- What are we trying to accomplish?
- How will we know that a change is an improvement?
- What changes can we make that will result in an improvement?

Practical steps for initiating process improvement projects can be found on the Institute for Healthcare Improvement website at http://www.ihi.org/IHI/Topics/Improvement/ImprovementMethods/HowToImprove/

Performance Reporting

Public Reporting of Data

An understanding of the multitude of regulatory agencies, public and private, that may require certain levels of performance or specific conditions to be met for payment and the ability to practice is essential in deciding how to monitor one's own practice and outcomes. Regulatory agencies may include federal and state governments, the Center for Medicare and Medicaid Services (CMS), The Joint Commission (TJC), private insurers, and payer groups (e.g., the Leapfrog group). Individual institutions may track indicators required by these agencies in different ways and often only speak of aggregate sets of data from specific patient groups. It is important to inquire as to whether outcome data related to care provided for patients or adverse events reported can be separated by primary care provider type (i.e., physician, NP, or PA) in order to determine the impact of NP practice and identify areas for specific improvement. This task may not always be easily accomplished, because of the array of care providers and specialties that may be involved with a patient's care in or outside of a hospital setting.

NPs must be aware of various health care report cards issued by insurance carriers and other organizations, which compile survey information from patients. This information is easily accessed by the health care consumer using the Internet. The methods of obtaining information and determining the criteria for evaluation are not always known to a provider, but may have the ability to influence the increasingly savvy health care consumer.

Organizational/Unit Reporting of Data

Quality dashboards can be a useful tool for evaluating outcomes. A dashboard is a summary document that displays important practice indicators for comparison of trends. For instance, an NP or a group of NPs in a specific area is interested in central line device days. Their current practice is to remove central lines as soon as they are no longer needed, in order to prevent bloodstream infections. Their institution has a goal for reducing bloodstream infections, and the NPs have directly associated themselves with placement and removal of central lines in their area. Daily, the NPs record placements and removals for central lines on all patients in their area. The days are counted from placement to removal, with a target of 4 days or less for the device to remain in place. A dashboard to reflect their outcomes might look like this:

MONTH	TOTAL CENTRAL LINES	CENTRAL LINE DEVICE DAYS
January	39	4.4
February	42	3.2
March	37	2.9

Another example of outcome measurement is tracking the time from admission to the intensive care unit to initiation of nutrition. The target may be postoperative day 1 for nutrition assessment. A dashboard could be developed to show the number of patients per month and whether the target was met. In this example, there is an additional column that explains why the target was not met. Columns A, B, and C would represent their most common reasons for not starting nutrition.

MONTH	TOTAL SPECIALTY SURGERY PATIENTS	NUTRITION STARTED WITHIN 24 HR OF SURGERY	IF GOAL NOT MET, WHY?			
			A	B	C	OTHER
January	39	35	2	1		1
February	42	40	1			1
March	37	32	3		1	1

Scorecards are also helpful when reviewing adherence to evidence-based practice guidelines. Often scorecards are generated as reports listing all providers and associated practice. For example, a blood transfusion scorecard could specify the provider, practice area, blood units ordered, and why. Using a scorecard can illustrate practice trends for comparison with those of other providers and practices.

Productivity measures such as new patient consults, subsequent day visits, critical care billing, and relative value units (RVU) can demonstrate the practitioner's understanding of billing, documentation, time management, and the resources required. Chart audit is the most frequently used tool to identify patterns and areas for improvement in documentation. Coding and billing reports itemized by the provider are excellent tools for monitoring financial data and work productivity. It is important to recognize that data collection can be an extremely time-consuming process. Therefore, identifying key resources to access data or selecting data sources that address the particular productivity measure can streamline the process. If data sources are not available, develop a simple tracking tool and collection process to ensure project completion and utilization of the data in a timely and efficient manner.

Tracking Performance

Tracking methods and outcomes data are readily available within each institution. It may be evident that traditional coding methods more often track physician outcomes rather than NP-specific outcomes. However, some physician tracking methods can be replicated for NP providers. Embracing existing data collection methods and technology can make the process of NP practice evaluation much easier (Rhoads, Ferguson, & Langford, 2006). For example, prescriptive practices and blood transfusion patterns can be tracked for both types of providers.

In some institutions where the NP is privileged as both admitting and covering provider, mortality, morbidity, and readmission rates can be tracked. Where the NP does not hold admitting privileges, and where data are physician specific, outcomes can be inferred by the association of the NP with a physician group or service. Specialty and subspecialty practices such as endocrinology, oncology, trauma, and critical care as well as age-related populations such as geriatrics or pediatrics will require practice-specific competency evaluation measures.

In 2006, the Society of Hospital Medicine's Benchmarks Committee published a white paper on measuring hospitalist performance. The committee set out to identify best practices in performance monitoring, as well as identify key performance metrics, including how they should be evaluated, presented, and used. The committee identified 10 key performance metrics—eight of which are categorized as operational and clinical—hospital costs, productivity, provider satisfaction, patient satisfaction, length of stay, mortality, readmission rates, and The Joint Commission (TJC) core measures—applicable to all health care providers. Classification of NP performance measures and instruments for measurement are presented in Exhibit 11.2. This classification system and tools for measurement can provide guidance in designing an NP-specific performance evaluation process to both measure success and stimulate professional practice improvement.

Accessing and Utilizing Data

A useful strategy for beginning data collection for the purpose of measuring a particular outcome is to compile a database specifically for patients cared for by the NP. When the NP has access to a database of patients for whom he or she has cared, questions or queries can be formulated, based on developed measures of quality (e.g., Joint Commission Core Measures, Centers for Medicaid and Medicare Services) or based on questions germane to a specific area of clinical practice or interest area of the NP.

When compiling or utilizing a database, special consideration must be given to the Health Information Portability and Protection Act (HIPPA) in terms of the purpose for gathering patient data. Allowable reasons for extracting patient information include treatment, payment, or operations. Outcomes measurement for the NP would typically be classified under the category of operations; however, individual institutions must be consulted regarding their processes and policies for the handling of patient information related to quality improvement. Approval of an Institutional Review Board (IRB) may be necessary if publication of an outcomes measurement or quality improvement project is undertaken.

Specific Outcome Metrics

The outcomes associated with NP practice may also be measured in terms of complication rates or prevention of adverse events. Examples of

EXHIBIT 11.2   Examples of NP Performance Measures and Tools for Measurement

Subjective Competency Assessment
- Self-review of core competencies
- Peer review of core competencies
- Adherence to evidence-based practice guidelines
- Development of evidence-based practice protocols
- Educational endeavors
- Incidences of misdiagnoses, unsafe practices, or off-treatment patterns
- Staff, patient, and family satisfaction
- Complaints from staff, patients, and families
- Process or systems improvement
- Project development
- Development of staff/patient education programs
- Mentoring students or orientees
- Consultation usage such as specialty team consultations when needed
- Resource utilization such as lab tests and diagnostics
- Timely ordering of interventions or therapies
- Patterns of pharmaceutical usage
- Local and national presentations and/or publications
- Leadership roles
- Committee involvement
- Maintenance of licensures and certifications
- Development of or adherence to hospital safety initiatives

Tools—Questionnaires, Surveys, Evaluation forms, Tests, Discussions, Direct Observance, Confidential reporting methods, Chart review

Technical Skills
- Complication rates
- Frequency of procedures performed
- Adherence to protocol and quality requirements

Tools— Skills Checklist, Simulation, Direct Observance, Logs

Outcomes Data
- Mortality rates
- Length of stay in hospital, ICU, or on a particular service or unit
- Blood transfusion rates
- Ventilator days
- Readmission rates
- Nosocomial infection rates
- Targeted device days (central lines, foley catheters)
- Percentages of adherence to evidence-based practice therapies

Tools—Dashboards, Scorecards, Graphs, Reports

Financial Productivity
- Compliance with coding and billing practices
- Consistency with documentation
- Abnormal billing patterns

Tools—Financial Reports, Graphs, Chart Audits

adverse events that have begun to be publicly reported in some areas of the United States are central-line-associated bloodstream infections (CLABSI), ventilator-associated pneumonia (VAP), hospital-acquired urinary tract infections, pressure ulcers, and hospital readmission. The NP can play an important role in preventing these complications through clinical practice and influence on patient care practices, such as ensuring that preventive strategies are being employed on at-risk patients and partnering with nursing staff to remove barriers to applying these strategies. The NP has an advantageous view of nursing and medical models of care which can be leveraged to improve overall patient outcomes. However, the collaborative system that is specific to the NP interferes with the ability to tease out the NP's individual impact on many clinical outcomes.

Measurement of satisfaction on the part of different consumer groups (e.g., patients, physicians, bedside nurses) is necessary in defining the unique contributions of the NP to patient care. Patient satisfaction is often measured by acute care institutions through contracted companies and/or internal surveys (e.g., the Press Ganey survey). Many of these surveys may not clearly identify the care provider who provided the majority of care to a patient, and the NP therefore is grouped together with all medical care providers. This is an area that is ripe for improvement with respect to abstracting patient satisfaction data for NPs. In this vein, it is also critically important that consumer education is continued to ensure that the consumer realizes what an NP is and how they deliver care. Despite the increasing presence of the NP role in all practice settings, the need for further education of health care consumers is clear. NPs, especially when unit-based, will often have significant accountability for the results of these surveys and the publicly reported Hospital Consumer Assessment of Healthcare Providers and Systems (HCAHPS).

Physician feedback on NP practice is not consistently collected or measured using a standard format. The perception of physicians likely varies based on practice settings, exposure to the role, and education on the uniqueness of the NP role, which differs from other nonphysician providers. The positive perception of NP practice by physicians in an individual practice setting can be critically important in allowing the NP to practice to the fullest extent of his or her role. It is the opinion of this author that the key to gaining positive acclaim in the realm of physicians is with clear outcome data that care of patients by the NP equals that of care provided by physicians.

The final goal is to optimize the system of care delivery by utilizing each team member's unique strengths. An additional strategy for sustaining a clear and enduring role in the health care of patients and partnering with physicians is to capitalize on assets that are traditional strengths of NPs, including expert complex care coordination, care of underserved populations, and holistic care, which takes the patient's medical, psychosocial, and spiritual needs into consideration. The NP should be encouraged to seek feedback about their impact on the management of such challenging patient populations.

With national and organizational imperatives to improve quality in patient care while remaining cost effective, NPs are being integrated into the inpatient environment. Therefore, it is critical that NP-sensitive measures be established to measure the value of the NP to the practice and to the institution. NPs must be aware of how their practice is evaluated. Developing an OPPE process that is clearly defined, manageable, consistently implemented, and practice-specific provides the foundation for individual practitioner performance evaluation. Clarifying data definitions and developing tools for collection can be complex to build, but they will be efficient and descriptive tools for consistent measurement. OPPE provides a clear and accurate assessment of the practitioner's competent practice.

A Comprehensive Practice Evaluation Process

It is clear that there are a variety of approaches and driving forces impacting the process of measuring NP outcomes. With a national impetus for health care quality advancement, patient safety, and improved patient outcomes, the hospital-based NPs performance in practice must be continuously monitored for quality assurance and improvement. But how does one accomplish this in the busy hospital setting. We will end this chapter with discussion on the factors that drive the institution to develop NP-specific measures and discuss the components of a comprehensive evaluation program.

PURPOSE AND DEFINITION OF NP PRACTICE EVALUATION

The purpose of performance evaluation is to identify trends in the NP's patient care, ensure quality, maintain patient safety, identify areas for improvement, and stimulate continual improvement of the practitioner's knowledge and skill and ability to translate evidence-based knowledge into practice. Performance evaluation is also a review of one's productivity, both work effort and financial productivity. The process of evaluation requires identification and assessment of outcomes that are specific to the NP's practice, and the development of tools to effectively measure these outcomes.

Measuring the value of the NP's practice in the hospital environment relies on core criteria for assessment and NP-sensitive indicators for quality (Kleinpell, 2009). If using TJC standards to define performance evaluation, then it is important to understand the core competencies and broadly develop a framework specific to NP practice. The evaluation program would further define the competency structure for critical care NPs with the subsequent development of value metrics to reflect these competencies (see Exhibit 11.3).

EXHIBIT 11.3   Sample of an Ongoing Professional Practice Subjective Competency Assessment Survey

COMPETENCY	PERFORMANCE LEVEL
Patient care: Provides patient care that is compassionate, appropriate, and effective for the promotion of health, prevention of illness, treatment of disease, and care at the end of life.	
Medical and clinical knowledge: Demonstrates knowledge of established and evolving biomedical, clinical, and social sciences, and the application of knowledge to patient care and the education of others.	
Practice-based learning and improvement: Able to use scientific evidence and methods to investigate, evaluate, and improve patient care practices.	
Interpersonal and communication skills: Demonstrates interpersonal and communication skills that establish and maintain professional relationships with patients, families, coworkers, and other members of the healthcare team.	
Professionalism: Demonstrates behaviors that reflect a commitment to continuous professional development, ethical practice, an understanding and sensitivity to *diversity and a responsible attitude toward patients, profession, and society. *The Joint Commission considers diversity to include race, culture, gender, religion, ethnic background, sexual preference, language, mental capacity, and physical disability.	
Systems-based practice: Demonstrates both an understanding of the contexts and systems in which health care is provided, and the ability to apply this knowledge to improve and optimize health care.	

Note: Levels signify as follows: 1 = Does not meet criteria for level; 2= meets criteria; 3 = exceeds criteria for level.
Source: Common Program Requirements (2007).

Significance: In light of the Licensure, Accreditation, Certification Education (LACE) movement, all NPs, regardless of specialty, must meet certain core competencies (APRN Consensus Work Group & the National Council of State Boards of Nursing APRN Advisory Committee, 2008). These core competencies have been recently updated by the National Organization for Nurse Practitioner Faculties and include basic requirements in knowledge inquiry, policy and process development, evidence-based practice application, quality, and leadership (National Organization for Nurse Practitioner Faculties, 2011). NPs are required to meet particular educational requirements, which are age- and population-focused before graduating and preparing for their specialty board certification. Once educated, licensed, and certified, an NP can seek employment.

During the credentialing and privileging process, core competencies are verified. And as the NP progresses in her practice, these competencies, such as use of clinical judgment, accuracy of interventions and expertise in technical skills, must be reviewed for advancing proficiency to ensure quality and patient safety. Effective evaluation processes should be implemented in every practice for ongoing appraisal of the NP's performance. From an organizational perspective, NP practice evaluation can demonstrate not only value to patients and practice, but also to the institution as a whole. On a global level, positive organizational NP practice evaluation can bring recognition to the overall contributions of NPs in health care.

Evolution

Assessing outcomes in nursing practice is not a new concept, as Florence Nightingale was the first known nurse to develop a process for outcomes assessment (Montalvo, 2007). Recently, the Institute of Medicine instituted its campaign to transform health care, specifying the transformation of the nursing profession as one initiative. They urged nurses in their respective roles to function to the full extent of their scope of practice, lead quality initiatives, produce evidence-based research, and translate this knowledge into evidence-based practice (Institute of Medicine of the National Academies, 2010). As the nursing role evolved into that of the NP, specific and sensitive measures for evaluating the NP were developed. However, many institutions continue to use existing nursing evaluations as a basis for conducting NP performance evaluation, despite the fact that staff nursing indicators are different from NP indicators. Alternatively, some evaluation processes have attempted to simply absorb the NP into the available metrics used for the physician provider group (i.e., measuring mortality and complication rates). This does not account for the unique background and education of the NP, who now has responsibility as an independent provider. Measurement systems must reflect the reality that NP practice is affected by a variety of independent variables. Use of inappropriate evaluation methods will lead to inaccurate data collection and incorrect conclusions. As the NP provider role evolves, it is important to establish an NP evaluation specific to NP outcomes, because the quality of NP practice affects patient care. In addition to their impact on patient safety and quality, NPs are increasingly scrutinized for their organizational value therefore requiring that measures used are accurate reflective of true NP practice.

Linking NPs to Quality Improvement and Cost Reduction

NP's scientific inquiry, knowledge, and application of evidence-based practice is essential in hospital-based practice. NPs who are actively involved in research and development of evidence-based guidelines for practice are actualizing a fundamental competency of scientific inquiry and application. Furthermore, adherence to these best practice standards can be a particular method of assessing quality in practice. Burns et al. (2003) reviewed a study in which NPs were involved in both the development and implementation of a program to improve clinical and financial outcomes of mechanically ventilated patients. Conclusions showed that through the implementation of this program, ventilator times, intensive care unit stays, and hospital length of stay, mortality rates and financial costs significantly decreased (Burns et al., 2003). Another study, about adding NPs to a postoperative cardiovascular care unit, revealed that cardiovascular surgeons in collaboration with NPs decreased length of stay and total costs (Meyer & Miers, 2005). The introductions of both these articles recognized the NPs' competency in critical care management and noted the decisions and actions of the NP groups to evoke positive changes in health care practice and quality improvement. Both studies cited specific outcome indicators to assess the NP's application of best practices. The impact of this and other studies supports the use of NPs in hospital-based settings and encourages development of methods for quantifying NP practice.

Developing a Professional Practice Evaluation Process for Critical Care ACNPs

It is clear that the impact of all independent providers must be evaluated on a continuous basis in order to assure that our patient care environment is safe. Therefore, development of an evaluation program that is effective in its goal to identify areas for improvement, advance NP competence, sustain quality of care, and improve patient outcomes is essential. A truly effective process would be one in which professional growth is prioritized. Performance evaluation programs and tools used to measure both performance and professional development can be lengthy and complex. Some evaluation processes may be too subjective while others appear driven by monetary compensation as the key incentive. An effective evaluation would include both subjective and objective measures of the practitioner's performance and would be designed to ascertain professional strengths, opportunities for growth, and short- and long-term goals. Performance indicators would focus on clinical competency and NPs' impact on the quality of patient care. The strongest evaluation tools are concise, user friendly, and reflective of factors specific to the quality and efficacy of the NP's professional practice.

There have been several suggestions for organization of general categories of measurement of professional practice. Kleinpell (2009) suggests the following four categories of assessment: care-related outcomes, patient-related outcomes, performance-related outcomes, and financial and economic outcomes. Burns (2009) suggests the use of aggregate data, financial outcomes, time-saving outcomes, and clinical outcomes. The model depicted in Figure 11.2 highlights four main categories for evaluating an NP's professional practice: competency review, clinical outcomes data, assessment of technical skills, and financial productivity. The competency review suggests assessment of competencies from the National Organization of Nurse Practitioner Faculties (2011) and Accreditation Council for Graduate Medical Education (Common Program Requirements, 2007). Instruments to evaluate performance are listed and include measures to extract both qualitative and quantitative data for assessment. Outcome measures are suggested and can be made practice specific.

Competency Assessment

In reality, competency assessment ties to all categories of performance evaluation and is measured using both quantitative and qualitative measures. Three of the categories (financial, clinical outcomes, and technical skills assessment), are more quantifiable measures. Objective data is easier to interpret but qualitative feedback also provides meaningful information regarding the practitioner's performance and impact on patient care. Qualitative review of performance should incorporate TJC's six general categories for practice assessment—patient care, medical/clinical knowledge, professionalism, practice-based learning and improvement, systems-based practice, and interpersonal and communication skills as they apply to NP practice. Practice specificity can often come from the answers during the subjective assessment. For example, if asking a staff nurse how the NP reflects professionalism in practice, the staff nurse will most likely describe the NP's professional practice as it applies to the particular area of the RN's practice. Examples of tools for qualitative measurement of NP competencies are shown in Figure 11.2. Layering NP core competency requirements over the six ACGME categories will create a comprehensive system for NP assessment.

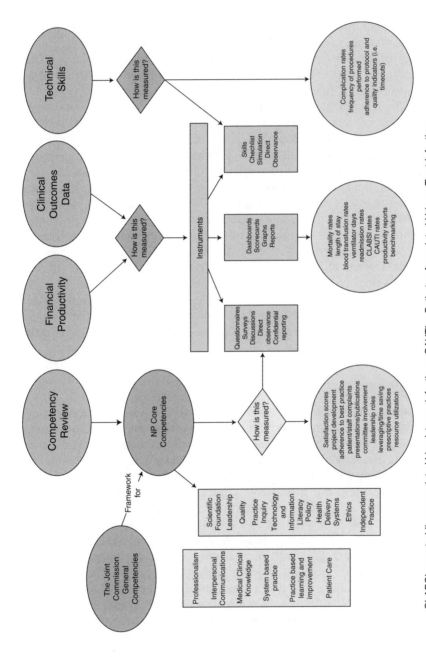

FIGURE 11.2 Implementation of Critical Care NP Professional Practice Evaluation.

Source: Used with permission by A. Kapu.

CLABSI = central-line-associated bloodstream infections; CAUTI = Catheter-Associated Urinary Tract Infection

Clinical Outcomes Data

With the reduction in resident duty hours and increased demands for quality and pay for performance, NPs have been integrated into critical care settings to provide coverage and quality improvement. With this rapid growth has come the increasing demand for quality indicators that are sensitive to NPs in this setting. Institutions, leaders, and practitioners are seeking indicators that are reliable and usable in quality improvement; one's that can be used to benchmark with other institutions. The subject is new and there are many avenues for exploration.

Although objective measures of an NP's practice can be difficult to define, when they are developed to be NP-sensitive metrics, they provide an accurate, ongoing assessment of quality in practice. The key for most institutions is to begin this process by examining the existing physician quality indicators and the tracking processes in place. Evaluation of the physician indicators will help to differentiate what is exclusive to the physician and what may be tailored to the NP. Mortality rates, readmission rates, and surgical complication rates may be difficult to differentiate by individual provider since the NP/physician model is a team-based one. Other indicators such as prescription patterns may be traced to the individual. Another indirect but popular method for tracking NP quality is that of tracking metrics pre- and post-integration of NPs into the organization. Some of these metrics might include: ICU and hospital readmission rates, mortality rates and ICU, and hospital length of stay.

Technical Skills

Evaluation of technical performance might be the easier process to define. It is a matter of simulation and direct observation of the practitioner performing these skills with documentation of technical and experiential proficiency. Most institutions require that the NP be privileged in specified procedures and thereby provide a framework for achieving such privileges. This may involve having an evidence-based, approved protocol for each procedure and a required number of procedures performed successfully under the supervision of a privileged provider for initial privileging. For maintenance of privileges, there may be a quantity of procedures required to be performed on a regular basis along with defined quality parameters. Quality parameters may include number of complications, use of "timeouts" which are recommended by The Joint Commission and maintaining accordance with the established evidence-based protocol (The Joint Commission, 2012). The entire team must understand the chosen mechanism for evaluation maintained competence and must be willing to make decisions of approval or revocation of skill based on these processes.

Financial Productivity

For most institutions, financial productivity tracking is already in place, specifically tracking charges, collections, applicable taxes and net revenue along with relative value units (RVUs), salary, and nonsalary expenses. Prior to establishing an NP program, it is fundamental to develop a pro forma or business case analysis. This can be reviewed periodically for comparison of projected versus actual productivity. This review can be most helpful in projecting realistic expectations, such as NP costs and collection rates, when adding new NP programs. Billing is based on services provided, however, this must be documented. The NP's documentation can be reviewed regularly for quality and compliance with billing and coding standards.

CONCLUSION

NPs are central figures within the hospital environment, providing quality and cost-effective care. Establishing an outcomes assessment plan measuring specific NP qualitative and quantitative outcomes is important. An effective evaluation program will optimize professional growth and improve quality of care, thereby illuminating the value of NPs to hospital-based practice, to the organization, and to health care as a whole.

With an increasing demand for transparency of quality and safety reporting by consumers and payers, organizations find themselves having to report measures of success to external agencies. This evaluation plan will likely be complex. But as organizations strategize to meet these demands, they increasingly turn to NPs as providers, integrating them into health systems to manage the continuum of patient care and processes that reflect quality and cost-efficient outcomes. NPs in turn must demonstrate competency in how well they perform when their key functions are aligned with organizational quality and safety strategies. Additionally, NPs must demonstrate to the organization that the care they provide is done so in a cost-efficient manner. Defining measurable specific quality, safety, and financial outcomes that align with organizational goals will support the continued integration of NPs into the health care team.

REFERENCES

ACGME. (2007). *Common program requirements: General competencies.* Retrieved from http://www.acgme.org/outcome/comp/GeneralCompetenciesStandards 21307.pdf

Burns, S. M. (2009). Selecting advanced practice nurse outcome measures. In R. M. Kleinpell (Ed.), *Outcome assessment in advanced practice nursing* (2nd ed., pp. 89–105). New York, NY: Springer Publishing.

Burns, S. M., Earven, S., Fisher, C., Lewis, R., Merrell, P., & Schubart, J. R. (2003). Implementation of an institutional program to improve clinical and financial outcomes of mechanically ventilated patients: One-year outcomes and lessons learned. *Critical Care Medicine, 31,* 2752–2763.

Donabedian, A. (1985). Twenty years of research on the quality of medical care: 1964–1984. *Evaluation & the Health Professions, 8*(3), 243–265.

Ingersoll, G. L., Witzel, P. A., & Smith, T. C. (2005). Using organizational mission, vision, and values to guide professional practice model development and measurement of nurse performance. *Journal of Nurisng Administration, 35*(2), 86–93.

Institute of Medicine. (2011). *The future of nursing: Leading change, advancing health.* Washington, DC: The National Academies Press.

Joint Commission of the National Academies, *Critical access hospital: 2012 national patient safety goals.* Retrieved January 20, 201, from http://www.jointcommis sion.org/standards_ information/npsgs.aspx

Kleinpell, R. M. (Ed.). (2009). Outcome assessment in advanced practice nursing (2nd ed.). New York, NY: Springer.

Langley, G. L., Nolan, K. M., Nolan, T. W., Norman, C. L., & Provost, L. P. (2009). *The improvement guide: A practical approach to enhancing organizational perform-ance* (2nd ed.). San Franscisco: Jossey-Bass Publication.

Leapfrog Group. Retrieved January 20, 2012, from http://www.leapfroggroup.org/ about_us

Measuring Nurse Practitioner Outcomes. (2006). *Dermatology Nursing. 18*(1):32-4, 37-8.

Meyer, S. C., & Miers, L. J. (2005). Effect of cardiovascular surgeon and acute care nurse practitioner collaboration on postoperative outcomes. *AACN Clinical Issues, 16,* 149–158.

Montalvo, I. (2007, September 30). The national database of nursing quality indi-cators [Journal article]. *The Online Journal of Issues in Nursing, 12*(3), doi: 10.3912/OJIN.Vol12No03Man02.

National Organization of Nurse Practitioner Faculties. (2011). *Nurse practitioners core competencies.* Retrieved January 20, 2012, from http://nonpf.com/associ ations/10789/files/IntegratedNPCoreCompsFINALApril2011.pdf

Newhouse, R. P., Stanik-Hutt, J., White, K. M., Johantgen, M., Bass, E. B., Zangaro, G., … Weiner, J. P. (2011). Advanced practice nurse outcome: 1990–2008. *Nursing Economics, 20*(5), 230–250.

Rhoads, J., Ferguson, L. A., & Langford, C. A. (2006). Measuring nurse practitioner outcomes. *Dermatology Nursing, 18*(1):32–4, 37–8.

Society of Hospital Medicine's Benchmarks Committee. (2006). *Measuring hospitalist performance: Metrics, reports and dashboards.* Retrieved from the Society of Hospital Medicine: www.hospitalmedicine.org/shmstore. Institute for Health-care Improvement, http://www.ihi.org/knowledge/Pages/HowtoImprove/ default.aspx accessed September 9, 2012.

12

Performance Improvement: Refining the Innovation

Kay Blum

> *When goals are not periodically revisited, reviewed, and defended, missions drift, and the goals of individual stakeholders can begin to dominate the agreed-upon system goals*
> KOTTKE, PRONK, AND ISHAM 2012

It is clear from discussions throughout this chapter that hospitals are complex, living organisms that are in a constant state of dynamic equilibrium. Even small changes in one part of the organization can affect function in other parts of the organization or in the organization as a whole. Attempts to simplify this complexity lead to underestimation of the effects of change. Change is a constant whether that change is evolutionary or revolutionary. Because the system is constantly changing, there must be constant attention to performance of the system so that the processes and strategies designed to support the quality functions of the system are at their peak at all times. Changes in the internal and external environments of the organization, market forces, regulations, as well as in the professionals and the patients they serve require dynamic and agile responses from the organization if it is to thrive in today's health care environment.

The decision to diffuse innovation within an organization demands evaluation of the intended and unintended consequences of that decision. The sustained success of the innovation frequently depends on the appraisal of and response to the results of that evaluation. This chapter describes the process of appraisal and refinement of a system of support for NP practice in the hospital setting.

ASSESSMENT AND EVALUATION

Whether in regard to patients or programs, assessment and evaluation are terms that are often used interchangeably. The meanings of the words and the associated processes are different, however, and need to be distinguished in relation to sustaining and refining NP practice in hospitals. Assessment is the systematic gathering of data about a program or person. Evaluation is the analysis and the attachment of value or meaning to the conclusions drawn from the assessment. This is not always an easy task and it is not always performed. Many times, data are collected on a regular basis as part of performance and quality improvement programs and are filed away without ever being analyzed, evaluated, and used as the foundation for real program refinement.

Assessment

The specifics of measuring progress and measuring success for individual NPs and the organization have been discussed previously (chapters 3 and 11). This section will focus on a schema or category of measurement that can describe the bigger picture of what goes into the assessment for program evaluation and how that differs from the metrics for individual success. Hundreds of quality and performance metrics have been proffered by numerous organizations whose mission is to guarantee the quality and safety of health care wherever it is practiced. Exhibit 12.1 lists just a few organizations that report quality measures. And while the availability of data is essential for decision makers, it is important to be selective since too much data can be distracting. How then does an organization choose the appropriate structural/organizational/system, process, and outcome metrics that appropriately reflect the value and sustainability of NP practice in the organization?

The method for conducting the assessment of your NP practice group should have been developed as part of the plan to implement NP practice in the organization, although often this is not the case. As with many statements that begin with the word "should," it may not have been. If the

---

EXHIBIT 12.1   Representative Quality Organizations That Publish Quality Indicators, Outcomes of Quality Measures, and Research on Quality in Health Care

Institute of Medicine
Priority Areas for National Action: Transforming Health Care Quality
The Joint Commission ORYX™
http://www.ahrq.gov/chtoolbx/emerging.htm#oryx
National Quality Measures Clearinghouse™
http://qualitymeasures.ahrq.gov/
Organizations publishing Report Cards on hospitals, physician practices, and nursing homes
http://www.ahrq.gov/qua/nqacmeas.htm
Centers for Medicare and Medicaid Services (CMS)
http://www.hospitalcompare.hhs.gov/hospital-search.aspx?
http://www.medicare.gov/HomeHealthCompare/search.aspx?
National Quality Forum
http://www.qualityforum.org/Home.aspx

EXHIBIT 12.2   Potential Data Sources for Analysis When Evaluating Quality and Safety Performance Indicators

Admissions database for demographics, ICD-9 admission codes, dates and times for admissions, geographic distribution of patients, sources of admissions

Infection Control database for hospital-acquired infections, catheter related bloodstream infections, reportable infections, endemic outbreaks

Electronic Health Records can often export spreadsheets or databases based on individual providers that will allow tracking of productivity by individual provider or provider class allowing NPs to demonstrate their collective productivity and utilization of resources as well as specific outcomes such as Length of stay, procedures and diagnostic requests.

Billing and financial databases are alternate sources of data about NP productivity

Data that is reported to CMS and the Joint Commission is also available internally for analysis so that core measures and HCAPS can be monitored internally

It is critical to remember that any administrative database is susceptible to error because of data entry. If the original data was not accurate, it will give inappropriate answers even if it was entered correctly. Data that consistently gives answers that are inconsistent with observation should be challenged.

---

implementation plan did not include an evaluation plan with specified metrics, then the first step in the process is to return to the reasons for integrating NP practice into the organization. What was the nature of the agenda setting and what goals were to be accomplished by NP practice? Where are you in the process of dissemination of the innovation? Is this an evaluation of the trial or of the final rollout Is this a preliminary evaluation or an ongoing evaluation? The stage and the maturity of the process will affect the frequency and, perhaps, the comprehensiveness of the evaluation.

In addition to evaluation of the program of NP practice in relation to organization goals and performance measures and individual NP performance, it is critical to look at the performance of NP leaders. In Chapter 3, the process of organizing and developing the structure and leadership model for supporting NP practice is described. That process needs monitoring, appraisal, and refinement as well to make it operate at optimum efficiency. The assessment of leaders is usually more challenging than any other because there are so many perspectives that can and should be included and most of them have both subjective and objective components. The concept of 360-degree assessment (US Office of Personnel Management 1997) has been proposed as a means of providing multiple perspectives on leader behavior and ability. By using multiple perspectives, the picture of the leaders is more complete and less susceptible to the bias of a single individual experience.

Quantitative and qualitative data are necessary to truly understand the impact of the integration of NP practice, its leadership, and its value to the organization. Evaluation of the innovation will likely be a challenging task. There will be parts that work and parts that do not work as well and need improvement. Over time, as aspects need revision in order to accommodate ongoing change, it will be as critical to understand why things work or do not work as that they work at all.

Evaluation of the Data

Through data analysis, patterns and associations can be identified in order to draw conclusions and support the development of an action plan. This process is limited by the knowledge, critical thinking abilities, and biases of the persons conducting the analysis and the quality of the data. The process and its outcome may further be limited by the evaluator's position in the system hierarchy. No single method of evaluation is better than any other method. There is no system that guarantees a better plan or outcome. Good analysis and pattern recognition requires discussion and the critical thinking of multiple stakeholders if it is to overcome bias and limited knowledge and experience. Sometimes even intuition or a hunch about the relationships between findings can lead to the identification of solvable problems that can be addressed.

A number of evaluation schemes have been described in the literature (Keller, Gare, Edenius, & Lindblad, 2009; Patton 2011). Traditionally *formative evaluation* has been used to fine-tune programs as they are developed and then a *summative evaluation* is used to determine the success or failure of the finished program in its steady state in meeting the objectives for which it was originally created. Patton (2011) describes the emergence of *developmental evaluation* to address program evaluation in situations where a steady state is never achieved. This phenomenon arose for him in programs where the changing context and demands required that the evaluation strategy designed to assess the effectiveness of the program be of similar complexity and volatility since no steady state was possible or desirable. In other words, the program he needed to evaluate could not stop evolving long enough for a summative evaluation to take place. A new kind of evaluation process needed to be created that would be more like the formative evaluation since the program being evaluated was acknowledging that it would never be finished and would always be developing and responding to changes in what was required. Developmental evaluation then needed to be designed into the project and made agile and responsive to changes in the project.

Keller and colleagues (2009) describe *realist evaluation*, where they take a more pragmatic approach to evaluation. Realist evaluation acknowledges that the assessment of parameters will return information about programs that is both positive and negative. It will identify components that work and do not work toward achievement of desired outcomes, it and accepts the fact that there are a host of desirable and undesirable, intentional and unintentional consequences of any innovation. With realist evaluation, the things that work are allowed to continue to work and attention is focused on how to address the things that do not meet the standards or objectives of the project.

One helpful systematic framework for analysis organizes indicators into system-based care process indicators and organizational structure support indicators for NP practice (Figure 12.1). With this system, organization-specific variables can be monitored on a regularly scheduled basis and reviewed by a designated group charged with analysis, oversight, and accountability for performance improvement. Failure to meet set or changing goals results in a root cause analysis and a problem-specific plan for refinement or reinvention to achieve to performance goals.

System-Based Indicators

System-based indicators have taken on increased meaning for the success of organizations with the advent of value-based purchasing by the Centers for Medicare and Medicaid Services (CMS). The publication of 30-day readmission rates, complication rates, and the Hospital Consumer Assessment of Healthcare Professionals and Systems (HCAHPS) has added great transparency to the quality of care for hospitals (HospitalCompare.hhs.gov). Changes in these numbers can be tracked as a general, though nonspecific, barometer of quality for evaluating programs and innovation in organizations. When NPs are hired as part of a program to specifically address a component of care addressed by a public measure, then monitoring of change in that measure over time should reflect the benefit of that program and the of NP practice included in it. It would be inappropriate, however, to base the judgment of the effectiveness of the NP solely on change in the publicly reported measure alone, but it is appropriate to include that value with others in the overall assessment of the complex assessment/evaluation of the innovation. It would be an oversimplification of a very complex problem to expect the NP to be the single solution to the problem, just as it would be inappropriate to seek a simple cause for the problem in the first place (Hines et al., 2008).

Both the organization and the processes that are measured by the publicly reported performance measures are complex. This makes it unlikely that the presence of NP practice alone would be sufficient to change that measure significantly, at least in the short term. However, over time, publicly reported measures such as 30-day readmission rates or hospital-acquired infections would be significantly affected by the combination of NP practice and changes in practice implemented by the NP. Even then, the performance improvement process would look at more variables than the publicly reported measures, to properly assess the issue and

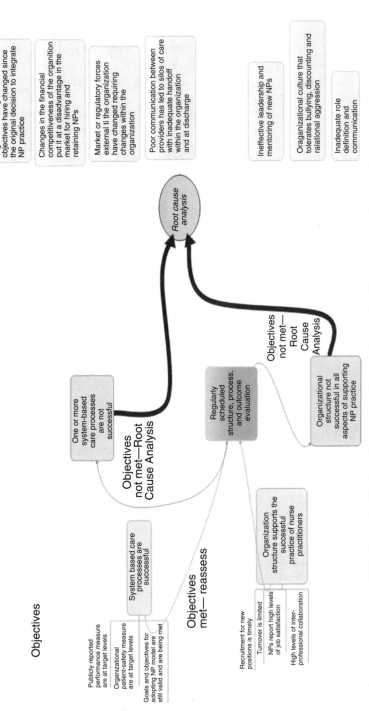

FIGURE 12.1 Systematic framework for analysis of performance improvement data.

present an accurate picture of the strategy and the process improvement that was necessary to achieve the goal.

No discussion of system-based objectives or organizational goals for safety and quality could be complete without including the principles of highly reliable organizations (HROs). Briefly, the translation of principles that guide the development of safety and quality in other high-risk industries (i.e., airline, defense) has been proposed as a means to assure a safer environment for patients and providers. The hypothesis is that if hospitals can be made into highly reliable organizations, then the processes will make them safer for both patients and the staff that care for them and the quality will increase. Quality care is more cost-effective care.

There are five major principles of HROs (Hines et al., 2008):

- *Sensitivity to operations*—regular, candid assessments of the state of the organization
- *Reluctance to simplify*—an acknowlegment of the complexity of the organization and a refusal to seek and accept oversimplified explanations and solutions to complex problems
- *Preoccupation with failure*—vigilant attention and follow-up to close calls where intentionally designed system "back-ups" prevented the problem from occurring. Planning ahead and focusing on what could go wrong instead of reacting to things that do go wrong.
- *Deference to expertise*—listening to the person with the most knowledge and expertise in the current situation independent of rank and position in the organization. This includes the ability to speak truth to power.
- *Commitment to Resilience*—developing the flexibility and agility to respond to emergencies and failures quickly and decisively when systems do fail.

The third category of system-based objectives focuses on the specific reason that the organization chose to implement NP practice. Chapter 8 describes the concept of collaboration and states that if the objectives for NP practice are not clear to everyone, and there is not agreement about that practice and commitment to the practice by physicians, NPs, and administration, the practice will not be collaborative and will not benefit patients, providers, or the organization and will ultimately fail. There must be planned, regularly scheduled monitoring of the assessment of achievement of benchmarks for those goals and adjustment in the plans if those benchmarks are not being met.

Successful NP Practice

The designation of system-based and successful NP practice categories is arbitrary since it is the philosophy of the authors that the two categories are inseparable and the success of the organization is inseparable from the success of the NP. The separation here is purely for convenience in organizing the data. The interrelatedness will be clear when the analysis and pattern identification is complete and an action plan emerges.

There will always be subjective evaluation of and by NPs of their practice and of the context in which they practice. This subjective evaluation has value and should never be discounted. It is however, subjective and cannot be generalized to the organization or to other NPs. It is critical, then, to look for other parameters that are better reflections of the organization as a healthy, nurturing environment for NP practice.

A hospital's reputation as NP-friendly spreads by word of mouth through social and professional networks. Individual professional working relationships within specific hospitals spread equally as well. Consequently, difficulty in recruiting locally for specific positions or for the hospital as a whole, high turnover, unresolved conflict, patient safety issues, and poor interprofessional collaboration are all individually and collectively warning signs that there are organizational barriers to successful NP practice. These barriers must be candidly evaluated and action must be taken to remedy them or the NP practice will not be successful and patient care will suffer. If on the other hand the environment for NP practice is good, then the question for performance improvement becomes one of how to expand and enhance the benefits of what is obviously a successful endeavor.

It is equally critical to be sure that culture is the problem with recruitment and not the recruitment process. A recruiter who is great at recruiting RNs for vacancies may not be as efficient at recruiting NPs. If turnover is low but recruitment is not as robust, then the discrepancy should cause the evaluators to look for alternate explanations. The evaluator must be careful not to assume that the first possible explanation is the only explanation or even a valid one. Premature closure of the analysis step prevents the process from working as it should.

ROOT CAUSE ANALYSIS

Root cause analysis (RCA) is a broad designation for strategies or approaches to determining the basic reasons why intended or unintended consequences occurred. This analysis is conducted as a foundation for an action plan to address correction of the causes, rather than the consequences themselves. The RCA can be used to explore successes or failures or both. Just as there are multiple approaches to assessment and evaluation, there are multiple approaches to RCA, and none is superior to the other. An approach that is systematic, comprehensive, and transparent will be useful if it is applied in a way that minimizes bias and power struggles and promotes open and candid discussion along the principles consistent with the definition of a highly reliable organization (Patton, 2011).

Figure 12.1 suggests some potential root causes for failure to meet the objectives of hospital-based NP practice. These are clearly general causes common to many hospital settings. An RCA for a specific hospital would have specific causes as a foundation for an action plan to deal with them. It would be unlikely that there would be a single root cause, given the complex nature of hospital organizations. Some categories of root causes follow here.

Change in Conditions

It is not unusual for conditions to change over the course of implementing an innovation such as NP practice in a complex and dynamic organization such as a hospital. Constant vigilance is required to maintain the relationship of evaluation criteria, performance measures, and organizational goals within the organization's efforts to be a force for good within the community. The careful exploration of forces inside and outside the organization may reveal changes that must be addressed if the organization is to be successful in achieving its goals, and these forces may or may not relate directly to the presence of NPs within the organization. Chief among these is the change in financial conditions in the organization. Poor financial management, merger with a larger organization, or change in financial philosophy can dramatically affect adoption decisions, support for previous decisions to adopt NP practice, and success in meeting publicly reported performance measures. Financial decisions can have an acute and profound effect on patient safety and quality as well, and for this reason alone Hines and colleagues (2008) point out that getting the Chief Financial Officer committed to the HRO philosophy is critical to its success.

Communication

For Rogers (2003) communication and diffusion are synonymous. Collaboration cannot happen without clear, respectful, and frequent communication. There can be no safety or continuity and, therefore, no quality of patient care without cogent, meaningful, systematic handoff from one provider to another. Good communication is no accident and must be pursued with diligence and attention to detail. The essential nature of good communication is reflected in all five characteristics of the highly reliable organization. Breakdown in communication is often identified as the primary reason for complex system failure.

Leadership

Leadership and management are two terms often used interchangeably, but incorrectly. Hines and colleagues (2008) identify four key aspects of executive leadership that are key to the success of HROs. First, the leader is accountable for the culture of the organization, and that culture is the foundation for the vision and strategy that leader uses to guide the organization. An open, transparent culture that promotes openness, courage, and learning will reflect a leader who values those traits. Second, transparency is critical to changing a culture that is closed and secretive. Problems cannot be corrected if they are not acknowledged or if people are afraid of taking responsibility for mistakes. A problem must be named and the name must be spoken aloud.

Third, safety must be the overarching strategy. Mistakes compound themselves and the organization devolves instead of improving its safety and quality profile. An organization where leadership tolerates anything short of a physically and psychologically safe environment for staff as well as patients will fail. And finally, leaders must own the climate for every subunit of the organization as well as the organization as a whole and be accountable for and to each member of that organization (Hines et al., 2008).

In reality, most administrators see themselves as managers and not leaders; accountable to the next higher level of management. This translates at many levels as a root cause for staff dissatisfaction, poor work adjustment, and high turnover of staff. Leadership development is not often distinguished from management training or considered, but may be a key factor in addressing performance improvement where NP practice is not meeting expectations. However, this is not inevitable.

Herrin and Spears (2007) have tied nurse leader competencies to lower turnover and higher quality outcomes. They document evidence that management practices in nursing are both strengths and threats to patient safety. Leader behavior is no less critical for NPs. How then do we improve the leadership abilities of those designated or chosen to lead us to a place of highest quality and reliable safety?

Leading people requires vision and creativity. Leadership cannot manifest without integrity, honesty, fairness, and respect. These qualities can be developed, but they require a culture that will sustain that development and that starts with the chief operating officer and permeates the organization. A number of programs are available commercially to help in the development of leaders. Exhibit 12.3 lists some of these programs.

EXHIBIT 12.3   Examples of Commercial Leadership Development Programs

Harvard ManageMentor
http://www.harvardmanagementor.org/
Leader Effectiveness Training
http://www.gordontraining.com/workplace-programs/
leader-effectiveness-training-l-e-t/

QUALITY IMPROVEMENT

There are a host of trademarked programs today that are marketed to hospital organizations as the answer to their quality and safety questions (Hines et al., 2008). These programs include Lean, Six Sigma, Lean Six Sigma, and others promising their system, if followed precisely, will lead to a new level of safety and quality. These programs bring with them impressive records from the world of manufacturing, where they have been very successful. Programs using these methods have been successful in addressing a number of problems in health care as well (Hines et al., 2008).

A word of caution is necessary here, however, because of the nature of this innovation—NP practice—and the characteristics of this organization—complex hospital environments with infinite variability (Yu & Hang, 2009). If one examines manufacturing, it becomes clear quickly that much of the process is quite predictable, so predictable in fact that it can be computerized and carried out by robots. The robotic process is often much more reliable and precise than the work completed by humans. This kind of precision is intuitively applicable to procedures in health care. It makes common sense that checklists, precision measurements, and fail-safes would improve safety and quality in procedure-oriented processes. It is not so clear that these same strategies would be as helpful in judgment-related processes where a number of variables with multiple potential responses need to be considered simultaneously.

Consequently, the performance improvement process in evaluating the impact of NPs on organization outcomes and organization structures on NP success is messy. It resists simplification and both success and failure have multiple etiologies and no single solutions. The NPs themselves may be the best source of solutions to the problems, and managers must have the confidence in themselves to defer to the NPs if necessary to identify and follow through on those solutions. At a minimum, NPs must be at the table for discussions that may impact the NP scope of practice or their clinical environment of care. The system must be robust enough to try new things, fail, and try again. Resilience is one of four qualities of an HRO. Successful performance improvement is system-focused, resilient, complex without resorting to oversimplification, and there is deference to the expertise to solve the problem wherever that expertise is.

Quality improvement for NP practice is an iterative process. Because of the complexity and dynamic nature of the interactions of NPs, patients, and the hospital organization, things are always changing. Things that work wonderfully today may not tomorrow, and things that do not achieve goals today may be successful in the future. Constant vigilance and tremendous optimism are critical for the resilience that is necessary to make the organization and NPs mutually successful.

SUMMARY

There is no question that every organizational decision made today must relate in some way to the safety and quality of the care that is provided by the people that make up that organization. That is especially true of the decision to integrate NPs into hospital-based practice. Each of the problems identified in Rogers' Agenda Setting Stage (2003) matched up with NP practice, as a solution relates in some way to the desire of the decision-making body to address an issue of safety or quality in the organization. Each of the structures and processes that have been discussed in this book that are directed at facilitating the transition of NPs from recruitment through expert status must be considered as part of any quality endeavor.

Performance or quality improvement cannot be an afterthought. It must be a priority of developmental planning for all innovation, but especially for NP practice. NP practice impacts every aspect of the organization and its commitment to being an HRO. NPs, as autonomous, accountable professionals, must have leadership roles providing the expertise for achieving that level of reliability.

If individual systems are not working, the NP should participate in the process of identifying the root cause of the issue(s). Diligent searches for root causes to be addressed for both successes and failures are critical in response to regular assessments and evaluation analyses. These assessments must be frequent, candid, qualitative discussions of difficult topics with accountability but not blame. The responsibility for the culture that promotes this kind of transparency starts at the top of the organization and demands nothing less from those accountable throughout the organizational chart.

Furthermore, each NP is accountable to each other NP for the quality of their own practice. No quality improvement program or strategy can replace the responsibility of the community of NPs to hold each other to acceptable standards of practice. No hierarchy of administration can relieve any community of NPs of the duty to care for each other and create a culture where each is safe from psychological and physical harm. No organization can relieve any community of NPs of the responsibility for the shared learning and professional socialization that only they can provide for each other. This is the essence of quality improvement and refinement of NP practice within the hospital organization.

REFERENCES

Braithwaite, J., Westbrook, J. I., Ranmuthugala, G., Cunningham, F., Plumb, J., Wiley, J., ... Debono, D. (2009). The development design, testing, refinement, simulation and application of an evaluation framework for communities of practice and social-professional networks. *BMC Health Services Research, 9,* 162. Retrieved February 27, 2012, from http://www.biomedcentral.com/1472-6963/9/162

Herrin, D., & Spears, P. (2007). Using nurse leader development to improve nurse retention and patient outcomes: A framework. *Nursing Administration Quarterly, 31*(3), 231–243.

Hines, S., Luna, K., Lofthus, J., Marquardt, M., & Stelmokas, D. (2008). *Becoming a high reliability organization: Operational advice for hospital leaders.* (Prepared by the Lewin Group under Contract No 290-04-0011.) *AHRQ Publication No. 08-0022.* Rockville, MD: Agency for Healthcare Research and Quality.

Keller, C., Gare, K., Edenius, M., & Lindblad, S. (2009). Designing for complex innovations in health care: Design theory and realist evaluation combined. *DESRIST 09 May 7–8. Proceedings of the 4th International Conference on Design Science Research in Information Systems and Technology.* Retrieved February 26, 2012, from http://dl.acm.org/citation.cfm?id=1555623.

Kottke, T. E., Pronk, N. P., & Isham, G. J. (2012). The simple health system rules that create value. *Preventing Chronic Disease 9*, 110179. Retrieved March 3, 2012, from http://www.cdc.gov/pcd/issues/2012/11_0179.htm

Patton, M. Q. (2011). *Developmental evaluation: Applying complexity concepts to enhance innovation and use.* New York: The Guilford Press.

Rogers, E. M. (2003). *Diffusion of innovation* (5th ed.). New York: The Free Press.

U.S. Office of Personnel Management. (1997). *360-degree assessment: An overview.* Developed with the assistance of Human Technology, Inc. of McLean, VA, under contract OPM-91-2958 with the U.S. Office of Personnel Management's Training Assistance Programs. Retrieved March 3, 2012, from http://www.opm.gov/perform/wppdf/360asess.pdf

Yu, D., & Hang, C. C. (2009). A reflective review of disruptive innovation theory. *International Journal of Management Reviews, 12*(4), 402.

13

Sustaining Success

Jennifer L. Titzer and Maria R. Shirey

Health care reform calls for patient-centered care, enhanced primary care with community-based services, and improved care continuity (Institute of Medicine, 2011). Implementing and sustaining these changes will require a consistent pipeline of competent and confident nurse practitioners, providing primary care services including health promotion, education, and assessment. The role of the nurse practitioner continues to evolve and expand as a result of increasing health care access challenges (American College of Physicians, 2009). In response to health care reform and demands, the number of nurse practitioner graduates has steadily increased over the last 20 years, making them the largest group of nonphysician primary care providers (American College of Physicians, 2009). To ensure a primed pipeline of competent nurse practitioners to meet health care challenges and the demand for primary care providers, strategic and deliberate succession planning is essential.

Health care reform and the aging population both indicate a need for strong nursing leaders. Nurse practitioners act as leaders in clinical practice, teaching, research, and health care policy; they direct and influence nursing practice using evidence-based guidelines (Carryer, Gardner, Dunn, & Gardner, 2007; McArthur, 2006). Nurse practitioners influence health care delivery systems on a local, regional, national, and global level; they do so without necessarily holding formal executive leadership positions (Carryer et al., 2007). Leadership does not require a specific position or title; rather it entails influencing others and acting with courage, competence, and confidence (Ulrich, 2009). Nurse practitioners in any setting require leadership and influencing skills, and these may be enhanced using formal succession planning efforts as the institution prepares for future management needs.

The expected increased demand for nurse practitioners and expanded nurse practitioner roles requires proactive and strategic succession planning. The purpose of this chapter is to define succession planning, review current health care succession planning evidence from the literature, and describe a practical nurse practitioner leadership succession planning model.

DEFINITION

Succession planning is a strategic process involving identification, development, and evaluation of intellectual capital to ensure leadership continuity within an organization.

Succession planning is a traditional method for transferring ownership in family businesses; however, it has become a common strategy for ensuring organizational leadership continuity (Carriere, Muise, Cummings, & Newburn-Cook, 2009). Succession planning focuses on proactively identifying high-potential individuals outside of formal leadership positions and preparing them for the future.

Talent management and leadership development are closely related yet different terms. Succession planning is a subcomponent of talent management and is a nursing leadership initiative, while talent management is more encompassing and is a human resource-driven initiative (Bersin, 2006). Succession planning is the deliberate development of internal talent through identification of high potentials, targeted formal education, and experiential learning opportunities. Leadership development is used synonymously with succession planning; however, their planning and objective setting differ. Succession planning is proactive and anticipatory of the organization's talent needs. Leadership development is more reactive and focuses on advancing the competency of individuals after they assume a particular role (Ponti, 2009).

EVIDENCE SUPPORTING SUCCESSION PLANNING

Literature specific to nurse practitioner succession planning is limited; however, the business and health care succession planning literature provide evidence supporting the need, common elements, and outcomes associated with this proactive process. A review of the health care literature reveals empirical outcomes related to nursing leadership succession planning at all levels is lacking and suggests research evaluating specific outcomes is much needed.

Needs Assessment

Owing to the projected nursing shortage that will ultimately impact future advance practice nursing and leadership positions, succession planning methods within health care have gained increasing attention. The Institute of Medicine (2011) recognizes the need for formal training supporting nursing role transitions; however, health care succession planning still lags behind other industries. Only one in four hospitals uses succession planning, in contrast to two out of three for-profit businesses (Ogden, 2010). Hospitals with deliberate succession plans most often focus on executive management and leadership levels.

Recognizing the need for succession planning beyond executive level positions, the National Center for Healthcare Leadership (2005) recommends organization-wide succession planning including front-line and clinical leadership roles. Maintaining a pipeline of capable leaders in all key positions, including the nurse practitioner role, is crucial for organizational sustainability. Not only is succession planning critical for nursing leadership, it can help support nurse practitioner's presence at the bedside.

Organizations that invest in succession planning and anticipate human capital needs have lower turnover rates (Roundeau, Williams, & Wagar, 2009), higher patient quality initiatives, and greater costs containments (National Center for Healthcare Leadership, 2011). Having a primed pipeline of internal talent for key roles increases leadership continuity, which supports a healthy work environment and reduces productive loss often associated with extended vacancy periods.

Succession Planning Elements

A review of business and health care succession literature enhances concept understanding and reveals common antecedents and attributes related to succession planning (Figure 13.1). Succession planning models described in the nursing leadership literature include deliberate organizational leadership succession plans, nurse leadership internships, and developmental programs for current nursing leaders. These same leadership programs, customized for advanced practice nurses, may have applicability to sustaining an influential nurse practitioner workforce.

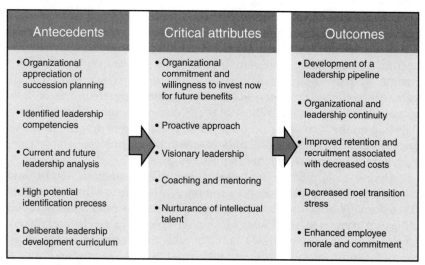

FIGURE 13.1   Succession planning in nursing: What is in a concept?

Succession planning antecedents include organizational appreciation of succession planning, strategic planning, identified leadership competencies, current and future leadership analysis, high potential identification processes, and a deliberate leadership development curriculum (Figure 13.1). Attributes of deliberate succession planning include an organizational commitment and willingness to invest now for future benefits, a proactive approach, visionary leadership, coaching and mentoring, and nurturance of intellectual talent. Nurse practitioners benefit from formal programs specifically designed to cultivate their leadership competencies and identify capable nurse practitioners for formal leadership role mentoring.

Outcomes of Succession Planning

Benefits of succession planning include the development of a leadership pipeline, organizational and leadership continuity, improved retention and recruitment, and decreased role transition stress (Figure 13.1). The potential succession planning outcomes address current organizational challenges such as reducing position vacancies, capitalizing internal intellectual talent, and enhancing employee commitment (Rothwell, 2010). As health care demands and complexity increase and the nursing workforce decreases, meeting these challenges through effective and efficient succession planning programs will be critical (National Center for Healthcare Leadership, 2011).

Individuals prepared to move into current and future key positions make up an organization's leadership pipeline (Charan, Drotter, & Noel, 2001). Similar terms describing a leadership pipeline are *leadership bench strength* and *talent pool*. Leadership bench strength is defined as "the organization's ability to fill vacancies from within" (Rothwell, 2010, p. 242). It is recommended that an organization have strong leadership bench strength with multifaceted individuals prepared to fit a variety of potential leadership roles, rather than having individuals being groomed for just one specific position. Succession planning increases internal leadership bench strength and the number of internal promotions, which consequently decreases recruiting costs and leadership vacancy times (Abrams & Bevilacqua, 2006; Collins & Collins, 2007; Wendler, Olson-Sitki, & Prater, 2009). Given the increasing need for nurse practitioners in the U.S. health care system, having nurse practitioners assuming formal leadership roles to prepare future nurse practitioner leaders is key.

Owing to familiarity with an organization's mission, values, and goals, internally developed and promoted candidates, when compared with externally hired candidates, have higher success rates and improved leadership competency (Blouin, McDonagh, Neistadt, & Helfand, 2006). Developing internal employees familiar with the strategies and goals of the organization supports the organizational culture, values, and atmosphere. Many times health care organizations do not worry about successors until a vacancy occurs. This type of passive leadership planning results in extended leadership vacancy periods. In the urgency of filling an unplanned vacancy, an unsuitable individual may be chosen, potentially disrupting the organization's culture and work environment. Strategic succession planning reduces leadership gaps and limits work environment disruptions. Having in place mechanisms to ensure an appropriate number of qualified nurse practitioner leaders is crucial for sustaining an adequate workforce and minimizing access-to-care difficulties.

Succession planning increases professional development and career advancement opportunities, which positively impacts employee morale, role transition, organization culture, and retention (Rothwell, 2010). Providing a nurturing environment and stimulating intellectual and professional development encourages nurse engagement (Mackoff & Triolo, 2008). Limited professional development and advancement opportunities may cause competent nurses to leave the organization, seeking outside positions. Succession planning demonstrates a commitment to current employees and increases nurse retention (McConnell, 2006). Succession planning is also a recruiting tool for high-potential individuals with goals of advancing into formal leadership positions. Organizations that are seen as committed to developing current intellectual talent are preferred workplace choices for motivated health care professionals (Abrams & Bevilacqua, 2006). In the absence of dedicated succession planning efforts, organizations risk their long-term survival (Currie, 2010).

IMPLICATIONS OF NURSE PRACTITIONER SUCCESSION PLANNING

As the face of health care evolves, all nurses will be called to lead organizations through inevitable challenges (Grossman & Valiga, 2009). Nurse practitioners, acting as teachers, patient advocates, role models, and problem solvers, are inherent leaders (McArthur, 2006). Ensuring a pipeline of competent and confident nurse practitioner requires deliberate and strategic succession planning.

Formal nurse practitioner education many times lacks crucial leadership training (Lewis, 2011). Historically, nurse leaders are selected based on their clinical reputation with the assumption their expertise will support a transition to more advanced roles. Lacking the proper education and training, leadership competency is gained from experience; this happens over time. During this transition, high levels of stress, reduced productivity, unhealthy work environments, decreased nurse satisfaction, and less than optimal patient outcomes are evident. With rapid health care system evolution, intentional succession planning enhancing recruitment, retention, and role transition becomes necessary (Hampel, Procter, & Deuter, 2010). The Institute of Medicine (2011) recommends that nurses take responsibility for their personal and professional growth. This requires seeking opportunities to expand leadership skills using mentoring, formal education, professional development conferences, and internships as possible venues. Given the Institute of Medicine (2011) recommendations for nurse practitioners to function at their full scope of practice, this shift requires leadership and entrepreneurial talent to tap into potential opportunities.

Mentoring and recognizing untapped leadership potential is the formal leader's responsibility (Grossman & Valiga, 2009). The formal leader must collect resources, provide them to their staff, and nurture the development of leadership skills. Mentors and coaches help emerging leaders build confidence, construct networks, and encourage professional engagement (Lewis, 2011). Mentors and coaches can be found through health care facilities, university faculty, and professional organizations. Mentoring requires current nurse practitioner leaders to recognize high-potential nurses and offer their time and expertise (Ulrich, 2009). Nurse practitioners who act as mentors and coaches strengthen the leadership pipeline, become professional role models (Lewis, 2011), and similarly contribute to succession planning efforts. In the absence of formal mentors, nurse practitioners must become resourceful, up to and including becoming their own mentors (Wellington, 2001).

Preparing for the increased demand for nurse practitioners in the future, health care organizations can collaborate with schools of nursing to identify high-potential nurses who aspire to advance practice roles. Clinical practice and faculty mentors can support these nurses through the formal educational process as well as providing experiential learning activities, facilitating their role transition. Close collaboration between academia and practice also help ensure that nurses seeking to be advance practice nurses understand the scope of practice and select the role that best fits their professional and personal goals. Working closely with academia, health care organizations have access to a pipeline of future advanced practice nurses, including nurse practitioners.

The Institute of Medicine (2011) recommends increasing the number of doctorally prepared nurses to prepare a pipeline of transformational advanced practice leaders who will help guide and shape health care reform. The doctorate of nursing practice (DNP) degree increases the advanced practice nurses' political skills, systems thinking, and business knowledge required to implement health care system changes (Petersen, 2011). The education and experience will increase nurses' confidence and facilitate leadership role transitions (Riley, 2011). Accordingly, pursuing the DNP should be a viable strategy for the nurse practitioner and is part of a full succession planning effort.

Professional organizations offer nurse practitioners personal and professional growth opportunities. Several organizations (ex Sigma theta tau has a Chiron program) including the American Academy of Nurse Practitioners (2011) offer mentorship programs that pair expert nurse practitioner fellows with novice nurse practitioners. The mentee identifies personal and professional needs and the mentor provides guidance and support. The program expands the novice nurse practitioner's professional network and provides continuing education opportunities, which could be incorporated into a full succession planning program.

Personal and professional growth is the responsibility of individual nurse practitioners; however, health care organizations also have a vested interest in developing the next generation of nurse practitioner leaders. Proactive, strategic, and deliberate succession planning provides novice nurse practitioners with opportunities to improve leadership competency and personal confidence. Developing a succession planning program requires organizational support and resource allocation. Similarly, the program should align with the organization's mission, vision, and values.

Succession Planning Model for Nurse Practitioners

Succession planning should follow a systematic approach that anticipates potential leadership voids and ensures well-prepared leaders are available to fill key positions and meet organizational needs (Redman, 2006). When cultivating talent at all levels is part of an organization's value system and strategic plan, chances are leader succession planning can occur seamlessly. Targeting the nurse practitioner workforce, practical models can be used to strategically plan for the future. One model useful for advanced practice nurses (APNs) is the succession model shown in Figure 13.2.

Overview of the Succession Planning Model

Figure 13.2 represents a five-step succession planning model, which "assumes systems framework of inputs and outputs that exist within both an internal (hospital) and external (community, region, state, and national levels influenced by regulatory and sociopolitical forces) environment" (Shirey, 2008, p. 215). Organizational factors, individual factors, development, execution, and evaluation/dissemination represent the five steps that occur within the internal environment. Although these five steps occur internal to the hospital environment, they also overlap with the external environment.

Step 1 in the model, organizational factors, encompasses commitment, vision, and assessment as key elements. Organizational commitment at the chief executive officer and hospital trustee level is required, as is vision and a current/future leadership needs assessment. To ensure access to patient care quality and safety, having in place a strong cadre of nurse practitioners who can impact patient outcomes is essential. The literature supports the positive relationship between APN practice and desirable outcomes, suggesting that investing in APN's makes business sense (Newhouse et al., 2011).

Step 2, individual factors, involves the identification of high-potential nurse practitioners for future roles within the organization. In evaluating

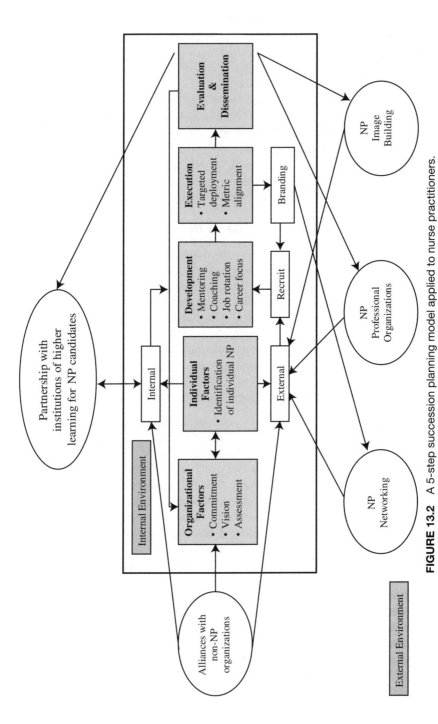

FIGURE 13.2 A 5-step succession planning model applied to nurse practitioners.

Source: Adapted from Shirey, M.R. (2008). Building the leadership development pipeline: A 5-step succession planning model. *Clinical Nurse Specialist,* 22(5), 214–217. Reprinted with permission from Wolters Kluwer Health.

the organization's mission, vision, and values along with the strategic plan and changing regulatory trends, it may become apparent that a new product or service needs to be deployed, and nurse practitioners are the most qualified to pursue these efforts. This situation could necessitate identification of individuals or groups of nurse practitioners who could be routed into the developmental phase of leadership development. It also could require that these individuals be provided with time allotted to perform the required tasks.

Step 3, development, entails the mentoring and coaching of nurse practitioners within a career continuum. The development step requires organizational support and investment to make available the human and financial resources (including release time) needed for successful role socialization. This step may also benefit from job rotation, which involves facilitating apprentice-like experiences needed to learn diverse components of a new role.

Step 4, execution, demands having a pre-formulated action plan with targeted metrics for implementing the leadership development efforts. The metrics used should align both organizational and individual needs, making for a mutually beneficial endeavor. The execution step done well could help the organization with marketing differentiation and thus branding itself as a desirable place for nurse practitioners to work and grow. There is economic value associated with branding a leadership succession planning program to develop nurse practitioners. This value may manifest itself in professional networking that improves recruitment and positive word of mouth for the institution.

Step 5, evaluation and dissemination, requires the creation of pre-determined metrics and comparing actual versus targeted succession planning program outcomes. This step also includes internal and external dissemination of program outcomes. Because the advanced practice nurse succession planning literature is scant (Currie, 2010; Currie & Grundy, 2011; Shirey, 2008), individuals must publish outcomes associated with these programs, thus sharing important findings with both the professional and lay community.

Real-World Model Application

Exhibit 13.1 is a case study that puts the various elements of the succession planning model (Figure 13.2) together into one meaningful whole. In this fictitious institution, a 350-bed acute care hospital, leaders complete a talent assessment demonstrating their commitment to succession planning (Step 1, organizational factors). In anticipating the need for two additional APNs to support a key health care clinic, the organizational leaders begin to address the model's individual factors (Step 2). Because the hospital has a formal succession planning program, they have in place a leadership development curriculum, mentoring, coaching, and experiential learning experiences (Step 3, development). Although the various developmental pieces are in place, the program has to be customized to meet the needs of nurse practitioners. The APN advisory council will enhance the existing program and target its deployment to address the needed nurse practitioner leadership essentials and related measurement targets (Step 4, execution). An evaluation tool based on identified competencies and including a self-assessment measure will be used to evaluate the program (Step 5, evaluation). The development of internal presentations and abstracts for submission to external venues demonstrates a focus on dissemination and completes Step 5 (dissemination) of the succession planning model.

EXHIBIT 13.1   Case Study Illustrating Application of the Succession Planning Model

A 350-bed acute care hospital conducts an annual evaluation of its current and anticipated internal intellectual capital needs. Included in this assessment are the advanced practice nurse positions. The hospital anticipates two additional advanced practice nurses will be required to support a new practitioner run health care clinic. The clinic currently employs three competent nurse practitioners. One of the nurse practitioners is a senior nurse practitioner and acts as the practice administrator. She also mentors the other nurse practitioners and shares leadership responsibility to help them gain experience. Hiring two new nurse practitioners will provide the senior nurse practitioner more time for administrative duties, mentoring, and coaching.

Evaluation of the advanced-practice nursing staff reveals three nurses interested in the positions. Although identified as high-potential nurse practitioners, they are novices with only one year of experience. Two nurse practitioner positions are anticipated; however, all three high-potential individuals will be placed in the succession plan. The hospital has a formal succession plan involving a formal leadership development curriculum, mentoring, coaching, and experiential learning experiences. Historically, nursing leadership has been the primary focus; however, the intellectual capital needs assessment demonstrates succession planning for advanced practice roles is needed here.

To develop a nurse practitioner succession planning program, the advanced practice nurse advisory council identified desired evidence-based leadership and clinical practice competencies. The competencies will guide the curriculum development and experiential learning activities. Leadership curriculum topics include self-reflection and personal strengths evaluation, communication skills, conflict resolution strategies, team dynamics, and interprofessional collaboration. Human resource, performance improvement, and financial management content is included in both didactic and experiential learning activities. The planned successors will participate in interviews, annual performance evaluations, and budgeting meetings. Each successor will work with mentors acting as change agents on a project with an emphasis on evidence-based practice. Nurse practitioner successors will

---

(*continued*)

> ### EXHIBIT 13.1   *(Continued)*
>
> also work on developing a personal and professional development plan while gaining an appreciation for their role and that of other collaborating health care providers. An evaluation tool, based on identified competencies and program objectives, will be used to assess nurse practitioner leadership competency progression.
>
> The identified high-potential nurse practitioners will complete a self-assessment and will be enrolled in a one-year succession planning program. During the program, experienced and expert nurse practitioners will mentor the more novice nurse practitioners. Upon program completion, the mentored nurse practitioners reassess their competencies using the same instrument they used before initiating the succession planning program. The competency assessment results are shared with the candidates and a summative program evaluation is completed. The hospital assesses its current and future advanced practice nurse need and then identifies high-potential individuals who can be placed in an ongoing succession planning cycle. This intentional approach to succession planning creates an advanced practice nursing pipeline, which addresses the health care organization's current and future human capital and patient-care needs. All program outcomes are then shared within and beyond the organization and are published to build the succession planning literature.

CONCLUSION

This chapter provides a definition for succession planning, including of a concept analysis and presents pertinent evidence to support a systematic process for nurse practitioner talent identification and development. Because nurse practitioners are key leaders in the clinical arena, developing this segment of the workforce must be deliberate and strategic. To ensure that a sustainable leadership succession planning effort is in place for nurse practitioners, the authors introduce a practical five-step succession planning framework, which can be applied in a variety of settings. To implement succession planning in health care requires recognition of such a plan's value, mobilization of resources to prepare for the future, and wherewithal to act with intention.

REFERENCES

Abrams, M., & Bevilacqua, L. (2006, April). Building a leadership infrastructure; the next step in the evolution of hospital systems. *Health Care Strategic Management, 24*(4), 1, 13–16.

American Academy of Nurse Practitioners. (2011). *AANP research and education.* Retrieved from http://www.aanp.org/AANPCMS2/ResearchEducation Accessed January 2012.

American College of Physicians. (2009). *Nurse practitioners in primary care*. Retrieved from http://www.acponline.org/advocacy/where_we_stand/policy/np_pc.pdf

Bersin, J. (2006). *Talent management, What is it? Why now?* Retrieved from http://www.bf.umich.edu/docs/KeyReferenceArticles.pdf

Blouin, A. S., McDonagh, K. J., Neistadt, A. M., & Helfand, B. (2006, June). Leading tomorrow's healthcare organizations: Strategies and tactics for effective succession planning. *The Journal of Nursing Administration*, 36(6), 325–330. Retrieved from http://journals.lww.com/jonajournal/pages/default.aspx

Carriere, B. K., Muise, M., Cummings, G., & Newburn-Cook, C. (2009, December 1). Healthcare succession planning: An integrative review. *The Journal of Nursing Administration*, 39(12), 548–555. Retrieved from http://journals.lww.com/jonajournal/pages/default.aspx

Carryer, J., Gardner, G., Dunn, S., & Gardner, A. (2007). The core role of the nurse practitioner: Practice, professionalism and clinical leadership. *Journal of Clinical Nursing*, 16(10), 1818–1825. doi:10.1111/j.1365-2702.2006.01823.x

Charan, R., Drotter, S., & Noel, J. (2001). *The leadership pipeline: How to build the leadership-powered company*. San Francisco, CA: John Wiley & Sons, Inc.

Collins, S. K., & Collins, K. S. (2007). Changing workforce demographics necessitates succession planning in health care. *The Health Care Manager*, 26(4), 318–325. Retrieved from http://journals.lww.com/healthcaremanagerjournal/pages/default.aspx

Currie, K. (2010). Succession planning for advanced nursing practice: Contingency or continuity? The Scottish experience. *Journal of Healthcare Leadership*, 2, 17–24.

Currie, K., & Grundy, M. (2011). Building foundations for the future: The NHS Scotland advanced practice succession planning development pathway. *Journal of Nursing Management*, 19(7), 933–942.

Grossman, S. C., & Valiga, T. M. (2009). *The new leadership challenge: Creating the future of nursing*. Philadelphia, PA: F.A. Davis Company.

Hampel, S., Procter, N., & Deuter, K. (2010). A model of succession planning for mental health nurse practitioners. *International Journal of Mental Health Nursing*, 19, 278–286. doi:10.111/j.1447-0349.2010.00668.x

Institute of Medicine. (2011). *The future of nursing: Leading change, advancing health*. Retrieved from http://www.iom.edu/Reports/2010/The-Future-of-Nursing-Leading-Change-Advancing-Health.aspx

Lewis, K. (2011). Nurse practitioner leaders: Are we missing the mark? *Nurse Leader*, 9(3), 31–35. doi:10.1016/j.mnl/2011.01.017

Mackoff, B. L., & Triolo, P. K. (2008). Why do nurse managers stay? Building a model of engagement. *The Journal of Nursing Administration*, 38(4), 166–171. Retrieved from http://journals.lww.com/jonajournal/pages/default.aspx

McArthur, D. B. (2006). The nurse practitioner as leader. *Journal of American Academy of Nurse Practitioners*, 18, 8–10. Retrieved from http://www.aanp.org/AANPCMS2/Publications

McConnell, C. R. (2006). Succession planning: Valable process or pointless exercise. *The Health Care Manager*, 25(1), 91–98. Retrieved from http://journals.lww.com/healthcaremanagerjournal/pages/default.aspx

National Center for Healthcare Leadership. (2005). *NCHL white paper on best practices in health leadership succession planning*. Retrieved from http://www.nchl.org/Documents/Ctrl_Hyperlink/doccopy3332_uid11172009427102.pdf

National Center for Healthcare Leadership. (2011). *National healthcare leadership survey implementation of best practices.* Retrieved from http://nchl.org/Docu ments/Ctrl_Hyperlink/doccopy5321_uid7282011150092.pdf

Newhouse, R. P., Stanik-Hutt, J., White, K. M., Johnatgen, M., Bass, E. B., Zangaro, G., ... Weiner, J. P. (2011). Advanced practice nurse outcomes 1990–2008: A systematic review. *Nursing Economics, 29*(5), 1–22.

Ogden, G. (2010). *Are you building your next generation of leaders?* Retrieved from http://nextlevel.gehealthcare.com/Are%20you%20building%20your%20next% 20generation%20of%20leaders.pdf

Petersen, S. (2011). Systems thinking, healthcare organizations, and the advanced practice nurse leader. In M. E. Zaccagnini, & K. W. White (Eds.), *The doctor of nursing practice essentials: A new model for advanced practice nursing* (pp. 37–57). Sudbury, MA: Jones & Bartlett Learning.

Ponti, M. D. (2009). Transition from leadership development to succession management. *Nursing Administration Quarterly, 33*(2), 125–141. Retrieved August 22, 2011, from http://www.bf.umich.edu/docs/KeyReferenceArticles.pdf

Redman, R. W. (2006). Leadership succession planning: An evidence-based approach for managing the future. *Journal of Nursing Administration, 36*(6), 292–297.

Rothwell, W. J. (2010). *Effective succession planning.* New York: American Management Association.

Riley, M. (2011). Emerging roles for the DNP. In M. E. Zaccagnini, & K. W. White (Eds.), *The doctor of nursing practice essentials: A new model for advanced practice nursing* (pp. 401–441). Sudbury, MA: Jones & Bartlett Learning.

Roundeau, K. V., Williams, E. S., & Wager, T. H. (2009). Developing human capital: What is the impact on nurse turnover? *Journal of Nursing Management, 17,* 739–749. doi:10.111/j.1365-2834.2009.00988.x

Shirey, M. R. (2008). Building the leadership development pipeline: A 5-step succession planning model. *Clinical Nurse Specialist, 22*(5), 214–217.

Ulrich, B. (2009). Mentoring the next generation of nurse leaders. *Nephrology Nursing Journal, 36*(1). Retrieved from http://findarticles.com/p/articles/ mi_m0ICF/is_1_36/ai_n31438354/?tag=content;col1

Wellington, S. (2001). *Be your own mentor.* New York, NY: Random House Publishers.

Wendler, M. C., Olson-Sitki, K., & Prater, M. (2009). Succession planning for RNs: Implementing a nurse management internship. *The Journal of Nursing Administration, 39*(7/8), 326–333. Retrieved from http://journals.lww.com/jonajournal/ pages/default.aspx

Epilogue

It gives me great pleasure to provide an epilogue for the book *Transitioning Into Hospital-Based Practice: A Guide for Nurse Practitioners.* Nurse practitioners (NPs) represent a growing segment of health care professionals who provide care to patients in a variety of settings, including hospital-based practice. This book provides NPs working in hospital-based practice with the resources and tools to develop a successful practice. The chapter authors are expert practitioners, educators, and administrators who share helpful information for maximizing the NP role in the hospital setting.

NP practice in the hospital setting has evolved over the past 20 years to include an impressive number of specialty-based practice roles as well as further development of traditional unit-based and collaborative practice models of care. Key to the continued success of the NP role is a clear understanding of role components and addressing barriers to practice, including those related to scope of practice. Although the NP role has been in existence for over 40 years, there continues to be uncertainty about the essential components that define NP practice. The Consensus Model for Advanced Practice Registered Nurse (APRN) Regulation outlines that licensure and scope of practice are based on graduate education within a defined patient population for the NP role. The model also identifies that services provided by NPs are not defined or limited by setting but rather by patient care needs. As the APRN Consensus Model is enacted by state boards of nursing, it will help to standardize regulation for NPs as well as ensure congruence between licensure, accreditation, certification, and education.

NP practice will continue to evolve, and this book provides valuable information that can be used by NPs to quantify the value of NP care as well as support continued role development. The Institute of Medicine Report on the Future of Nursing highlighted the important role of NPs and included the recommendation that they should be able to practice to the full extent of their education and training. In working to ensure the success of NPs entering the workforce and continued expansion of the NP role, it is resources such as this book that will help to ensure successful integration and growth of the NP role.

—Ruth Kleinpell
Chicago, Illinois

Appendices

A

Part I: NP Job Description Template*

Title: Nurse Practitioner   **Grade:**

FLSA Status: **Job Code:**

Department: **Location:**

I. GENERAL POSITION SUMMARY (*PROVIDE A BRIEF LINE POSITION OVERVIEW*)

To maintain and advance its position as a leading health care system, UMMC must have a dynamic and seamless process of delivering care that results in superior clinical and financial outcomes. Through their involvement in the management of patient care, nurse practitioners have responsibility for diagnosing and treating patients in collaboration with physician colleagues. Nurse Practitioners provide continuity, facilitating and coordinating communication between the health care team and patient and families and coordinating care to ensure quality of care, cost effective care, appropriate length of stay, and patient safety. The Nurse Practitioner is a direct link between the medical staff to the health care team and patient and families. The Nurse Practitioner serves as a link integrating relevant research and best practices in collaboration with specialty team of providers.

II. PRINCIPAL RESPONSIBILITIES

The following statements are designed to describe the general nature and level of work being performed by the provider assigned to this classification. This description is not intended to be an exhaustive list of all job responsibilities performed by this individual. A detailed description specific to performance functions will be described in the Nurse Practitioner's collaborative written agreement.

A. Clinical Responsibilities

    i. Performs comprehensive history and physical assessments for patients admitted/scheduled to *(assigned practice setting)*
    ii. Obtains and interprets appropriate diagnostic tests within the scope of the individual practice setting

---

iii. Establishes medical diagnosis based on history, assessment, and diagnostic findings

iv. Designs, implements, and documents appropriate treatment plans including prescriptions of medications based on a comprehensive review of History of Present Illness (HPI) and diagnostic results

v. Communicates plan of care with the patients and family members. Performs patient and family instruction related to the plan of care, disease process, new treatment plans, and medication regimens.

vi. Initiates appropriate referrals and specialty consultations or other agency involvement as needed

vii. Counsels and educates patients in health maintenance and health promotion activities. Provides primary, secondary, and tertiary preventive care services

viii. Communicates plan of care with appropriate providers including:

☐ Collaborative physician
☐ Primary care provider
☐ Referring provider
☐ Other _____

B. Education Responsibilities

i. Provides formal and informal educational programs for other members of the health care team

ii. Participates in mentoring activities

iii. Promotes understanding of *(disease process of specialty area)* throughout hospital and outpatient practice.

iv. Functions as a clinical resource for other team members including interns, residents, fellows, nurses, and medical students.

v. Provides community education and outreach related to disease-specific processes

vi. Acts as a community health resource for specialty disease entity

C. Research Responsibilities

i. Industry Sponsored Research
1. Screens patients for potential inclusion into approved clinical trials
2. Enrolls appropriate patients into clinical trials following rules of human subjects research and protocol design
3. Serves as a clinical trial subinvestigator
4. Obtains appropriate written consent for patient enrollment
5. Provides ongoing education regarding risk/benefits of inclusion into research protocols, study aims, study activities and follow-up schedules.

6. Provides ongoing patient evaluation for adverse events and patient responses to therapy
7. Serves as a liaison between study sponsor and department
8. Oversees all interactions with institutional review board (IRB)

ii. Advanced Practice Research

1. Pursues independent nursing research
2. Designs and implements research protocols
3. Creates appropriate consent forms
4. Reports research findings through abstracts, manuscripts, and poster presentations

D. Administrative Responsibilities

i. Supervision of ancillary staff including annual reviews
ii. Attends various department and division meetings as required
iii. Maintains compliance and regulatory documentation for administrative purposes and reimbursement for services
iv. Participates in and leads quality assurance activities (i.e., chart reviews, peer review) and establishes standards of practice

E. Professional Development

i. Serves on department, hospital, and community committees
ii. Maintains professional licensure, certification, and collaborative agreement as required by the Maryland State Board of Nursing and national certifying organizations
iii. Participates in department educational opportunities (i.e., journal clubs, grand rounds, etc.)
iv. Participates in local, regional, and national professional opportunities
v. Pursues educational opportunities for professional growth (i.e., continuing education units (CEUs), update conferences)

III. QUALIFICATIONS

(A) Masters degree in nursing or equivalent
(B) Registered and in good standing with the Maryland State Board of Nursing
(C) National Certification
(D) DEA and CDS eligible
(E) CPR/ACLS/BCLS as required
(F) Maintains updated hospital safety and other mandatory training
(G) Updated immunizations as recommended per practice area

Part II: Applying the Job description Template to Specialty Practice

Children's Heart Program PNP

Title: Nurse Practitioner	Grade:
FLSA Status:	Job Code:
Department:	Location:

I. GENERAL POSITION SUMMARY

To maintain and advance its position as a leading health care system, UMM must have a dynamic and seamless process of delivering care that results in superior clinical and financial outcomes. Through their involvement in the management of patient care, nurse practitioners have responsibility for diagnosing and treating patients in collaboration with physician colleagues. Nurse Practitioners provide continuity, facilitating and coordinating communication between the health care team and patient and families and coordinating care to ensure quality of care, cost effective care, appropriate length of stay, and patient safety. The Nurse Practitioner is a direct link between the medical staff to health care team and patient and families. The Nurse Practitioner serves as a link integrating relevant research and best practices.

The Pediatric Nurse Practitioner in the Children's Heart Program provides an advanced level of comprehensive health care to children with cardiac problems in the inpatient and outpatient care settings in collaboration with a specialty team of providers.

II. PRINCIPAL RESPONSIBILITIES

The following statements are designed to describe the general nature and level of work being performed by the provider assigned to this classification. This description is not intended to be an exhaustive list of all job responsibilities performed by this individual.

A. Clinical Responsibilities (75%)

Inpatient Clinical Responsibilities
    i. Performs comprehensive history and physical assessment for patients admitted to the cardiology service or post-cardiac interventional procedure.
    ii. Orders, obtains and interprets appropriate diagnostic tests.
    iii. Establishes medical diagnosis based on history, assessment, and diagnostic findings.

    iv. Designs, orders and documents appropriate treatment plans/plans of care including prescriptions of medications based on a comprehensive review of HPI and diagnostic results.

    v. Initiates protocols/clinical pathways, evaluates the plan of care, ensuring timely intervention.

    vi. Collaborates with cardiologists regarding admission, discharge and transfer decisions.

    vii. Presents patients to the cardiologist on am rounds.

    viii. Communicates plan of care with appropriate providers including the collaborative physician, the primary care provider, the referring provider, the nursing staff, and the case manager.

    ix. Communicates plan of care with the patients and family members. Provides patient and family instruction related to the plan of care, cardiac disease process, new treatment plans, and medication regimens.

    x. Counsels and educates patients and family members in cardiac disease process, health maintenance and health promotion activities. Provides primary, secondary, and tertiary preventive care services.

    xi. Initiates appropriate referrals and specialty consultations or other agency involvement as needed.

    xii. Facilitates patient flow. Collaborates with the multidisciplinary team including case management, ensuring appropriate and timely discharge.

    xiii. Provides specialty consultation.

    xiv. Coordinates care for patients admitted for cardiac catherization/EPS including pre-procedural history and physical assessment, moderate sedation, recovery monitoring, and discharge process.

    xv. Advocates for patients, ensuring patient/family participation in care, knowledge of treatment options, and understanding of patient rights.

    xvi. Considers the holistic needs of patients and orchestrates resources (i.e., pain service, palliative care).

Outpatient Clinical Responsibilities

    i. Performs comprehensive history and physical assessments for patients scheduled for cardiac catheterization or new patients scheduled in the cardiology clinic. Appropriate history taking and physical examination are also done for each patient visit.

    ii. Obtains and interprets appropriate diagnostic tests in collaboration with the cardiologist.

    iii. Follow monthly laboratory data required on patients including INR results and post-transplant laboratory test results and review with physician.

    iv. Establishes medical diagnoses for common health problems and reviews diagnoses with collaborating cardiologist.

    v. Prescribes medications as authorized per collaborative agreement.

vi. Counsels and educates patients and families in health maintenance, diet, and exercise, as well as, in the management and prevention of illness.

vii. Provides follow-up or coordination of care for follow-up after consultation with the cardiologist as needed.

viii. Refers patients to appropriate licensed physicians, or other health care providers/agencies as needed. Refers patients to physician specialists in all areas of the hospital or community whenever appropriate.

ix. Establish an NP panel of patients, i.e., murmur evaluation.

Supports Outpatient Coordination of Care Responsibilities

i. Daily triage of parent phone calls with appropriate documentation and phone log. Consult with physician as indicated.

ii. Complete prescription refills.

iii. Complete letters/school forms as needed for parents.

iv. Retrieve dental or surgical clearance information for physicians as needed.

B. Education Responsibilities (10%)

i. Provides formal and informal educational programs for other members of the health care team consistent with evidence-based practice standards.

ii. Participates in mentoring activities. Precepts students.

iii. Promotes understanding of pediatric cardiovascular disease processes.

iv. Functions as a clinical resource for other team members including but not limited to interns, residents, fellows, nurses, and medical students.

v. Provides community education, health promotion and outreach.

vi. Acts as a community health resource for pediatric cardiovascular specialty disease entity.

C. Clinical Leadership/Outcomes (5%)

i. Works with physician leaders and hospital administration to achieve service specific outcome targets for key metrics including clinical outcomes, length of stay (LOS), cost of care and patient satisfaction.

ii. Participates in performance improvement activities aimed at improving clinical outcomes and minimizing variation.

iii. In collaboration with physician leadership and the multidisciplinary team, develops clinical pathways.

iv. Participates in and leads quality assurance activities (i.e., chart reviews, peer review) and establishes standard of practice.

v. Advances the patient care delivery process through the application of research, evidence-based practice standards, and industry best practices.

vi. Advises and influences hospital level policy and procedure that improves the delivery of care.

vii. Introduces and evaluates new patient care delivery systems, models of care and therapeutic and preventive interventions that target patient needs not met by current care delivery strategies.

viii. Actively participates and contributes to various department and division meetings and organizational initiatives.

ix. Maintains compliance and regulatory documentation for administrative purposes and reimbursement for services.

D. Customer Service

i. Models and upholds a customer service focus to all internal and external customers.

ii. Demonstrates respect for all people in the work environment.

iii. Ensures confidentiality of patient information.

E. Professional Development (10%)

i. Serves on department, hospital and community committees.

ii. Maintains professional licensure, certification, and collaborative agreement as required by the Maryland State Board of Nursing and national certifying organizations

iii. Participates in department educational opportunities (i.e., journal clubs, grand rounds, etc.).

iv. Participates in and presents at local, regional, and national professional organizations.

v. Pursues educational opportunities for professional growth (i.e., CEUs, update conferences).

vi. Promotes the organization to all customers. Acts as a loyal and supportive informed spokesperson for the hospital.

III. QUALIFICATIONS

A. Masters degree in Nursing or equivalent

B. Registered and in good standing with the Maryland State Board of Nursing

C. National Certification by ANCC or PNCB as Pediatric Nurse Practitioner

D. DEA and CDS eligible

E. CPR/PALS/BCLS as required

F. Maintains updated hospital safety and other mandatory training

G. Updated immunizations as recommended per practice area

B

Examples of Start-up Activities Initiated Upon Acceptance of Position*

NURSE PRACTITIONER: CHECKLIST OF START-UP ITEMS

Please note that most of the required forms are included on the Nurse Practitioner computer drive.

Hospital telephone extensions are provided below for various departments listed as 8-XXXX. To call from outside the hospital, please dial 410-XXX-XXXX)

KEY PAPERWORK

Please complete as soon as possible. These forms should be your first priority upon acceptance of employment and receipt of this computer drive.

ITEM	CONTACT	DATE COMPLETED
Complete documents in the following sequence		
Maryland Board of Nursing	1. **Submit to Maryland Board of Nursing if new graduate NP or out-of-state NP:** • National NP Certification—must be aligned with practice site, (i.e., inpatient pediatric setting—pediatric acute care NP certification) • Apply for Maryland NP certification • www.mbon.org 2. **NP Attestation filed when have MD NP certification** • **Instructions:** http://www.mbon.org/adv_prac/attestation_instructions.pdf (Saved in MBON Folder 1) • **NP Attestation Form:** http://www.mbon.org/adv_prac/attestation_form.pdf (Saved in MBON Folder 1) • **NP Attestation Addendum** http://www.mbon.org/adv_prac/attestation_addendum.pdf (Saved in MBON Folder 1) • **NP Addendum New Procedure and Competency Checklist** http://www.mbon.org/adv_prac/attestation_competency.pdf (Saved in MBON Folder 1)	

---

*Reproduced with the permission of the University of Maryland Medical Center.

ITEM	CONTACT	DATE COMPLETED
Apply for Controlled Substance Licensure—need both CDS & DEA to prescribe controlled substances *Must complete CDS application before DEA as need this # to apply for DEA license*		
CDS (Maryland Controlled Drug Substances)	http://www.dhmh.state.md.us/drugcont/ 410.764.2890 Must be completed before DEA (Saved in Controlled Substance Application Folder.)	
Federal DEA (Drug Enforcement Administration)	http://www.deadiversion.usdoj.gov/drugreg/index.html 410-962-7580	
Complete hospital credentialing packet, above documents must be included		
Hospital Credential and Privileging	UMMS Medical Staff Office http://www.umm.edu/med_staff_services/index.html (Forms attached in Medical Staff Credentialing Folder.)	
Apply for NPI & PECOS after credentialing approved by medical staff office		
National Provider Identification #	http://nppes.cms.hhs.gov or 1-800-465-3203	
	Provider Enrollment Chain and Ownership System (PECOS) form—call Advanced Practice Office Manager for assistance in completing form	

COMPUTER/TECHNOLOGY ACCESS

Forms are included on the computer drive provided to you by Nurse Recruitment (see the "Computer Access and Information Forms" folder). Forms applicable to your area of practice should be submitted to your Director/Manager at your earliest convenience.

ITEM	CONTACT	DATE COMPLETED
Need hospital e-mail address to complete most applications		
E-mail account	Service Administrator (Novell and Groupwise Access Request Form – Saved in: Computer Access and Information Forms folder 4)	
NP will have "medical student" provider access to power chart until credentialing approved—supervisor contacts IT for change in status		

ITEM	CONTACT	DATE COMPLETED
Power chart (UMMC electronic medical record)	Call Help Desk – 8-XXXX (Account Request Form Saved in: Computer Access and Information Forms folder 4) Power Chart access requires: 1. Filling out a form and 2. Successful completion of an exam with the score of 80 and higher. The exam can be taken online by accessing: http://www.xxxxxxxx.com Username: xxxxx Password: xxxxxx	
Horizon HPF (scanned prior medical records)	Call Help Desk – 8-XXXX (Horizon Patient Folder Form attached)	
IMPAX (radiology files)	IMPAX administrator or contact Radiology (IMPAX user guide Saved in: Computer Access and Information Forms folder 4)	
Telephone Dictation and OTIS (online discharge/ transfer summaries)	Medical Records – 8-XXXX	
VPN (remote intranet access)	Help Desk – 8-XXXX (VPN request Form Saved in: Computer Access and Information Forms folder 4.)	
Phone Directory/ Voicemail/Long distance phone access	Telecommunications 8-XXXX	
EPIC (**outpatient electronic medical record**)	Help Desk – 8-XXXX (Account Request Form Saved in: Computer Access and Information Forms folder 4)	
Firstnet (**Emergency Department only**)	Help Desk – 8-XXXX (Account Request Form Saved in: Computer Access and Information Forms folder 4)	
Accupedia (pediatric continuous medication infusions) **PEDS ONLY**	Pediatric Pharmacy 8-XXXX	

ITEM	CONTACT	DATE COMPLETED
Pediatric TPN program **PEDS ONLY**	Pediatric Pharmacy 8-XXXX For pediatric providers only (Pediatric TPN Request Form Saved in: Computer Access and Information Forms folder 4)	

OTHER INFORMATION

ITEM	CONTACT	DATE COMPLETED
Health Sciences Library	Electronic resources and journals can be access via intranet. UMMS ID badge permits access to Health Sciences Library. (See Health Sciences Library Folder for additional information)	
Much more information	Hospital Intranet http://xxxxxxxxxx	
Orientation Framework/ Evaluation	See "Orientation Framework" form in "Informational Documents" folder.	
Unit-based Orientation Forms	Provided by Manager/Director	
Useful Websites	See "Useful Websites" form in "Informational Documents" folder.	

OFFICE & BUSINESS SUPPLIES

ITEM	CONTACT	DATE COMPLETED
Office keys	Contact Service line Office Manager	
Business Cards	Contact Advanced Practice Office	
Pager	Contact Advanced Practice Office	
Lab Coats	Contact Advanced Practice Office	
Scrubs	Contact Linens Service	

Reproduced with permission of the University of Maryland Medical Center

C

Clinical Orientation Timeline Template*

ORIENTATION WEEK	ACTIVITIES/TASKS FOR ENTRY LEVEL NPs	ACTIVITIES/TASKS FOR OUTPATIENT BASED PROVIDERS	ACTIVITIES/TASKS FOR EXPERIENCED NPs
Week 1	Three day Hospital Orientation Power chart module /prescriber training class Healthstream modules Paxis/PIM/email/dictation Day 3: APN Orientation Day 4: Unit/Service Operations Day 5: Observation of Service/Unit Rounds **Feedback and Goal Setting**	2 day Hospital Orientation Power chart module /prescriber training class Healthstream modules Paxis/PIM/email/dictation Day 3: APN Orientation Day 4: Unit/Service Operations Day 5: Observation of Service/Unit Rounds **Feedback and Goal Setting**	2 day Hospital Orientation Power chart module /prescriber training class Healthstream modules Paxis/PIM/email/dictation Day 3: APN Orientation Day 4: Unit/Service Operations Day 5:Observation of Service/Unit Rounds **Feedback and Goal Setting**
Week 2	**Shadow NP/MD Preceptor** Activities to Include the daily routine of the service: Rounds Documentation Assessment/Order Entry Presentation Plan of Care D/C Process Patient Education **One Day/Week: Didactic Content:** Self Learning Simulation Medication Safety Diagnosis Specific **Feedback and Goal Setting**	Completion of Reimbursement and Insurance Provider Contracts with Practice Managers. **One Day/Week: Didactic Content:** Self Learning Simulation Medication Safety Diagnosis Specific **Feedback and Goal Setting**	**Shadow NP/MD Preceptor** Activities to Include the daily routine of the service: Rounds Documentation Assessment/Order Entry Presentation Plan of Care D/C Process Patient Education **One Day/Week: Didactic Content:** Self Learning Simulation Medication Safety Diagnosis Specific **Feedback and Goal Setting**
Week 3	**Patient Care Delivery/ Management with Supervision of 1-2 patients** Activities to Include the daily routine of the service: Rounds	**Patient Care Delivery with Supervision of 1-2 Patients** Activities to include: the outpatient routine of the service: clinic or practice environment Assessment	**Patient Care Delivery/ Management with Limited Supervision of 1-2 patients** Activities to Include the daily routine of the service: Rounds

(Continued)

(Continued)

ORIENTATION WEEK	ACTIVITIES/TASKS FOR ENTRY LEVEL NPs	ACTIVITIES/TASKS FOR OUTPATIENT BASED PROVIDERS	ACTIVITIES/TASKS FOR EXPERIENCED NPs
	Documentation	Presentation	Documentation
	Assessment/Order Entry	Coding/Billing	Assessment/Order Entry
	Presentation	Documentation	Presentation
	Plan of Care	**One Day/Week: Didactic Content:**	Plan of Care
	D/C Process	Self Learning	D/C Process
	Patient Education	Simulation	Patient Education
	One Day/Week: Didactic Content:	Medication Safety	**One Day/Week: Didactic Content:**
	Self Learning	Diagnosis Specific	Self Learning
	Simulation	**Feedback and Goal Setting**	Simulation
	Medication Safety		Medication Safety
	Diagnosis Specific		Diagnosis Specific
	Feedback and Goal Setting		**Feedback and Goal Setting**
Week 4	**Patient Care Delivery/ Management with Supervision of 1-2 patients**	**Patient Care Delivery with Supervision of 1-2 Patients**	**Patient Care Delivery/ Management with minimal supervision of 3-4 patients**
	Activities to Include the daily routine of the service:	Activities to include: the outpatient routine of the service: clinic or practice environment	Activities to Include the daily routine of the service:
	Rounds	Assessment	Rounds
	Documentation	Presentation	Documentation
	Assessment/Order Entry	Coding/Billing	Assessment/Order Entry
	Presentation	Documentation	Presentation
	Plan of Care	**Non Unit based Educational Opportunity:**	Plan of Care
	D/C Process	OR	D/C Process
	Patient Education	Radiology	Patient Education
	Non Unit based Educational Opportunity:	Specialty Training	**Non Unit based Educational Opportunity:**
	OR	Outpatient Clinics/ Processes	OR
	Radiology	**Moderate Sedation Training**	Radiology
	Specialty Training	**Begin to perform procedures, as appropriate with supervision**	Specialty Training
	Outpatient Clinics/ Processes	**Feedback and Goal Setting**	Outpatient Clinics/ Processes
	Moderate Sedation Training	**Self Evaluation and Reflection**	**Moderate Sedation Training**
	Begin to perform procedures, as appropriate with supervision	**Modification of Timeline as needed**	**Begin to perform procedures, as appropriate with supervision**
	Feedback and Goal Setting		**Feedback and Goal Setting**
	Self Evaluation and Reflection		**Self Evaluation and Reflection**
	Modification of Timeline as needed		**Modification of Timeline as needed**
Week 5	**Patient Care Delivery/ Management with**	**Patient Care Delivery with Supervision of Half**	**Patient Care Delivery/ Management with**

(Continued)

(Continued)

ORIENTATION WEEK	ACTIVITIES/TASKS FOR ENTRY LEVEL NPs	ACTIVITIES/TASKS FOR OUTPATIENT BASED PROVIDERS	ACTIVITIES/TASKS FOR EXPERIENCED NPs
	Supervision of half of expected patient load Activities to Include the daily routine of the service: Rounds Documentation Assessment/Order Entry Presentation Procedures Plan of Care D/C Process Patient Education **One Day/Week: Didactic Content:** Self Learning Simulation Medication Safety Diagnosis Specific **Feedback and Goal Setting**	**Panel of Outpatient Patients** Activities to include: the outpatient routine of the service: clinic or practice environment Assessment Presentation Coding/Billing Documentation **Feedback and Goal Setting**	**Minimal supervision of expected patient load** Activities to Include the daily routine of the service: Rounds Documentation Assessment/Order Entry Presentation Procedures Plan of Care D/C Process Patient Education **Feedback and Goal Setting**
Week 6	**Patient Care Delivery/ Management with Supervision of half of expected patient load** Activities to Include the daily routine of the service: Rounds Documentation Assessment/Order Entry Presentation Plan of Care D/C Process Patient Education **One Day/Week: Didactic Content:** Self Learning Simulation Medication Safety Diagnosis Specific **Feedback and Goal Setting**	**Patient Care Delivery with Supervision of Half Panel of Outpatient Patients** Activities to include: the outpatient routine of the service: clinic or practice environment Assessment Presentation Coding/Billing Documentation **Feedback and Goal Setting**	**Patient Care Delivery/ Management with Minimal supervision of expected patient load** Activities to Include the daily routine of the service: Rounds Documentation Assessment/Order Entry Presentation Procedures Plan of Care D/C Process Patient Education **Feedback and Goal Setting**
Week 7	**Patient Care Delivery/ Management with Supervision of half of expected patient load** Activities to Include the daily routine of the service:	**Patient Care Delivery with Supervision of Half Panel of Outpatient Patients** Activities to include: the outpatient routine of the service: clinic or	**Patient Care Delivery/ Management with Minimal supervision of expected patient load** Activities to Include the daily routine of the service:

(Continued)

(Continued)

ORIENTATION WEEK	ACTIVITIES/TASKS FOR ENTRY LEVEL NPs	ACTIVITIES/TASKS FOR OUTPATIENT BASED PROVIDERS	ACTIVITIES/TASKS FOR EXPERIENCED NPs
	Rounds Documentation Assessment/Order Entry Presentation Plan of Care D/C Process Patient Education **One Day/Week: Didactic Content:** Self Learning Simulation Medication Safety Diagnosis Specific **Feedback and Goal Setting**	practice environment Assessment Presentation Coding/Billing Documentation **Feedback and Goal Setting**	Rounds Documentation Assessment/Order Entry Presentation Procedures Plan of Care D/C Process Patient Education **Feedback and Goal Setting**
Week 8	**Patient Care Delivery/ Management with Supervision of half of expected patient load** Activities to Include the daily routine of the service: Rounds Documentation Assessment/Order Entry Presentation Procedures Plan of Care D/C Process Patient Education **Non Unit based Educational Opportunity:** OR Radiology Specialty Training Outpatient Clinics/ Processes **Feedback and Goal Setting**	**Patient Care Delivery with Supervision of $\frac{3}{4}$ to Full Panel of Outpatient Patients** Activities to include: the outpatient routine of the service: clinic or practice environment Assessment Presentation Coding/Billing Documentation **Feedback and Goal Setting**	**Patient Care Delivery/ Management with Minimal supervision of expected patient load** Activities to Include the daily routine of the service: Rounds Documentation Assessment/Order Entry Presentation Procedures Plan of Care D/C Process Patient Education **Feedback and Goal Setting**
Week 9	**Patient Care Delivery/ Management with Limited Supervision of half of expected load** Activities to Include the daily routine of the service: Rounds Documentation Assessment/Order Entry	**Patient Care Delivery with Minimal Supervision of $\frac{3}{4}$ to Full Panel of Outpatient Patients** Activities to include: the outpatient routine of the service: clinic or practice environment Assessment Presentation	Orientation is complete when credentialing by the Medical staff office is confirmed. **Program Evaluation** **Transition plan**

(Continued)

(Continued)

ORIENTATION WEEK	ACTIVITIES/TASKS FOR ENTRY LEVEL NPs	ACTIVITIES/TASKS FOR OUTPATIENT BASED PROVIDERS	ACTIVITIES/TASKS FOR EXPERIENCED NPs
	Presentation Procedures Plan of Care D/C Process Patient Education **One Day/Week: Didactic Content:** Self Learning Simulation Medication Safety Diagnosis Specific **Feedback and Goal Setting**	Coding/Billing Documentation **Feedback and Goal Setting**	
Week 10	**Patient Care Delivery/ Management with Limited Supervision of half of expected patient load** Activities to Include the daily routine of the service: Rounds Documentation Assessment/Order Entry Presentation Procedures Plan of Care D/C Process Patient Education **One Day/Week: Didactic Content:** Self Learning Simulation Medication Safety Diagnosis Specific **Feedback and Goal Setting**	**Patient Care Delivery with Minimal Supervision of $\frac{3}{4}$ to Full Panel of Outpatient Patients** Activities to include: the outpatient routine of the service: clinic or practice environment Assessment Presentation Coding/Billing Documentation **Feedback and Goal Setting**	
Week 11	**Patient Care Delivery/ Management with Limited Supervision of full expected patient load** Activities to Include the daily routine of the service: Rounds Documentation Assessment/Order Entry Presentation Procedures Plan of Care	**Patient Care Delivery with Minimal Supervision of $\frac{3}{4}$ to Full Panel of Outpatient Patients** Activities to include: the outpatient routine of the service: clinic or practice environment Assessment Presentation Coding/Billing Documentation **Feedback and Goal Setting**	

(Continued)

(Continued)

ORIENTATION WEEK	ACTIVITIES/TASKS FOR ENTRY LEVEL NPs	ACTIVITIES/TASKS FOR OUTPATIENT BASED PROVIDERS	ACTIVITIES/TASKS FOR EXPERIENCED NPs
	D/C Process Patient Education **Feedback and Goal Setting**		
Week 12	**Patient Care Delivery/ Management with Limited Supervision of full expected patient load** Activities to Include the daily routine of the service: Rounds Documentation Assessment/Order Entry Presentation Procedures Plan of Care D/C Process Patient Education **Program evaluation** **Transition plan**	**Patient Care Delivery with Minimal Supervision of $\frac{3}{4}$ to Full Panel of Outpatient Patients** Activities to include: the outpatient routine of the service: clinic or practice environment Assessment Presentation Coding/Billing Documentation **Program Evaluation** **Transition plan**	

D

Peer Review Evaluation Tool and Self-Evaluation Tool*

NURSE PRACTITIONER PEER REVIEW/
SELF EVALUATION FORM

INSTRUCTIONS FOR COMPLETION

The attached form can be used as a peer review or self evaluation tool to evaluate nurse practitioner performance. The Organizational Competencies section references a distinct set of skills and behaviors that the organization has deemed pertinent for this role throughout the organization. The Performance Standards section references the specific duties assigned to **Nurse Practitioners** throughout our program. Additionally, the rating criteria are defined below to assist you with the completion of this evaluation. Thank you for your prompt completion of this form.

RATING CRITERIA

Unacceptable: performance does not meet job requirements.
Developing: demonstrates a level of skills and competency; however, results do not consistently meet job requirements.
Competent: results are good. Performance is consistent with job requirements.
Excelling: results often exceed job requirements. Employee consistently demonstrates skills and competency in meeting job requirements and can apply skill and competency in new situations or in unique ways.
Role Model: results significantly exceed job expectations. Consistently demonstrates that he/she is an expert in meeting job requirements and can be

---

*Reproduced with the permission of the University of Maryland Medical Center.

used as a role model/mentor on an organizational level. *Must identify instances when consistently and significantly exceeds expectations.*

Organizational Competencies

Technical Excellence: applies one's skills to perform the job, grows job-related skills, and stays current on changes that affect the ability to perform.

- ☐ Unacceptable
- ☐ Developing
- ☐ Competent
- ☐ Excelling
- ☐ Role Model

Comments: _____

_____

Initiative, Problem Solving, and Flexibility: Uses good judgment to solve problems and make decisions, adapts to change, and takes responsibility for getting the job done.

- ☐ Unacceptable
- ☐ Developing
- ☐ Competent
- ☐ Excelling
- ☐ Role Model

Comments: _____

_____

Team Work and Communication: Works effectively as part of a team by treating others with respect, seeking and providing coaching, using good communication skills, and resolving personal conflicts.

- ☐ Unacceptable
- ☐ Developing
- ☐ Competent
- ☐ Excelling
- ☐ Role Model

Comments: _____

_____

Service Excellence: Desires to serve others by understanding customer needs, meeting and exceeding expectations, and treating customers with respect.

☐ Unacceptable
☐ Developing
☐ Competent
☐ Excelling
☐ Role Model

Comments: _____
_____

Performance and Resource Management: Meets job's expectations and deadlines, participates in improving work processes, seeks input regarding own performance, and provides constructive performance feedback to others.

☐ Unacceptable
☐ Developing
☐ Competent
☐ Excelling
☐ Role Model

Comments: _____
_____

Performance Standards

Performs comprehensive physical assessments of patients

☐ Unacceptable
☐ Developing
☐ Competent
☐ Excelling
☐ Role Model

Comments: _____
_____

Establishes medical diagnoses for common short-term or chronic stable health problems

☐ Unacceptable
☐ Developing
☐ Competent
☐ Excelling
☐ Role Model

Comments: _____
_____

Orders appropriate labs or diagnostic tests; interprets tests accurately

☐ Unacceptable
☐ Developing
☐ Competent
☐ Excelling
☐ Role Model

Comments: _____

_____

Evaluates patients' physical and emotional responses to drugs and treatment.

☐ Unacceptable
☐ Developing
☐ Competent
☐ Excelling
☐ Role Model

Comments: _____

_____

Engages in teaching patients, family & hospital staff.

☐ Unacceptable
☐ Developing
☐ Competent
☐ Excelling
☐ Role Model

Comments: _____

_____

Appropriately prescribes drugs; seeks guidance from attendings or pharmacists on medication management

☐ Unacceptable
☐ Developing
☐ Competent
☐ Excelling
☐ Role Model

Comments: _____

_____

Manages discharge process; identifies discharges in timely manner; troubleshoots discharge issues.

☐ Unacceptable
☐ Developing
☐ Competent
☐ Excelling
☐ Role Model

Comments: _____
_____

General Comments:

NP Signature: _____

E

Example of Nurse Practitioner Clinical Competencies*

Pediatric Intermediate Care (IMC) Nurse Practitioner Cognitive & Technical Competencies

The nurse practitioner orientation is an individualized process based on one's previous experiences and will be tailored to meet the needs of the particular orientee. The following cognitive competency goals were developed to establish a common knowledge base for all practitioners.

Nurse Practitioner:_____

Competency Goal: Comprehensive patient management of diagnoses commonly encountered in the pediatric intermediate care (PIMC) setting.

<u>**Learning Content:**</u>

Pediatric Intermediate Care NP Cognitive Competencies

DIAGNOSIS PLANS FOR MANAGEMENT &	PATHOPHYSIOLOGY	DIAGNOSIS & DIFFERENTIAL	STABILIZATION INTERVENTIONS & WORK-UP	MANAGEMENT	POTENTIAL COMPLICATIONS	PATIENT & FAMILY EDUCATION
	DOCUMENT DATE OF DISCUSSION & PRECEPTOR INITIALS					
General:						
Mild Traumatic injuries						
Child abuse and neglect						
Anaphylaxis						
Toxic Ingestions						
Acute respiratory distress						
Cardiovascular:						
S/P Cardiac Catheterization						
S/P Ablation						
CHF						
SVT						
Pericarditis						
Acute hemodynamic instability						

DIAGNOSIS PLANS FOR MANAGEMENT &	PATHOPHYSIOLOGY	DIAGNOSIS & DIFFERENTIAL	STABILIZATION INTERVENTIONS & WORK-UP	MANAGEMENT	POTENTIAL COMPLICATIONS	PATIENT & FAMILY EDUCATION
	DOCUMENT DATE OF DISCUSSION & PRECEPTOR INITIALS					
ENT:						
Foreign body						
Obstructive sleep apnea						
Post-op ENT management						
Upper airway obstruction						
Metabolic:						
Acid/base disturbances						
DI/SIADH/CSW						
Hyperkalemia						
Hypocalcemia						
Hyponatremia						
Hypoglycemia						
Moderate dehydration						

Index